The Dispersal of Government Work from London

Presented to Parliament
by the Prime Minister and Minister for the Civil Service
by Command of Her Majesty
June 1973

LONDON
HER MAJESTY'S STATIONERY OFFICE
£1·30 net
Cmnd. 5322

THE DISPERSAL OF GOVERNMENT WORK FROM LONDON

CONTENTS

THE DISPERSAL OF GOVERNMENT WORK FROM LONDON:

STATEMENT BY THE GOVERNMENT

The Government is indebted to Sir Henry Hardman for his review of the possibility of dispersing more of its work from London and for his comprehensive presentation of the issues involved; it is also grateful for the work of Departments and associated bodies which took part in the review, and for the contributions made to the exercise by the Institute for Operational Research, the Tavistock Institute of Human Relations (Human Resources Centre) and the Joint Unit for Planning Research at University College, London.

2. Sir Henry Hardman presented his report as a basis for discussion and for eventual decisions. It poses complex questions, and while the recommendations are a most valuable starting point, the Government will not take final decisions until there has been an opportunity to consider each on its merits and all in the light of the issues raised by the report. The Government now publishes Sir Henry Hardman's report, as office location policies, whether in the private or the public sector, are a matter of general interest and it believes that the material it contains will be the best background to any public discussion there may be in the coming months.

The scope of the review

3. Dispersal is not new to the Civil Service. Apart from the relocations before or during the war, there has been a considerable movement of work away from London. This has been most marked during the last ten years, following the last dispersal review, undertaken by Sir Gilbert Flemming in 1962–63. As a result, over a third (some 57,000) of all headquarters staffs already work outside London; some 23,600 posts have moved since 1963 while, under current plans for further dispersal, some 6,800 more are due to leave the capital. In addition, some 10,000 posts in new Government organizations have been set up outside London and some 10,600 more are due to follow. In the non-industrial Civil Service as a whole, 7 staff in 10 work outside London. The regional distribution of the dispersed work is set out below. It will be seen that well over half this work has gone to, or is planned for, the assisted areas particularly Scotland and Wales which will each have received some 11,000 posts.

4. In the past, dispersal has been substantially of work which is relatively self-contained and can be done anywhere. Sir Henry Hardman's review, in considering the possibility of taking the dispersal process a stage further, has been concerned largely with work of a different character, namely the formulation of policy, and its implementation, at higher levels. He has examined some 86,000 posts in Government departments and in offices which, while not part of the central machinery of Government, are closely associated with it, e.g. the Research Councils. Such work cannot be done outside London without some loss of effectiveness in the services provided for Ministers, Parliament and the public, whether individuals or organizations. Sir Henry Hardman has therefore been considering how much could be moved at what price in lost efficiency and has concluded that, if the Government were prepared to bear some loss,

some 30,000 posts could be dispersed, over a period of years, from 20 Departments and other bodies. The Ministers concerned will be considering how far the effect on their Departments is an acceptable price to pay for the benefits of easing recruitment and accommodation problems in London and of creating new office work opportunities elsewhere. In reaching its final decisions, the Government will take full account of the evidence presented by Sir Henry Hardman on the criterion of operational efficiency and of the arguments raised in the discussion of his report.

5. The second main criterion which has guided the Government is the desirability of improving the opportunities for office employment outside London especially, so far as possible, in cities within the assisted areas and in new and expanding towns. Accordingly, as well as considering the possibility of sending more work from a Department to its existing dispersal centre or centres, for which there are good reasons as described in the report, or to regional administration centres, the Government invited Sir Henry Hardman to consider the scope for sending work to specified places. Sir Henry Hardman has consequently suggested, as part of his principal recommendations, a distribution of the 30,000 posts between a number of different places. This distribution is also set out below.

Consultation

6. While in principle endorsing Sir Henry Hardman's view that few rather than many locations should be selected, the Government now wishes to consider his recommendations further before making final decisions. In doing so, it will want to consider the implications of the proposal, not only for the organization and management of the Departments affected, but also for the staff concerned. It is accordingly inviting staff to give their opinions through the National and Departmental Whitley Council machinery. It expects to reach and announce decisions during the autumn in the light of these and other opinions which will no doubt be put to it. While it considers the report to be cogently and authoritatively argued, the Government is not committed to the precise scale or to the pattern of dispersal proposed by Sir Henry Hardman. Whatever decisions it finally takes, the Government will wish to consider with the utmost care the needs of staff who have to move with their work. In the meantime, however, it has already given its approval to the dispersal of the Science Research Council and the Natural Environment Research Council to Swindon, following consultations between the Management and Staff Sides of these bodies.

Civil Service Department,
Whitehall,
London SW1A 2AZ.
13th June 1973.

DISTRIBUTION OF THE NON-INDUSTRIAL CIVIL SERVICE AND OF WORK SITED OUTSIDE LONDON UNDER DISPERSAL AND NEW OFFICE POLICIES SINCE MAY 1963, TOGETHER WITH WORK NOW PROPOSED FOR DISPERSAL BY SIR HENRY HARDMAN: *NUMBER OF POSTS* (1ST APRIL 1973)

Region	Location	Non-Industrial Civil Service work at location (a)	Work dispersed; new offices created (included in column (a)) (b)	Further dispersal and new offices already planned (c)	Additions proposed in Hardman's "Recommended" solution[1] (d)
Scotland	... ...		6,758	4,383	1,177
	Glasgow	11,420	3,896	3,204	1,177
Northern	... ...		3,749	691	2,110
	Newcastle	15,635	706	84	500
	Teesside	1,900	230	115	1,610
North West	... ...		6,020	1,914	6,276
	Liverpool[2]	9,785	1,858	1,485	2,000
	Manchester[3] ...	13,495	2,424	330	1,390
	Central Lancashire New Town[4] ...	3,370	—	—	2,886
Yorkshire and Humberside	... ...		878	860	—
Wales	... ...	} 8,165	4,077	5,540	5,542[5]
	Cardiff		1,217	200	5,542[5]
	Newport				
West Midlands	... ...		279	—	—
East Midlands	... ...		794	92	—
East Anglia	... ...		1,192	—	737
	Norwich	3,175	1,103	—	737
South West	... ...		1,385	1,017	3,487
	Plymouth	5,900	256	674	1,660
	Bristol	4,725	—	—	1,248
	Swindon	655	—	—	579
South East	... ...		8,634	1,475	12,098
	Basingstoke	1,100[6]	601	650	300
	Milton Keynes (Bletchley)	145	—	—	10,890
	Southend	2,985	1,971	228	500
	Sunningdale	225	—	—	50
	Teddington	Not available	—	—	358

[1] Included for illustrative purposes and without prejudice to final decisions.
[2] Including Birkenhead, Bootle, Crosby, Litherland and Wallasey.
[3] Within a 12-mile radius of Manchester Town Hall.
[4] Preston area.
[5] This includes some 1,500 posts which the Government indicated (Hansard, Vol. 830, No. 55, Written Answers Col. 367) would be dispersed to Cardiff, the occupying Departments being decided in the light of the results of the location review. Excluded from column (c).
[6] Excludes Forestry Commission, which is to move to Edinburgh.

A Review
of the possibility of
dispersing more Government
work from London

REPORT

by

SIR HENRY HARDMAN, KCB

February 1973

A REVIEW OF THE POSSIBILITY OF DISPERSING MORE GOVERNMENT WORK FROM LONDON

CONTENTS

305375

A 2

A REVIEW OF THE POSSIBILITY OF DISPERSING MORE GOVERNMENT WORK FROM LONDON

REPORT BY SIR HENRY HARDMAN, K C B

Origins, scope and findings of the review

1. The White Paper on the Reorganisation of Central Government (Cmnd. 4506) of October 1970 announced a review of the location of Government work, with particular reference to the possibility of dispersing more of it from London.

2. I was appointed to lead the review. The Civil Service Department appointed a substantial team of officials to carry it out and on them the burden of the work has fallen. But I take full responsibility for the recommendations which follow. I gratefully acknowledge the assistance that I have had in reaching them, not only from the Civil Service Department but from the Departments and organisations under review.

3. The work under review was chiefly that of the headquarters of Departments in London. It covered some 86,000 posts. The procedure involved the application of operational research techniques and the consideration of a mass of information and conflicting interests. The details of the method and of these considerations are set out in the appendices. This main section of the report concentrates on those points which Ministers will want to have chiefly in mind in making decisions on which work is to be dispersed and to where.

4. My recommendations are given in the later paragraphs of the report and set out in detail, Department by Department, in Appendix 9. But, in summary, of the various courses which I suggest Ministers might consider, the one I would recommend involves the dispersal from London to a comparatively small number of receiving locations of some 31,000 jobs.

The past and the present

5. Dispersal of civil service work from London is not new. The civil service has an outstanding record of office dispersal, especially long-distance dispersal. The history is summarised in Appendix 1. Furthermore, much civil service work has never been done in London. The outcome is that the overwhelming majority of civil service work is now done outside the London area. Definitions are notoriously difficult. But in broad terms the situation is as follows (the figures relate to October 1972).

6. The civil service totals 690,000 staff. Of these, 500,200 jobs are in the non-industrial civil service. Again, out of this total, for the non-industrial civil service 356,500 or 70 per cent are located outside London, defined as more than 16 miles from Charing Cross.

7. Of the 143,700 civil servants in London, 47,800 are employed in regional or local offices. These can broadly be defined as those dealing with work for the London area or providing a necessary over-the-counter service for the public in London coresponding to similar services elsewhere in the country. Of the remainder, roughly 78,000 civil service staff were

5

subject to the review, those excluded being employed on work which could not be moved from London, including the Cabinet Office and such national institutions as museums and galleries. The 78,000 staff under review, the more dispersable of whom already serve in offices in the suburbs to which they were dispersed as a result of the last major dispersal review in 1963, include virtually all those carrying out the main policy work in the main national departments of Government. Indeed they can, for the most part, truly be called headquarters staff. Many of them either directly, or as support staff, are involved in providing advice to and doing work for Ministers. Earlier dispersals have already sent from London staff engaged on large operations of a clerical type. The scope for further dispersal must therefore be limited. Also subject to the review were some 3,000 members of Her Majesty's Forces in the Ministry of Defence and roughly 5,000 non-civil service staff in organisations wholly or partly publicly financed and based in London. Thus the review covered a total of some 86,000 staff (details are given in Appendices 1 and 2).

The economics of dispersal

8. Ministers have said that the study should have regard to two main factors. These are the efficiency of Government operations and the needs of regional policy. A major consideration must therefore be the economic effects of dispersing civil servants from London. This phrase includes the resource effects, the changes in the pattern of Government expenditure, and the effects on civil service numbers. The calculations are set out in Appendix 3, but in summary the conclusions are as follows.

9. It is the resource effects to which most attention should be paid. Here there are common misconceptions. The major points are as follows. There is little multiplier effect from moving civil service jobs from London to less favoured economic areas. There is unlikely to be any substantial effect on registered unemployment. The new jobs created, those filled by local recruitment, will from their nature in many cases go to women. And many of these women, in turn, will not be registered as unemployed. Altogether, the resource gain from the changed location of the work in employment terms is only likely to be a few hundred pounds per job per annum. More important is the effect from using less costly provincial accommodation. This is substantial and real, although of course it is greater on moving from central rather than suburban London. Adding all the factors together, the resource gain in current discounted value terms of the move of a civil service job from London to the provinces averages about a total of £5,500. In other words, if the 31,000 jobs recommended for dispersal were moved, the resource gain would total about £170 million.

10. Perhaps most noteworthy, the above figure holds good with surprisingly little variation from one area to another. It is the change from London to elsewhere which matters. And this is because it is the difference in costs of office accommodation between central London and elsewhere which is the dominant feature.

11. The exchequer cash flow argument is somewhat less important. In practice it is again paying for accommodation which is the dominant feature. Not surprisingly, the initial provision of new accommodation in the dispersed

locations will mean at first that there is an increased burden on the exchequer. For the size of dispersal recommended this might run at £2–£8$\frac{1}{2}$ million a year in any of the early years. That is presuming the approval of a dispersal programme in 1973, with the first substantial dispersals taking place in 1975. But savings should offset expenditure to produce net savings by about 1980. By 1981 there could well be a saving of the order of £6 million a year and the figure would increase very substantially in following years.

12. The third element is civil service manpower. This is much more difficult to quantify, for the reasons set out in Appendix 3. The most likely outcome is that dispersal will cause some increases in staff. In the short term the increases are, on average, likely to be of the order of 60 posts for every 1,000 dispersed. These increases are accounted for by the appointment of staff to manage the dispersal move, additional operational staff, larger training complements and the preparatory recruitment of staff for double-banking at the dispersal locations while the work is still being done in London. Much of this increase will be temporary and the longer term permanent needs should be much lower, since dispersal management units will not be required and much of the temporary reinforcement of staff should cease to be needed; additions will however be necessary to provide liaison offices in London in some instances. According to Departments' provisional estimates the permanent need is likely to average about 30 posts for every 1,000 dispersed. Looked at in a different way, the figures suggest that the permanent staff increase for those Departments required to disperse will be less than an average of 1·5 per cent of their present London Headquarters staff.

13. Taking these considerations together, therefore, there is some case for dispersal in terms of a saving of resources and, in time, in terms of exchequer expenditure. But the resource gain, great though it is, does not provide an overwhelming argument for dispersal. There need to be other considerations to justify the loss of efficiency which dispersal involves.

14. It is here that considerations of regional policy are important. Governments, for many years, have accepted the need to help the less favoured areas in the country. The dispersal of office jobs, of the type which the civil service provides, can be used to redress the imbalance of work in such areas. In doing this, they contribute more than the straight financial effect of importing such extra work. And they can perhaps provide, to some extent, a Government presence in the regions. Such considerations cannot be quantified. But Ministers will want to have them, as well as the direct resource implications, in mind in forming a judgment on civil service dispersal.

The communications study

15. The above paragraphs give the economic background against which decisions on dispersal must be taken. They show the case for dispersal, but equally they imply restraints. These are explained in greater detail later. But first it is necessary to explain how the study was carried out.

16. The work studied was essentially that of headquarters offices of Government Departments amongst which policy work predominated. The

305375   A 4 initial stage was a study of the communications of staff involved (see Appendix 4). This meant a measurement of the frequency of their meetings and of their need to have meetings. It covered contacts within Government and outside.

17. The results of these studies gave an initial measure of the relative dispersability of blocks of work. Again this was measured both with regard to their separation from their own and other Government Departments and from other organisations in London. From this evidence groups of blocks of work were then selected which at first sight seemed dispersable and proposals were put to Departments for dispersing various combinations. This process is described in Appendix 6. It was at this stage also that Departments had initial consultations with their Departmental Staff Sides.

Receiving locations

18. While the communications study described in the preceding paragraphs was carried out, separate consideration was given to possible receiving areas. Necessarily, in the earlier stages of the review possible receiving locations had to be considered separately from numbers because, until the later stages of the review, there was no indication as to the possible numbers which might be involved. But some considerations were identifiable and dominant. First, there were the interests of regional policy. These suggested locations in assisted areas. The second consideration was the efficiency of the operation of Government Departments. This review was not concerned with separate executive blocks of work which could function on their own. Much of that work has already been dispersed. It was much more concerned with policy work where the effects of splitting an organisation between London and elsewhere were more likely to be keenly felt in a Department's operations and not least in its services to its Ministers. As such, where dispersal was justified, there was greater need than in past dispersals for quick communication to London, especially given the assumptions that Ministers and their personal staffs would have to stay in London. All this pointed to the need to choose important regional centres with good travel facilities to London and preferably to other major centres.

19. Third, some Departments already have headquarters work dispersed to particular locations. In these cases it would be sensible to consider building on the existing dispersed work in the same location, both for reasons of economy in services and because of the need to provide viable blocks of work to give reasonable careers to staff without an undue amount of movement. Indeed, this last point links with one of the most important considerations in the dispersal study, a point which has found general agreement amongst all those concerned. This is the need for whatever dispersal is decided upon to take the form of the movement of reasonable numbers of staff to a few locations rather than spreading out the same number of staff over a large number of locations, each of which would only receive a very small number of jobs. To scatter staff over a large number of towns in this way would be inefficient in terms of the operation of Departments, bad for the staff concerned in prospects and career management and of limited use to regional policy. It is most important for the success of an efficient dispersal policy that the receiving locations should be as few in number as possible.

20. Against this background Ministers considered in the summer of 1972 possible locations for dispersed Government work. They authorised further study of the possible receiving capacity of the locations which they chose as preferred receiving locations against the criteria set out above. A note on these locations appears in Appendix 5. The recommended distribution of Government work between them is set out in later sections of this report and is further explained in Appendix 9.

The approach to making recommendations

21. When the fact-finding stages had been completed, it was necessary to bring together the issues referred to so far. The results of the communications study, showing what were theoretically possible blocks of work for dispersal, had to be considered against the economic factors, the organisation of Departments, the management of staff and the preferred receiving locations. And this approach had to be done Department by Department. For it should never be forgotten that Government is organised in terms of Departments. They form, each under their own Ministers, the units through which Government operates. If the efficient functioning of Government is to be preserved, then it is the efficient functioning of each Department which has to be preserved. There can be no such thing as the dispersal of Government, unless the whole of Government were to be transferred to some different town, which is not within my terms of reference. So the study of dispersal is the study of the dispersability of each Department. The proposals are therefore essentially proposals for each Department.

22. It will be clear, however, from the detailed consideration of each Department set out in Appendix 9 that, although Departments were entitled to full consideration of their special needs, none could be treated completely in isolation. It was necessary to consider where dispersed blocks of work from each Department could go in relation to those from other Departments. To do this a method was used which is akin to cost-benefit analysis. It is explained in Appendix 6. But just to call it a cost-benefit analysis would give a wrong impression. To have used a straight application of cost-benefit analysis techniques, with money values being put on all elements, would have given an unreliable picture. The damage to the efficient operation of a Department cannot be measured simply in terms of the extra hours of travelling and other financial costs involved in the dispersal and by setting these directly against the resource gains from a move to particular locations. For that reason a technique was used, explained in Appendix 6, by which different weighting could be given to the amount of communication damage which would be suffered in a Department at different levels of dispersal. A series of comparisons was made with the resource gain for moves to different locations. For purposes of comparison between Departments, one set of calculations was always carried out using the same distance. The reason for this is that communications damage increases with greater distances of move from London whereas, as explained above, the resource gain varies remarkably little for areas outside London. Then finally the relative dispersability of different blocks of work from different Departments was compared so as to suggest a possible allocation between the preferred receiving locations.

Qualitative factors in the judgment

23. If the above procedure had been followed exclusively, it would have been a mechanistic approach. The operational research techniques involved have enabled large volumes of information to be considered. But decisions on information so analysed must be taken with qualitative factors in mind. One obvious qualification is that Departmental organisation constantly changes. Many Departments have had reorganisations during the course of the communications study. Far more changes are bound to occur over the period of five to ten years, which is the shortest practical time in which to envisage the carrying out of a large-scale dispersal programme. In addition there are a number of factors, all of which must modify the simple recommendations for dispersal which would otherwise come from a mechanistic approach.

24. Perhaps first there is the consideration of the operation of London as the national capital. The operation of central government in its true policy-forming sense lies naturally there. Without the building of a Canberra or an Ottawa it is in London that the majority of the work with which this review has been concerned must stay. Even though little policy work may be dispersed, there will be strains on Ministers. They will be separated from officials to whom they are used to turning, and need to turn, for urgent and sustained personal briefing. This is closely associated with relations with the legislature. While these are chiefly conducted by Ministers, speedy response is fundamental. This is not just a question of particular items of Parliamentary business but reaction to the whole range of demands and needs of the legislature. Then there is the characteristic of Government operation through Departments as noted above. The White Paper on the Reorganisation of Central Government of October 1970 set out the arguments for the importance of bringing together functions of government which are related. While bringing together means chiefly the unity of a Department under a single Minister, it has the important secondary meaning of physical co-location of connected work. This is difficult to achieve in London. Dispersal makes it impossible. There is also the importance of working contacts between Government and the public. This is not just access by the public to local offices. In London the majority of contacts are with organisations often representative of important features of national life which have their headquarters in London. Such contacts would be weakened by dispersal and it is perhaps the loss of the informal contacts, which could not so easily be replaced as the formal meetings, that would do the greater harm.

25. All the above add up to an unquantifiable but very powerful argument against disrupting Government operations by moving staff away from the central area of policy making, which must remain in London. No amount of improvement in telecommunications, or increased travel, or increased staff could offset the strains and inefficiencies which would come from dispersal of the type of work covered by this review. As will be seen later, I have decided to recommend for dispersal some 31,000 jobs. Since roughly half would comprise staff who move with their jobs, this would mean the creation in all of about 15,000 new jobs in the receiving locations. There

must always be some doubt about the evaluation of the benefits to be gained from dispersal as against the disruption to the service to Ministers and to the community in general which it would entail.

26. But if Ministers do decide in favour of such a dispersal (and I must emphasise that my recommendations are essentially a basis for discussion), then a final and most important consideration is that of the civil service staff themselves. Increased dispersal, even if it is confined to a few locations, will mean an increase in the degree of movement which is imposed upon a man in his career. Some of the burden will fall on senior staff, relatively few of whom have so far been affected by it. The later enforced move back to London may well impose the bigger hardship than the initial move away. Extra consideration will have to be given to career management in the conditions which dispersal will impose. The implications for the families of dispersed civil servants must be considered, with recognition that wives and husbands often both have jobs. Finally, there are the problems of those remaining in London. Consideration needs to be given to phasing moves so as to avoid redundancies.

27. All these factors have to be taken into account in recommending blocks of work for dispersal. Their effects can be mitigated, though not completely offset, if improvements can be made in two areas, both of which I recommend for urgent study if a dispersal programme is to be pursued. The first of these is telecommunications as described in Appendix 7. Straightforward improvements in the telephone service are an essential if policy work is to be dispersed. There are other improvements which should be considered as set out in the Appendix. But these are necessarily more for the longer term future.

28. The second consideration is more important. Studies carried out as part of the review by the Tavistock Institute of Human Relations suggested a number of points on which changes were desirable in arrangements for helping staff in dispersal moves. Although I do not dwell upon the point here, I consider it most important that improvements should be made in this area—such as help with purchase of houses—and my recommendations are set out in detail, together with a summary of the Tavistock Report, in Appendix 8.

Recommendations

29. With so many conflicting considerations, some quantifiable but many necessarily subject qualitiative judgments, it is impossible to say that there is a single right proposal for the dispersal of Government work from London. Ministers will want to consider all the factors set out in the preceding paragraphs and elaborated in the appendices to the report. These factors do not point to any one solution and it would be wrong to say there is a right solution. But they do suggest that there are resource gains to be had from dispersal and that there are widely varying relative degrees of dispersability amongst the work which has been reviewed. Furthermore decisions can only be taken against the yardstick of a set of proposals. And since this review has covered all the issues involved both in terms of numbers and places, it is right to recommend a solution as a starting point for Ministerial consideration.

30. I would therefore recommend the dispersal set out in the following table. As will be seen from the details given in Appendix 9, these are not just numbers for each Department but the number of staff involved in particular blocks of work. Necessarily these proposals, even where they have resulted from discussion with Departments, are related to Departmental organisation as it existed at the time of the review. Recommendations and indeed decisions must relate to organisation as it is. Given that Governmental organisation is never static, some variation in the number of posts which actually get moved in five to ten years time or even later when the dispersal is carried out is inevitable. This should in no way invalidate the taking of decisions on numbers and places now, provided that those decisions are related to currently identifiable blocks of work. Similarly, while the numbers in my recommendations are precise to the extent that they relate to defined blocks of work, the decisions which Ministers finally announce might better be presented in round terms, given that the numbers of staff in the blocks of work to be dispersed will be subject to change. The suggested receiving locations are those chosen by Ministers, including those selected by Departments whose work is already in part dispersed (see paragraph 19).

RECOMMENDED DISPERSAL

Department	Number of posts in blocks of work to be dispersed	Suggested receiving location
Ministry of Agriculture, Fisheries and Food	1,250	Manchester
Agricultural Research Council	140	Manchester
Civil Service Department	707 comprising	
	357	Norwich
	300	Basingstoke
	50	Sunningdale
Her Majesty's Customs and Excise	500	Southend
Ministry of Defence	10,890	Milton Keynes
Department of Employment	1,540 comprising	
	1,400	Liverpool
	140	Plymouth (with Home Office)
Department of the Environment (DOE) ...	1,248	Bristol
DOE (Property Services Agency)	4,100	Cardiff
Foreign and Commonwealth Office (FCO) ...	986	Central Lancashire New Town (Preston-Leyland-Chorley)
FCO (Overseas Development Administration)	1,177	Glasgow
Department of Health and Social Security ...	1,480 comprising	
	500	Newcastle
	980	Central Lancashire New Town
Home Office	1,437	Plymouth
Criminal Injuries Compensation Board ...	83	Plymouth
Board of Inland Revenue	1,610	Teesside
Natural Environment Research Council ...	191	Swindon
Office of Population Censuses and Surveys ...	920	Central Lancashire New Town
Science Research Council	388	Swindon
Her Majesty's Stationery Office	380	Norwich
Department of Trade and Industry	1,800 comprising	
	1,442	Cardiff/Newport
(Laboratory of the Government Chemist)	358	Teddington
Export Credits Guarantee Department ...	600	Liverpool
Total	31,427	

31. I should draw attention to my reservations about Glasgow. This is the city in the list approved by Ministers which is most distant from London. This distance does constrain the amount of work which can be dispersed with tolerable loss of efficiency. There is however another constraint. The number of Departments which have United Kingdom, as opposed to England and Wales, responsibilities is limited. For these reasons, the only *prima facie* candidates for relocation in Scotland are the Ministry of Defence, the social security side of the Department of Health and Social Security, the Foreign and Commonwealth Office, including the Overseas Development Administration, and the Department of Trade and Industry. Of these, as argued in Appendix 9, Part 2, the MOD's most obvious area of dispersal is along the westerly axis from London, while the FCO work proposed for dispersal is allocated to Central Lancashire New Town, and even there it would incur a level of damage more severe than I regard as desirable (Appendix 9, Part 1). DHSS already has dispersal centres in the North West and North East (Blackpool and Newcastle) and it is sensible that further dispersal should be sited at or near these centres. And, as indicated in Appendix 9, Part 2, two large elements of the DTI work recommended for dispersal must, for statutory reasons, remain in England and Wales; they are too large for it to be sensible in management terms to split off the other two elements and send them elsewhere. This reduces the field to the ODA and illustrates the dilemma of the balance to be struck between regional policy and efficiency. As Appendix 9 (Parts 1 and 2) indicates, the recommendation that work from ODA should be sent to Glasgow would place a severe strain on the Administration. I recommend it as a solution only with serious misgivings and only because otherwise there is no work from London which could go to Scotland at all. Indeed, Ministers may well feel that that is the right solution, given that Glasgow has done well out of dispersal so far (having received the largest dispersal of the previous exercise, the National Savings Bank, which will total some 7,000 posts). If no work is to go to Glasgow from London, the most sensible course would be to consider the dispersal to Glasgow of parts of the Scottish Office from Edinburgh.

32. While the table in paragraph 30 sets out the solution I would commend, it needs to be read against this qualification and those expressed elsewhere in this report. It should also be considered against the information on London as the communications centre of the country and of the examples of work proposed for dispersal in Appendix 10, which give an insight into the effect of dispersal. To give Ministers an appreciation of what is implied, and what would be the effect of giving greater weight to the efficiency of Government operation, I suggest an alternative solution. It is a redistribution of the same total dispersal from London but to less distant places. Furthermore, I have in this solution tried as far as possible to propose locations which should be acceptable to Departments. In this solution the communications damage is reduced by $8\frac{1}{2}$ per cent compared with that of the main recommendations, while the resource gain is down by less than 1 per cent. On this revised proposal the possible solution would be as follows.

FIRST ALTERNATIVE—THE " EFFICIENT " SOLUTION

Department	Number of posts in blocks of work to be dispersed	Suggested receiving location
Ministry of Agriculture, Fisheries and Food	1,250	Coventry
Agricultural Research Council	140	Coventry
Civil Service Department	707	
	comprising	
	357	Norwich
	300	Basingstoke
	50	Sunningdale
Her Majesty's Customs and Excise	500	Southend
Ministry of Defence	10,890	Milton Keynes
Department of Employment	1,540	
	comprising	
	1,400	Liverpool
	140	Liverpool (with Home Office)
Department of the Environment (DOE) ...	1,248	Bristol
DOE (Property Services Agency)	4,100	Cardiff
Foreign and Commonwealth Office (FCO) ...	986	Bristol
FCO (Overseas Development Administration)	1,177	Manchester
Department of Health and Social Security ...	1,480	
	comprising	
	500	Newcastle
	980	Central Lancashire New Town
Home Office	1,437	Liverpool
Criminal Injuries Compensation Board ...	83	Liverpool
Board of Inland Revenue	1,610	Leeds
Natural Environment Research Council ...	191	Swindon
Office of Population Censuses and Surveys ...	920	Titchfield
Science Research Council	388	Swindon
Her Majesty's Stationery Office	380	Norwich
Department of Trade and Industry	1,800	
	comprising	
	1,442	Cardiff/Newport
(Laboratory of the Government Chemist)	358	Teddington
Export Credits Guarantee Department ...	600	Cardiff
Total	31,427	

33. As against the above proposals, which would cause less damage to
the operation of Departments than my recommended solution, it would also
be possible to suggest a different solution, which would mean a greater
degree of damage than in my recommended solution. The presumption would
be the need to disperse a given number of jobs to a list of receiving locations
within assisted areas; this would mean imposing a minimum dispersal of
some fixed number of posts to each of certain receiving locations. Taking
this approach I put forward as a second alternative the following.

SECOND ALTERNATIVE—THE " REGIONAL " SOLUTION

Department	Number of posts in blocks of work to be dispersed	Suggested receiving location
Ministry of Agriculture, Fisheries and Food	1,250	Liverpool
Agricultural Research Council	140	Liverpool
Civil Service Department	707	
	comprising	
	357	Norwich
	300	Basingstoke
	50	Sunningdale
Her Majesty's Customs and Excise	500	Southend

Department	Number of posts in blocks of work to be dispersed	Suggested receiving location
Ministry of Defence	10,890 comprising	
	6,218	Cardiff
	4,672	Milton Keynes
Department of Employment	1,540 comprising	
	1,400	Liverpool
	140	Plymouth (with Home Office)
Department of the Environment (DOE) ...	1,248	Bristol
DOE (Property Services Agency)	4,100	Teesside
Foreign and Commonwealth Office (FCO) ...	986	Liverpool
FCO (Overseas Development Administration)	1,177	Glasgow
Department of Health and Social Security ...	1,480 comprising	
	500	Newcastle
	980	Central Lancashire New Town
Home Office	1,437	Plymouth
Criminal Injuries Compensation Board ...	83	Plymouth
Board of Inland Revenue	1,610	Plymouth
Natural Environment Research Council ...	191	Swindon
Office of Population Censuses and Surveys...	920	Central Lancashire New Town
Science Research Council	388	Swindon
Her Majesty's Stationery Office	380	Norwich
Department of Trade and Industry	1,800 comprising	
	1,142	Newcastle
	300	Newport
(Laboratory of the Government Chemist)	358	Teddington
Export Credits Guarantee Department ...	600	Glasgow
Total	31,427	

34. In this possible solution the resource gain is only $1\frac{1}{2}$ per cent higher than in my recommended solution but the damage is 22 per cent higher—and approaching 34 per cent higher than in the so-called "efficient" solution. Moreover, the solution involves the harmful division of both the MOD and DTI.

Conclusion

35. The small increase in resource gain for the last solution set out above over the increased damage which it would do to the operations of Government is notable. I could not recommend such a solution. But the needs of regional policy, albeit the small variation in resource gain which occurs as between any move outside London, do suggest dispersal proposals more widely scattered through the country than in the case of the "efficient" solution, which concentrated on the efficiency of Government operation. Hence I come back to recommending the solution set out in paragraph 30. But it is essentially for Ministers to decide.

HENRY HARDMAN

Civil Service Department,
    Whitehall,
        London, S.W.1.

February 1973.

LIST OF APPENDICES

Registry of Friendly Societies
Gaming Board for Great Britain
Government Actuary's Department
Department of Health and Social Security
Home-Grown Cereals Authority
Home Office
Immigration Appeal Tribunal
Central Office of Information
Board of Inland Revenue
Lord Chancellor's Department
Medical Research Council
National Debt Office
National Economic Development Office
Natural Environment Research Council
Office of Population Censuses and Surveys
Ministry of Posts and Telecommunications
Potato Marketing Board
Public Works Loan Board
Race Relations Board
Office of the Registrar of Restrictive Trading Agreements
Science Research Council
Social Science Research Council
Her Majesty's Stationery Office
Central Statistical Office
Department of Trade and Industry
Registry of Trade Unions and Employers' Associations
Her Majesty's Treasury
Treasury Solicitor's Department
University Grants Committee

10. EXAMPLES OF WORK RECOMMENDED AND NOT RECOMMENDED FOR DISPERSAL.

11. THE LOCATIONS AS TRAVEL CENTRES.

THE DISTRIBUTION OF THE NON-INDUSTRIAL CIVIL SERVICE AND OF DISPERSED WORK

(a) Note on the distribution of the non-industrial Civil Service*

1. The non-industrial Civil Service consists of some 500,200 staff, serving in the three types of office shown in Table 1 (1).

Table 1 (1)

Office	Number	Percentage
Headquarters	153,760	30·7
Regional	24,018	4·8
Local and other offices ...	322,400	64·5

Note

Headquarters offices are Ministerial offices, the supporting policy-making branches and other branches serving the whole of a Department on functions of a national (that is, non-regional and non-local) character. Such offices are normally in London, Cardiff or Edinburgh, but may be located elsewhere as a result of dispersal.

Regional, Area or Command offices are responsible to Departmental Headquarters offices for local offices or other establishments.

Local offices and other establishments : "Local offices" (including any separately located sub-units) represent Departments at the local level in the administration or implementation of national policy; they may be responsible to either Departmental Headquarters or regional offices. "Other establishments" may be directly responsible to Departmental Headquarters, or to regional, area or command offices; they normally perform a special function, not associated with the nationwide administration of policy (*e.g.* research and development establishments).

2. The biggest number of staff is in local offices of, for example, the Departments of Employment and Health and Social Security, and is included in the "local and other offices" category given above.

* Source: Civil Service Department.
Date: 1 October 1972.

3. The geographical distribution of staff is as follows:

Table 1 (2)

	Headquarters staff		Non-Headquarters staff		All staff	
	Number	Number as percentage of total CS staff	Number	Number as percentage of total CS staff	Number	Number as percentage of total CS staff
London (Inner and Outer)	95,886	19·2	47,824	9·6	143,710	28·8
Rest of South East Region	11,562	2·3	70,128	14·0	81,690	16·3
Rest of the UK ...	45,335	9·0	221,031	44·2	266,366	53·2
Locations outside the UK	977	0·2	7,435	1·5	8,412	1·7
Totals ...	153,760	30·7	346,418	69·3	500,178	100·0

4. The geographical distribution of Headquarters staff is as follows:

Table 1 (3)

	Number	Percentage
Inner London	85,744	55·8
Outer London	10,142	6·6
Elsewhere	57,874	37·6
	153,760	100·0

(b) Non-industrial Civil Service and Population : Distribution by Region‡

Table 1 (4)

Region	*Population		†Non-industrial Civil Service				All staff	
			Headquarters staff		Non-Headquarters staff			
	Number ('000s)	Per-centage	Number	Per-centage	Number	Per-centage	Number	Per-centage
Scotland ...	5,224	9·7	10,332	6·8	31,566	9·5	41,898	8·6
Northern ...	3,292	6·1	13,745	9·0	18,025	5·4	31,770	6·6
North West ...	6,729	12·5	8,430	5·5	37,465	11·3	45,895	9·5
Yorkshire/ Humberside	4,792	8·9	2,213	1·5	22,201	6·7	24,414	5·0
East Midlands	3,385	6·3	189	0·1	17,579	5·3	17,768	3·7
West Midlands	5,103	9·5	503	0·3	23,463	7·1	23,966	4·9
East Anglia ...	1,665	3·1	1,240	0·8	9,281	2·8	10,521	2·2
South East ...	17,143	31·8	107,448	70·6	117,952	35·5	225,400	46·5
South West ...	3,771	7·0	6,574	4·3	35,628	10·7	42,202	8·7
Wales ...	2,724	5·1	1,452	1·0	19,392	5·8	20,844	4·3
Great Britain	53,828	100·0	152,126	100·0	332,552	100·0	484,678	100·0

* Source: Census 1971, Great Britain, Advance Analysis (HMSO 1972).

† Source: Civil Service Department.

‡ Excludes figures for Northern Ireland and locations outside the United Kingdom.

Date: 1 October 1972.

(c) Distribution of dispersed work

Note on dispersal history

5. The present review is the third major dispersal initiative in the last 35 years. Although there had been some earlier dispersal of Headquarters work, the first sizeable initiative was mounted in anticipation of the attack on London in 1940. Numerous Government offices were removed to such locations as Bath, Blackpool, Colwyn Bay and Harrogate where accommodation could readily be found, usually in hotels. Moves were also contemplated which would displace staff close to the very centre of Government activity but the Prime Minister decided against this on the grounds that the effect on efficiency and morale would be too damaging.* At the end of the war some of the offices were recalled to London, but others stayed put, the most notable example being the Ministry of Defence offices at Bath.

6. The second initiative came in 1962 when the then Government invited Sir Gilbert Flemming to consider the scope for dispersing Headquarters work. At that time, there were some 31,360 Headquarters posts outside London and some 7,480 more were due to go, a total of

* Minute to Sir Edward Bridges, 14 September 1940, *The Second World War*, W. S. Churchill, Cassell, Vol. 2, Chapter XVII.

38,840. The Post Office, then still a Government Department, accounted for some 11,500 of these. Sir Gilbert Flemming accordingly reviewed some 95,000 posts. He recommended the dispersal of some 14,000 from the London area and of some 5,500 to the outskirts of London. He also made recommendations on Departments in the Defence area, but attached no figures to those.

7. The essence of Sir Gilbert Flemming's approach was to identify self-contained units of executive work which could be separated from London and from the rest of the Government operation fairly readily and without an intolerable loss of efficiency.

8. The Government instituted a dispersal programme based on the Flemming recommendations in summer 1963. Their successors took two additional steps. First, they decided in 1965 that whenever a new organisation was to be set up it should if possible be located outside London: the Investment Grants Organisation and the Land Commission are examples of this. Second, they decided in 1967 that, wherever possible, preference should be given, in choosing locations, to the assisted areas.

9. The distribution of dispersed work, whatever the date of the dispersal decision, is set out below. The completion of existing dispersal plans and the results of decisions taken by Governments in and since 1963 are separately identified. The salient features of dispersal over the last 10 years are that

(a) 22,525 posts have been dispersed
(b) 7,840 posts are awaiting dispersal
(c) 9,490 new posts have been set up outside London
(d) 10,370 new posts are to be set up outside London

⎫
⎬ 50,225 posts
⎭

10. These figures do not include dispersal from the Post Office, which ceased to be a Government Department in 1969, or offices which were set up by the Labour Government and have been abolished. Nor do they include the relocation of work within the London area (i.e. within 16 miles of Charing Cross), resulting from Sir Gilbert Flemming's recommendations of 1963.

11. A regional analysis is also given below of the distribution of work dispersed, and of " new organisation " work set up outside London, since 1963. One significant point is that the bulk of the work is not going to locations in the south, i.e. in the South East and South West Regions. Independent commentators have observed that the Government has set a good example on " the question of office dispersal, and particularly with respect to long distance decentralisation ".*

---

* Office Dispersal and Regional Policy. J. Rhodes and A. Kan, Cambridge University Press, 1971 (page 113).

Distribution (by Departments) of relocated work

(excluding the headquarters of the Scottish and Welsh Offices in Edinburgh and Cardiff respectively)

12.   In Table 1 (5), details are given, by Departments, of the numbers of posts located or to be located outside London under dispersal policies.

A   This comprises work which has already been dispersed, the bulk of it in Headquarters offices, under decisions taken on or before 1 October 1972.

B   This comprises work which, on 1 October, was awaiting dispersal under decisions taken since Sir G. Flemming's report of May 1963.

C   This comprises work in new Government organisations which, on 1 October 1972, had been established or were to be established outside London under the policy initiative of 1965 (see paragraph 8 above); in most cases these organisations are of a national Headquarters character.

Table 1 (5)

Department Location	A		B	C	
	Dispersed work			New office work	
	1	2	3	4	5
	No. of posts dispersed before May 1963	No. of posts dispersed May 1963–October 1972	No. of posts awaiting dispersal, 1 October 1972	Established by 1 October 1972: No. of posts	To be set up after 1 October 1972: No. of posts
Ministry of Agriculture, Fisheries and Food					
Guildford	1,080				
Reading				54	246
Charity Commission					
Liverpool		104			
Civil Service Department					
Basingstoke		601			
Edinburgh				121*	69*
Crown Estate Office					
Bracknell		40			
Customs and Excise					
Lytham St. Anne's	} 250				
Southend					
Rayleigh		15			
Southend		1,171	53	540	442

Department Location	A Dispersed work		B	C New office work	
	1 No. of posts dispersed before May 1963	2 No. of posts dispersed May 1963–October 1972	3 No. of posts awaiting dispersal, 1 October 1972	4 Established by 1 October 1972: No. of posts	5 To be set up after 1 October 1972: No. of posts
Ministry of Defence (Admiralty)					
Bath	4,580				
(Air Ministry)					
Bracknell					
Cheadle Hulme					
Harrogate	} 2,030				
Worcester					
(War Office)					
Leeds	150				
MOD					
Bath		268	350		
Blandford		14			
Carlisle		71			
Gloucester		34			
Harrogate		246			
Portsdown			25		
Quedgeley		9			
Taunton		248			
Worcester		231			
Ministry of Defence (Procurement Executive) (Ministry of Aviation)					
Broxbourne					
Harefield					
Liverpool	} 610				
Reading					
MOD					
Bedford		30			
Farnborough		70			
Liverpool		75			
Reading		18			
Department of Education and Science					
Darlington		640			
Department of Employment					
Runcorn		744			
Department of the Environment (Ministry of Transport)					
Cardiff					
Hemel Hempstead	} 380				

Department	Location	A Dispersed work		B	C New office work	
		1 No. of posts dispersed before May 1963	2 No. of posts dispersed May 1963–October 1972	3 No. of posts awaiting dispersal, 1 October 1972	4 Established by 1 October 1972: No. of posts	5 To be set up after 1 October 1972: No. of posts
DOE						
	Crowthorne		568*			
	Hastings		750			
	Hemel Hempstead		43			
	Liverpool		233			
	Swansea				1,543	5,017
FCO (ODA)						
	Basingstoke			650		
Forestry Commission						
	Basingstoke	145 (to be relocated in Edinburgh)				
DHSS (MPNI)						
	Blackpool	} 10,860				
	Newcastle					
DHSS						
	Billingham				35	
	Blackpool				25	
	Cumbernauld				136	
	Fleetwood		331		69	
	Reading				127	
Home Office						
	Birmingham		3			
	Bristol		3			
	Corby		76			
	Manchester		2			
	Redhill		8			
Inland Revenue						
	Cardiff	} 2,600				
	Edinburgh					
	Liverpool					
	Worthing					
	Bootle		450*		1,200	1,380†
	Bradford		252*			
	Cardiff		50*			
	Crewe		23*			800
	Cumbernauld					
	East Kilbride				1,540	
	Edinburgh		1,003*	188*		
	Exeter		30*			
	Gateshead		221*			
	Leeds		89*			
	Manchester		2,178*	335*		
	Middlesbrough		195*			
	Newcastle		109*			
	Newport		80*			
	Plymouth		50*			
	Portsmouth		163*	185*		
	Sheffield		85*			

Department Location	A		B	C	
	Dispersed work			New office work	
	1	2	3	4	5
	No. of posts dispersed before May 1963	No. of posts dispersed May 1963– October 1972	No. of posts awaiting dispersal, 1 October 1972	Established by 1 October 1972: No of posts	To be set up after 1 October 1972: No. of posts
Inland Revenue–contd.					
Shipley		196*	55*		
Southampton		247*			
Stoke		45*			
Washington		41*	160*		
Worthing		365			
Land Registry					
Croydon				390*	
Durham				176*	424*
Gloucester				488*	212*
Harrow				591*	
Lytham St. Anne's		50	175	527*	98*
Nottingham				535*	140*
Plymouth				152*	448*
Stevenage				390*	60*
Swansea				109*	441*
Tunbridge Wells				690*	
Department for National Savings					
Durham		1,835			
Glasgow		3,681	3,319		
Ordnance Survey					
Southampton	1,730	700			
Passport Office					
Newport		87			
Peterborough		89			
Paymaster General's Office					
Crawley		606			
Office of Population Censuses and Surveys					
Southport / Titchfield / Worthy Down	750				
Titchfield		180	200		
Royal Mint					
Llantrisant		167	276		
Her Majesty's Stationery Office					
Basildon	140	488			
Gateshead				54*	91*
Norwich		1,103			

Department Location	A		B	C	
	Dispersed work			New office work	
	1	2	3	4	5
	No. of posts dispersed before May 1963	No. of posts dispersed May 1963–October 1972	No. of posts awaiting dispersal, 1 October 1972	Established by 1 October 1972: No. of posts	To be set up after 1 October 1972: No. of posts
Department of Trade and Industry					
Billingham					115*
Bootle					105*
Cardiff			80		180*
Glasgow					100*
Leicester		50			
Liverpool		36			
Newport		790	290		
Totals of non-industrial staff (rounded)	25,200	22,500	6,300‡	9,500	10,400

*Non-Headquarters posts. (There may be a few cases where a figure so marked includes a small number of Headquarters posts.)

† Additional number of posts under original automation programme. Suspended indefinitely following review of personal tax system.

‡ In addition, the Government has indicated (Hansard, Vol. 830, No. 55, Col. 367 WA) that some 1,500 posts are to be dispersed to Cardiff and that the occupying Departments would be decided in the light of the results of the location review.

Source: Civil Service Department.

Date: 1 October 1972.

Regional distribution of re-located work

13. Table 1 (6) gives the regional distribution of re-located work set out by parent Departments in Table 1 (5); it excludes work dispersed before the completion of Sir Gilbert Flemming's review in May 1963 (Table 1 (5), Col. 1).

X comprises the work in columns 2 and 4 of Table 1 (5), *i.e.* number of posts dispersed May 1963–1 October 1972 plus number of posts in newly established offices 1965–1 October 1972.

Y comprises the work in columns 3 and 5 of Table 1 (5), *i.e.* number of posts on 1 October 1972 awaiting dispersal or the establishment of new offices under decisions already taken.

Table 1 (6)

Region	Location	X		Y	
		No. of posts placed outside London (see note X above)	Percentage of overall total placed outside London	No. of posts to be placed outside London (see note Y above)	Percentage of overall total to be placed outside London
		1	2	3	4
SCOTLAND					
	Cumbernauld	136		800	
	East Kilbride	1,540			
	Edinburgh	1,124		257	
	Glasgow	3,681		3,419	
		6,481	20·2%	4,476	24·6%
NORTHERN					
	Billingham	35		115	
	Carlisle	71			
	Darlington	640			
	Durham	2,011		424	
	Gateshead	275		91	
	Middlesbrough	195			
	Newcastle	109			
	Washington	41		160	
		3,377	10·5%	790	4·3%
NORTH WEST					
	Blackpool	25			
	Bootle	1,650		1,485	
	Crewe	23			
	Fleetwood	400			
	Liverpool	448			
	Lytham	527		98	
	Manchester	2,180		335	
	Runcorn	744			
		5,997	18·7%	1,918	10·5%
YORKSHIRE AND HUMBERSIDE					
	Bradford	252			
	Harrogate	246			
	Leeds	89			
	Shipley	196		55	
		783	2·4%	55	0·3%

Region	Location	No. of posts placed outside London (see note X above) 1	Percentage of overall total placed outside London 2	No. of posts to be placed outside London (see note Y above) 3	Percentage of overall total to be placed outside London 4
		X		**Y**	
WALES					
	Cardiff	50		1,760	
	Llantrisant	167		276	
	Newport	957		290	
	Swansea	1,652		5,458	
		2,826	8·8%	7,784	42·7%
EAST MIDLANDS					
	Corby	76			
	Leicester	50			
	Nottingham	535		140	
	Sheffield	85			
		746	2·3%	140	0·8%
WEST MIDLANDS					
	Birmingham	3			
	Stoke	45			
	Worcester	231			
		279	0·9%	0	
EAST ANGLIA					
	Norwich	1,103			
	Peterborough	89			
		1,192	3·7%	0	
SOUTH WEST					
	Bath	268		350	
	Bristol	3			
	Exeter	30			
	Gloucester	522		212	
	Plymouth	252		623	
	Quedgeley	9			
	Taunton	248			
		1,332	4·2%	1,185	6·5%
SOUTH EAST					
	Basildon	488			
	Basingstoke	746		650	
	Bedford	30			
	Blandford	14			
	Bracknell	40			
	Crawley	606			
	Crowthorne	568			
	Croydon	390			
	Farnborough	70			
	Harrow	591			
	Hastings	750			
	Hemel Hempstead	43			
	Portsdown			25	
	Portsmouth	163		185	
	Rayleigh	15			

Region	Location	X		Y	
		No. of posts placed outside London (see note X above) 1	Percentage of overall total placed outside London 2	No. of posts to be placed outside London (see note Y above) 3	Percentage of overall total to be placed outside London 4
SOUTH EAST—*continued*	Reading	199		246	
	Redhill	8			
	Southampton	947			
	Southend	1,711		495	
	Stevenage	390		60	
	Titchfield	180		200	
	Tunbridge Wells	690			
	Worthing	365			
		9,004	28·1%	1,861	10·2%
	Total	32,017	100%	18,209	100%

Source: Civil Service Department.
Date: 1 October 1972.

THE COVERAGE OF THE REVIEW

(a) Government and other offices subject to dispersal policy

1. A note on the different types of Civil Service offices is given in Appendix 1. It is headquarters offices in London (*i.e.* within 16 miles of Charing Cross) which are the principal object of dispersal policy, but it also extends to non-Government bodies (*e.g.* the Arts Council), which are financed wholly or substantially by public funds and have their headquarters offices in London. The main work of the location review was accordingly concerned with such offices and organisations; it excluded most of the regional offices in London, all local offices and most non-headquarters establishments in the London area. The public corporations, which are not formally subject to dispersal policy, were also excluded. Lists of offices included and excluded are given below.

2. On 1 January 1971, when the review began, there was a total of some 97,000 non-industrial Civil Service posts in headquarters offices in London. Between 1 January, 1971 and 1 September, 1972 (although 1,780 headquarters posts were dispersed), this total increased to some 100,500; of these, however, some 5,000 (see below, (c) (iii)) had ceased to be Government posts for various reasons, including the effect of the 1972 Superannuation Act and the hiving off of certain Department of Trade and Industry work to form the Civil Aviation Authority. This left some 95,500 Civil Service posts, made up as follows:

Posts in headquarters blocks under review (at
    time of communications study) ... ...   78,200 (see (b) below)

Posts in headquarters blocks *not* under
    review   ... ...   11,100 (see (c) (i) below)

Balance

(1) Increase of posts in headquarters blocks
    under review between dates of com-
    munications studies and 1 September 1972

(2) parts of Departmental Headquarters *not*
    under review (see (c) (ii) below) for which
    individual statistics are not available
    Total (1 + 2)   6,200

Grand Total   95,500

3. The review covered the following posts:

Civil Service headquarters posts ... ...   78,233 (see (b))

Headquarters posts occupied by members of
    Her Majesty's Forces ... ...   3,069 (see (b))

Headquarters posts not part of the Civil
    Service ... ...   4,831 (see (b))

    86,133

(b) Headquarters of Government Departments and Other Bodies included in the Location Review*

Departments and other bodies included in the Review	Civil Service headquarters staff under review	Non-Civil Service headquarters staff under review
CABINET OFFICE		
Central Statistical Office	225	
AGRICULTURE, FISHERIES AND FOOD		
Ministry of Agriculture, Fisheries and Food ...	3,285	
Central Council for Agricultural and Horticultural Co-operation		32
Home-Grown Cereals Authority		49
Potato Marketing Board		46
CHANCELLOR OF THE EXCHEQUER		
Treasury...	1,068	
Customs and Excise	2,000	
Inland Revenue	3,942	
Government Actuary's Department...	56	
National Debt Office	58	
Registry of Friendly Societies	102	
Treasury Solicitor's Department	340	
EDUCATION AND SCIENCE		
Department of Education and Science	1,361	
University Grants Committee	119	
Agricultural Research Council		140
Arts Council		134
British Film Institute		173
Medical Research Council...		305
Natural Environment Research Council		191
Science Research Council		388
Social Science Research Council		112
EMPLOYMENT		
Department of Employment	2,788	
ENVIRONMENT		
Department of the Environment including Country- side Commission	12,545	
Agrement Board		26
Centre for Environmental Studies		53
Council for Small Industries in Rural Areas ...		131
Development Commission		28
Housing Corporation		26
Historic Buildings Council		11
Location of Offices Bureau		13
Executive Sports Council		114
FOREIGN AND COMMONWEALTH		
Foreign and Commonwealth Office	2,395	
FCO—Overseas Development Administration ...	1,426	
Directorate of Overseas Survey	381	
Centre for Educational Development Overseas ...		68
Council for Technical Education and Training for Overseas Countries		25
Inter-University Council		66
British Council		1,420
HOME OFFICE		
Home Office	3,831	
Community Relations Commission		54
Criminal Injuries Compensation Board		83
Gaming Board		42
Immigration Appeal Tribunal		36
Race Relations Board		31

32

Departments and other bodies included in the Review	Civil Service headquarters staff under review	Non-Civil Service headquarters staff under review
LORD CHANCELLOR		
Lord Chancellor's Department	235	
LORD PRIVY SEAL		
Civil Service Department	1,948	
Including:		
Civil Service Council for Further Education		
Civil Service Sports Council		
Government Hospitality Fund		
Central Office of Information	1,298	
Her Majesty's Stationery Office	481	
POSTS AND TELECOMMUNICATIONS		
Ministry of Posts and Telecommunications	396	
SOCIAL SERVICES		
Department of Health and Social Security	5,571	
Health Education Council		62
Office of Population Censuses and Surveys ...	920	
TRADE AND INDUSTRY		
Department of Trade and Industry	9,290	
British Tourist Authority		203
English Tourist Board		89
Export Credits Guarantee Department	1,480	
DEFENCE		
Ministry of Defence	23,400†	
SMALL DEPARTMENTS AND OTHER BODIES		
Charity Commission	200	
Civil Service Pay Research Unit	46	
Office of the Registrar of Restrictive Trading Agreements	71	
Registry of Trade Unions and Employers' Associations	44	
Exchequer and Audit Department		418
National Economic Development Office ...		215
Public Works Loan Board		47
Gross Totals	81,302	4,831
Less posts held by members of Her Majesty's Forces	3,069	
Net Totals	78,233	4,831

Notes:
  * These figures show the numbers of staff under review in each Department or organisation etc. at the time when the communications study was undertaken. As such, they are not identical with published figures for a particular date.
  † The MOD figure includes 3,069 posts held by members of Her Majesty's Forces.

305375

B

(c) Government Offices in London excluded from the Review

(i) Departments

	Civil Service headquarters posts in London on 1 October 1972
Cabinet Office (excluding Central Statistical Office)	390
Courts, Lord Chancellor's Department	1,776
Crown Estate Office	75
Customs and Excise:	
Part of Accountant and Comptroller General's Office and Training Centres*	53
Ministry of Defence:	
Naval Supply and Stores Staff*	350
Directorate-General of Defence Contracts*	25
Director of Public Prosecutions	146
Education and Science:	
Science Museum	366
Victoria and Albert Museum	583
Foreign and Commonwealth Office:	
Overseas Development Administration Scientific Units*	650
Her Majesty's Stationery Office:	
Presses, Binderies, Warehouses, etc., non-industrial staff	652
Land Registry:	
Land Charges and Agricultural Credits Department*	175
Law Officers' Department	15
Lord Advocate's Department (Scotland)	10
Manpower Economics, Office of	43
National Savings, Department for:	
Headquarters, London	150
National Savings Committee Headquarters	250
National Savings Bank*	3,500
Ordnance Survey	18
Parliamentary Counsel	40
Paymaster General's Office	12
Population Censuses and Surveys:	
Microfilm Work*	200
Privy Council Office	32
Public Record Office	318
Public Trustee Office	549
Royal Mint:	
Mint and Decimal Coinage Factory*	276
Scottish Office	26
Department of Trade and Industry:	
Business Statistics Office*	290
Part of Insolvency Service Headquarters*	80
Welsh Office	23
	11,073

* To be dispersed under existing plans for dispersal.
Source: Civil Service Department.

(ii) Headquarters posts in the parts of Departments listed below were also excluded from the Review

PRIME MINISTER'S OFFICE

MINISTRY OF AGRICULTURE, FISHERIES AND FOOD
Royal Botanic Gardens, Kew
Salmon and Freshwater Fisheries Laboratory (to be relocated near Salisbury)

MINISTRY OF DEFENCE
Admiralty Research Laboratory, Teddington
British Forces Broadcasting Service, Head Office
Explosives Research and Development Establishment, Waltham Abbey
Mapping and Charting Establishment
National Army Museum
Royal Air Force Museum
Royal Army Medical College
Royal College of Defence Studies
Royal Hospital, Chelsea
" Soldier " Magazine

DEPARTMENT OF EMPLOYMENT
Duchess of Gloucester House
Office of the Wages Councils

DEPARTMENT OF THE ENVIRONMENT
Building Research Station, Watford
Fire Research Station, Boreham Wood
Material Testing Laboratory, Stanmore

FOREIGN AND COMMONWEALTH OFFICE
India Office Library and Records

DEPARTMENT OF HEALTH AND SOCIAL SECURITY
Public Health Laboratory Service Board
Central Public Health Laboratory

INLAND REVENUE
Special Commissioners of Income Tax

LAW COMMISSION

DEPARTMENT OF TRADE AND INDUSTRY
Metrication Board
National Physical Laboratory, Teddington
Office of the Queen's Award to Industry
Patent Office and Industrial Property and Copyright Department

35

(iii) London headquarters staff, designated Civil Service staff on 1 January 1971 (when the Review began), excluded from the Review*

	Non-Civil Service headquarters posts in London on 1 September 1972
British Museum	1,306
British Museum (Natural History)	541
Imperial War Museum	163
London Museum	87
National Gallery	203
National Maritime Museum	181
National Portrait Gallery	69
Tate Gallery	214
Wallace Collection	63
Royal Fine Art Commission	4
Historical Manuscripts Commission	17
Standing Commission on Museums and Galleries	3
Royal Commission on Historical Monuments (England) ...	52
Commission on the Constitution...	14
Royal Commission on Environmental Pollution	5
Parliamentary Commissioner for Administration	50
Commission on Industrial Relations	118
Monopolies Commission	27
Civil Aviation Authority	1,500†
	4,617

* The figures in this table were obtained from the Civil Service Department for 1 September 1972 by which time the posts were no longer part of the Civil Service, in some cases as a result of the provisions of the Superannuation Act, 1972.

† This figure relates to 1 April 1972, the vesting day of the Civil Aviation Authority.

THE RESOURCE AND EXCHEQUER EFFECTS OF DISPERSAL AND ITS CONSEQUENCES FOR CIVIL SERVICE MANPOWER

Resource gain and social benefit attributable to dispersal

1. It is usually claimed that dispersal of Government work confers substantial advantages in terms of Exchequer savings and the creation of both new or varied employment opportunities and a multiplier effect in the receiving location. In the trade-off which has been attempted between damage to efficiency and economic gains, costs and benefits have been interpreted entirely in terms of their net impact on the real resources of the economy as a whole and not in terms of their effects on the cash flows of central Government. For instance, where the creation of jobs in areas of underemployment is expected to result in the bringing into employment of people who would otherwise have been out of work, there is a resource gain and, as a result of their higher taxpaying capacity and lower entitlement to social security benefits, an Exchequer gain. These cannot be added together. It is the value of new net output which represents the gain to the nation as a whole, whereas the Exchequer effects are relevant mainly to the distribution of income, not to its total size. There will need to be estimates of the overall effect on the Exchequer of any given proposals and an attempt at this has been made (see paragraph 13 onwards). These would take into account such items as rent savings and construction costs, etc., as well as the items mentioned above, but the economic element of the case for dispersal does not rest on changes in the pattern of Government spending; it rests on the resource gain to the nation as a whole. And so this is the measure which has been used. The main features of the analysis are set out in the following paragraphs.

2. The non-industrial civil service uses people, office space, various forms of communications and very little else (*e.g.* scarcely any capital equipment). Neither telecommunications nor physical communications have turned out to be major items on the cost side of the equation. Inter-city rail travel could conceivably be a fairly large item in Exchequer cash terms, but its resource costs are very low. More civil servants travelling are not going to affect significantly British Rail's main items of expenditure. This leaves staff costs and office space, both of which could be expected to be cheaper in locations other than central London.

3. The maximum possible resource saving which can occur as a result of employing staff in alternative locations is equal, in principle, to the total costs of employing a man otherwise unemployed. If it is assumed that vacancies likely to be filled by otherwise unemployed people will be at Clerical Officer level and below, rather than for more senior posts, this gives a maximum saving of around £1,400 per job per annum.

4. Savings of this magnitude will not accrue from the average dispersed job, however. There are two main reasons for this. First, a large proportion of the jobs created in new locations would of necessity be filled by staff moving in post. There is a saving involved here to the extent that the cost of living is lower outside London, but this is a sum of the order of a very few hundred pounds per annum rather than well over a thousand.

37

Second, such evidence as is available suggests that although new jobs can have an impact on unemployment that is far from negligible, their main effect (and certainly their main direct effect) is to attract workers away from other employers. One of the reasons for this is no doubt simply that the unemployed are not a homogeneous group and are not always able directly to fill whatever vacancies arise.

5. This has a bearing on the analysis used in the present exercise because, whereas most of the unemployment register is normally composed of men, and mostly of men whose aptitudes and experience are more suitable for work in a branch of engineering, mining, or construction, or in the manual side of the service sector (*e.g.* transport), it is clear that almost all the vacancies created by dispersal would be non-manual, that most of them demand some level of academic qualification, and that a majority are at present filled by women. All of this suggests (although it is impossible to be dogmatic) that the main impact of dispersal on unemployment will be via the large numbers of unemployed women who do not register as unemployed and whose numbers can be estimated only from census data. Further support for this view comes from the simple observation that married women are especially likely not only to be suitable for office work but also to remain unemployed without migrating simply because wives stay with husbands and there is nothing to prevent the situation arising where the husband is in a job while the wife is left without any appropriate employment opportunities for prolonged periods. (The most notable case in point is probably Teesside, where male unemployment is normally quite low but where the "hidden female labour reserve" is among the highest in the country.) In many potential receiving locations there is no reason to expect to employ any substantial numbers of unemployed, either men or women.

6. The conclusion to all this is that, even in areas of the greatest economic need, resource gains (as a result of staff movement) of more than a few hundred pounds per annum cannot confidently be expected to flow from the removal of the average job to the average receiving location. Furthermore, this figure does not alter much, no matter what the geographical situation. This is because there is a fairly large saving on house prices, commuting costs and staff costs (*i.e.* the London salary weighting) for any move beyond, roughly, the Outer Metropolitan Area; subsequent variations between areas (including the employment of the otherwise unemployed) are dwarfed by this. So the staff costs item in the analysis ends with resource gain for a job dispersed from London of £300–£400 per annum.

7. The second main item, office costs, presents a very different picture. It was estimated that the average square foot of letting space in central London offices occupied by the Government was worth (at 1971 price levels) about £5–£7 whereas a typical figure in equally well placed sites in provincial towns and cities would be about £1. This saving of around £5 per square foot has to be multiplied by 150 or so to take into account the floorspace used by the typical officer, giving £750 per annum.

8. So far, then, the major items in the analysis are savings in staff costs and savings in office costs, but the latter dominate the former. There is also remarkably little to allow a convincing discrimination between different locations outside London on cost grounds.

9. A number of other items was also taken into account. These were the cost of moving staff, differentials in local authority rates (a substantial but rather uncertain element treated in principle as an addition to rent), working wives' loss of income and possible unemployment, and local income/multiplier effects. The last of these is worth a brief description. It is often assumed that multiplier effects of various sorts are a vital part of a cost-benefit analysis which deals with regions, but the only really substantial source of multiplier effects from the dispersal of Government work is the importation of staff and their spending power. The proportion of their income which ends up being spent on value added locally, whether on goods or services, is, however, quite small. Most of it is either taxed away or flows quickly outside any given region. For instance, the purchase of a £100 washing machine at a local electrical goods shop will result in a sum of far less than £100 going to people who live locally. Most will go to the manufacturers of the machine and to the Government, as it would have done no matter where the machine was actually purchased.

10. Furthermore, since the economic case for dispersal is the net gain to the whole nation, the Government can take credit only for that part of local value added which has the effect of using otherwise unused resources, or resources which are cheaper than in London. The net result is that the multiplier effect, on any reasonable assumptions, can contribute very little to the overall benefits of dispersal.

11. It may therefore be seen that the dominant feature of the net benefits of dispersal is differentials in the market value of office space. This results essentially from the very high levels of rent reached in central London, partly as a result of the Office Development Permit policy introduced in 1965. The conclusions on the economic value of dispersal are accordingly sensitive to substantial re-estimates of the probable future course of London rents. Continued high London rents have been assumed, but without any continuing increase in real terms at anything like the annual rate of increase between 1966 and 1971.

12. Any actual dispersal pattern decided upon could not realistically be expected to result in job movement until, say, the middle of the decade. Once begun, it will not be completed for several years. For working purposes, it has therefore been assumed that dispersal would begin in 1975 and would have its movement spread out in equal stages for 10 years until 1984. The final discounted gain in resource terms for each job removed from London varies from £3,000–£8,000; this variation is explained mainly by variations in office rents between different parts of London. For reasons explained above, gain does not vary much from one area to another. An example is given in Table 3 (1).

Exchequer implications
13. As just indicated, the analysis of the costs and benefits of dispersal for the purposes of selecting dispersal proposals was (with the Treasury's agreement) carried out in terms of real effects on the whole community. However, it also is necessary to make an attempt to summarise the impact in terms of financial costs as more commonly understood.

39

14. It seems fair to assume that an analysis of the annual flows rather than single discounted sums is called for, mainly because this enables the results to be seen in a budgetary context. Table 3 (2) thus covers each of the 10 years from the assumed date of the first dispersal to the programme's assumed conclusion. Other assumptions have to be made before the analysis can proceed, however. First, it is necessary to define which items ought in practice to be counted as part of the impact on the Exchequer, since there is no agreed doctrine on this. For instance, as noted in paragraph 1, the relief of unemployment has an effect on cash flows both because of the resultant fall in social security payments and because of the increase in taxable capacity of the persons concerned, yet it is not clear whether these would normally be recognised as part of the reckoning in Exchequer terms. They are in any case highly uncertain quantities and could not in fact make a large difference to the overall picture (though it is worth noting that the effect would be to increase the financial attractions of dispersal), so they have not been included in the reckoning.

15. Another awkward case is exemplified by rail fares. Since British Rail is a nationalised industry, it seems logical to argue that what the Exchequer lost on extra rail fares it would gain by having to finance a smaller British Rail deficit, except to the extent that the costs of running the railway system really are increased by the extra traffic generated by dispersal. In other words, it is argued that resource costs and Exchequer costs can be regarded as identical in this case and, since the estimate of the resource costs involved was minimal, they have again been ignored in the assessment of Exchequer implications.

16. Ideally, the costs of extra telecommunications equipment and use should have been taken into account. Conventional telephone costs are likely to be a trivial item, but it is not so clear how much might be spent on more sophisticated equipment; indeed, how much is spent is largely optional. Because of this, and because it is probable that use of such equipment would create savings in staff time at least of the same magnitude as the cost of the equipment, it has not been considered necessary to include an estimate in the analysis.

17. The items which have been included are as follows:
   (a) Office rents
   (b) Site and office construction costs
   (c) Transfer grants to staff
   (d) Salary differentials

Rents and construction costs

18. This part of the estimate is greatly affected simply by the assumed split, at receiving locations, between occupation of leased and of Crown built offices. There is no easy way of predicting this, but Table 3 (2) makes the working assumption that Crown offices are used to the maximum extent, compatible with the first moves occurring in 1975. If it is estimated that it will typically take five years from its acquisition to completion, this

40

implies that with sites acquired in mid-1973, say, it would be 1978 before dispersed work could move into Crown buildings and that dispersals in 1975–77 inclusive would be housed in leased accommodation. Since it is also assumed, for the purpose of this analysis, that dispersal takes place in 10 equal stages between 1975 and 1984 this implies a 70/30 split between Crown and leased accommodation.

19. The Department of the Environment has estimated that typical site costs per job in the provinces might be of the order of £700 (though this presupposes good central locations) and that construction costs might be of the order of £3,000 per job. Site costs incurred in years before 1975 are not covered by Table 3 (2). Assuming (as the Appendix does) 30,000 dispersed jobs, this would imply site costs totalling £2·1 million in 1973 and 1974 as well as from 1975 to 1977, but no offsetting gains in these early years unless some small dispersals got under way more quickly than is assumed.

20. Typical rents in provincial locations are taken as £1·20 per square foot.

21. Turning to the savings from vacating premises in London, one is faced with the apparent difficulty that average rents actually paid on the leased part of the estate are of the order of only £1.50–£2 per square foot. It does not follow, however, that the savings to the Exchequer of vacating premises will only be of this order. There are two main reasons for this. First, even if the civil service only vacated the older property held on long leases (*i.e.* that which makes the average as low as it is) it would none the less be possible in most cases to sub-let at current market rates or obtain a substantial premium for surrender. Second, dispersal would enable estate managers to cease or slow down the search for the new premises which are constantly required to cater for growth plus the cessation of old leases. New premises are currently being obtained at an average figure of about £7.50 per square foot.

22. Taking these two factors into account, it seems not unreasonable to estimate an average Exchequer gain of around £6 per square foot (not £7.50, since some of the long low-rent leases might be associated with older premises which would not command rentals as high as the new premises which are currently being acquired). We have assumed that Crown buildings being erected in London would go ahead regardless of dispersal, since the financial case for having them is so strong; thus there would be no saving of construction costs.

Transfer costs

23. It has been assumed that it costs an average of £1,000 to cover the costs of an officer on permanent transfer and that half of the staff in post do transfer with the work. In itself, the resultant cost is not very great in relation to benefits, but it is worth bearing in mind that if as a result of the present review it were necessary to concede a more generous treatment to transferred staff than at present and if (as seems inescapable) the new treatment were to apply to *all* officers on permanent transfer every year, then the additional costs could be fairly substantial. For instance, if

even an extra £100 per officer were applied to the 10,000 or so officers who are involved in permanent transfer every year, this would give a total of £1 million per annum (and again would probably commence before any dispersals got under way).

Salary costs

24. The only item here is the saving of the London salary weighting. In most cases it is the Inner London weighting of £175 per annum that is involved. No doubt this will rise slightly over time in real terms, but it has been assumed static for ease of exposition.

Conclusions

25. Table 3 (2) shows net costs arising in the first few years of dispersal (plus site costs and possibly transfer costs arising in the previous two years). The account is in the black by 1980 (the sixth year of dispersal) and net gains rise to well over £23 million per annum by the end of the assumed programme. They would be higher than this to the extent that specific transfer grants cease after 1984 (adding £1·5 million to the savings) and lower to the extent that concessions were made on transfer allowances generally.

26. The conclusion that annual savings of this magnitude should be arising from 1984 onwards is not open to very substantial modification by different asumptions about the split between leasing and Crown building, since by definition the building programme would still have to be completed by 1984. Clearly, however, the net costs in the early years would be further increased if Crown buildings were used for a higher proportion of dispersed work, but given the time lags involved in new buildings this would also tend to mean delaying the entire dispersal programme, thus eroding the economic justification somewhat by postponing the resource benefits further into the future.*

Consequences of dispersal for civil service manpower

27. It is difficult to generalise about the manpower implications of dispersal before Departments receive Ministerial decisions on numbers and locations. It is only when Departments have a definite decision to disperse certain areas of work to a particular place and to a certain timetable that they will be able to assess the manpower implications accurately.

---

* *Note on the Research Councils by Sir Henry Hardman*

The dispersal of the three Research Councils included in my recommendations would require financial assistance from the Government, over and above the provisions of the Science Budget, the purpose of which is to promote research and development in their respective areas. Although dispersal may in time yield savings on operating costs, the moves themselves will produce additional short-term costs, over and above the Councils' normal administrative costs. It would be unreasonable to expect the Councils to meet these within their existing budgets and I accordingly recommend that the agreed costs of the move should be met by the Government. I also recommend that the Councils should have access to the services of the Property Services Agency in relation to the procurement of offices at their dispersal locations.

28. A preliminary appraisal has been carried out, however, on the basis of the recommendations made in the report. This suggests that in the short term there are likely to be increases in the manpower required, of the order of an average of 60 posts for every 1,000 to be dispersed. This would comprise staff engaged on dispersal management (as indicated in Appendix 8, on the provision of support services for staff) and staff to plan the move and to minimise its disruptive effects on work prior to and during dispersal. It would also cover the training of new staff taken on at the dispersal location. In the longer term, it is likely that there would be a permanent increase in staff to compensate for loss of official time through travel to and from the dispersal location, to provide for liaison offices in London and as a result of easier recruitment at the dispersal location. This increase, which would come after dispersal had been implemented, would probably be an average of 30 posts for every 1,000 dispersed. Both the shorter and longer-term implications are considered in some detail in paragraphs 30–33.

29. The present review has not included a study of the manpower effects of the dispersals of the 1960s and it is in any event too soon to gauge with any certainty the long-term effect of many of them. Moreover, such a study would have encountered serious difficulties. First, records have not been kept in a form which would easily enable this element in a dispersed Department's manpower changes to be isolated; superficially relevant changes could well mask other causes. Second, past dispersal could be of limited relevance to future dispersal. The units dispersed hitherto have usually been selected on the grounds that they constituted readily separable blocks of " executive " work, not closely linked with policy formulation in London. The recommendations in the present report are founded on different principles. It must also be doubtful whether experience of the units of the Scottish Office and of the Welsh Office in London, because of the special nature of their role and coverage, can be regarded as a guide to the long-term size of the rear links which certain Departments might need to leave in London. At a later stage, however, individual Departments may be able to rely on previous dispersal experience as some guide to their requirements for carrying through the next round of dispersal.

30. To take the short term first, most factors must operate towards increasing manpower. First, all Departments which disperse work will need to set up a dispersal unit with support services for planning the operation, discussing it with staff representatives and actually carrying it out. The work would include the proper management of the staff affected, the transfer of some staff to other work in London, the setting up of the new offices in the regions and recruitment and training of new staff. Much of this work will have to be carried on both in London and at the dispersal locations, with a considerable amount of travelling in between. Similarly, the normal Departmental work will be affected in the transitional period. The support services especially, but also those in operational units responsible for carrying out the Department's policies, are likely to need some reinforcement, since it will be important to ensure smooth functioning simultaneously in the old offices and the new to prevent any disruption to Departmental work and services.

31. It is likely that Departments will begin to appoint staff to the dispersal management units very soon after decisions are taken, except perhaps in cases where the dispersal is to take place at a later stage in the programme. Departments' provisional assessments suggest that such units will account for an average of a quarter of the short-term increases in staff, *i.e.* in the region of 15 posts for every 1,000 dispersed. The remaining 45 posts per 1,000 will consist largely of reinforcements to the operational units, including an element of duplication during the transitional period of dispersal and new staff being trained to replace staff who are not dispersing with their work. In most cases, these operational increases will begin two or three years before dispersal and build up to a peak during the period of the transfer of work. The bulk of the short-term increases are likely to be temporary. Dispersal management units will cease to function after dispersal has been implemented and personnel sections will take over any continuing tasks related to the management and planning of dispersed work. Similarly, when dispersed work has settled down in its new location, the temporary reinforcement and duplication of work in operational units and the numbers of new staff undergoing training to replace those not dispersing should reduce fairly rapidly.

32. In the longer term, it is very likely that dispersal will necessitate a permanent increase in manpower, even after discounting any savings of staff in London. Increases are likely to be due largely to three factors. First, the separation of units in a Department leads to loss of official time in travelling between locations for discussions with Ministers and senior officials, in the parent Departments as well as other Departments in London, and maintaining other essential contacts. With larger scale dispersals it would be realistic to assume journeys in the opposite direction on a not dissimilar scale. This hits hardest at the more senior levels but it is probably realistic to accept that the strain cannot be taken up by individuals and that in practice some extra staff will be required. The need for this should be mitigated, but will by no means be removed, by modern telecommunications; consideration will have to be given, Department by Department, to the benefits in terms of efficiency and the savings of staff time to be set against the capital cost or rental. Also, in many cases liaison offices in London will be required to deal with the co-ordination of business with London and provide necessary services to Ministers. These could be somewhat on the lines of the units kept in Whitehall by the Scottish and Welsh Offices, though not with an identical purpose. These operational requirements are likely to account for a very large part of the longer-term staff increases. Second, increases in staff could arise from improved recruitment. Many Departments cannot recruit as well as they would wish in London and their agreed staff ceilings inevitably come to reflect this inhibition, among other factors. If this inhibition were removed there would be strong pressure for numbers to rise correspondingly. Indeed, one or two Departments have mentioned the expectation of this as a positive attraction in dispersal. Third, there are likely to be smaller increases as a result of providing office services to the dispersed office, *i.e.* messengers, office keepers, etc. It will be necessary for many Departments to increase numbers of staff in these areas in order to maintain efficient services; it will not be sufficient simply to disperse a part of existing office service units in London. In addition, a few

Departments may need to provide specialist or professional support to operational units both in London and the dispersal location and similar considerations will apply.

33. These increases should be partially offset by some savings in staff. First, it is to be hoped that there will be a decrease in the numbers of buildings now in use in London and thus in the services required for each of them. If the number of buildings drops because work now housed in separate offices in London is brought together in fewer buildings elsewhere, economies of scale may result in a reduced demand for such suppporting staff as telephonists, messengers, registry staff and custodial and cleaning staff. Second, easier recruitment, particularly of typing, secretarial and clerical staff should produce better quality which, in the long run, should slightly reduce the overall need. Taken together, the savings in these two areas are unlikely to be substantial, however, and the provisional assessments by Departments suggest that there will be a longer-term net increase of staff of around an average of 30 posts for every 1,000 dispersed.

34. No more than a very approximate assessment of the long-term manpower implications can thus be safely hazarded but, as with the short-term, the foregoing are among the factors which individual Departments will need to take into account in making firmer assessments. In the event, it is likely that the needs of different Departments will not be precisely comparable. This is principally because of two major factors which need to be taken into account. These are the distance over which dispersal is required and the proportion of non-mobile staff in the areas of work to be dispersed. As explained in Appendix 6, greater distance in general leads to greater loss of official time in travel (and the net loss of time will vary between Departments even over the same distance according to the number of essential face-to-face links with contacts in London) and this, in turn, will lead to the need for greater compensation in the form of extra staff. Also, distance is likely to affect staff turnover prior to and during dispersal. The results of the study of the human aspects of dispersal (Appendix 8) suggest that it is possible that the great bulk of non-mobile staff would prefer not to disperse, particularly to unpopular locations (largely those most distant from London). The greater the distance of dispersal and the larger the proportion of non-mobile staff, the greater will be the turnover of staff, so that for affected Departments the recruitment and training of new staff may well be well above the provisional average suggested in paragraph 31. Conversely, Departments required to disperse over a relatively short distance are likely to require fewer additional staff. But there are other influences on the position of individual Departments. Some may be dispersed to locations where they already have a dispersed office; some may be dispersed *in toto,* necessitating the creation of a liaison office in London; some Departments may eventually have more scope for savings of staff in London through reduced fragmentation; and, finally, experience in recruiting staff in London differs between Departments so that the scope for filling vacant posts after dispersal will also differ. All of these factors may lead to higher or lower increases as a result of dispersal than the overall average.

35. The preceding paragraph underlines the impossibility of reaching an accurate assessment at this stage of the manpower implications of dispersal and the need to consider the issue Department by Department after decisions have been taken.

TABLE 3 (1)

The following table is an example of the analysis in the paper. It is based on a hypothetical block of work in central London consisting of 100 jobs—half at Executive Officer level and above, and half below Executive Officer level. Newcastle is used as a typical development area receiving location. The working assumption is that 75 per cent of the more senior grades and 25 per cent of the junior grades transfer in post to the new location. Staff are assumed to require an average of 150 square feet of space each.

Item	Cost (−) or Benefit (+) £	Percentage of total
Differential cost of office space (assuming requirements total 15,000 sq. ft)	+400,200	60
Differential cost of rates on office premises	+126,450	19
Miscellaneous extra costs (mainly communications)	−14,800	−2
Differential house prices for transferred employees	+50,500	8
Differential commuting costs for transferred employees ...	+33,500	5
Cost of moving transferred employees	−21,000	−3
Loss of wives' income	−27,200	−4
Income-multiplier gain created by transferred employees ...	+22,825	3
Differential cost of filling local vacancies (including relief of unemployment)	+92,550	14
Total	+663,025	100

TABLE 3 (2) EXCHEQUER COSTS AND BENEFITS ASSUMING 30,000 JOBS DISPERSED

£'000

	Cost (−) or Benefit (+)	1975	1976	1977	1978	1979	1980	1981	1982	1983	1984
Saving in London rent[1] ...	+	—	2,700	5,400	8,100	10,800	13,500	16,200	18,900	21,600	24,300
Cost of rented accommodation in typical provincial location[1]	−	540	1,080	1,620	1,620	1,620	1,620	1,620	1,620	1,620	1,620
Site costs in typical provincial location	−	2,100	2,100	2,100	2,100	2,100	—	—	—	—	—
Construction costs in typical provincial location[2] ...	−	3,000	6,000	9,000	9,000	9,000	9,000	9,000	6,000	3,000	—
Transfer allowances	−	1,500	1,500	1,500	1,500	1,500	1,500	1,500	1,500	1,500	1,500
Salary costs (saving of London weighting on the 50 per cent of the staff recruited locally)	+	263	525	788	1,050	1,313	1,575	1,838	2,100	2,363	2,625
Cost or Benefit		−6,877	−7,455	−8,032	−5,070	−2,107	+2,955	+5,655	+11,880	+17,843	+23,810

(1) Assumes 150 sq. ft per job and a lag of one year between the release of London premises and realisation of savings in rental.

(2) Assumes the £3,000 per job to be spread in three equal stages over the last three years of the total time from site purchase to completion.

APPENDIX 4

THE STUDY OF COMMUNICATIONS PATTERNS

Introduction

1. The effect of earlier dispersal exercises has been to remove from London some work which is wholly or relatively self-contained, leaving behind staff working on policy business in support of Ministers, at the senior levels of Departmental organisation and management, and in such offices of public access as the Companies Registration Office and the Passport Office.

2. The character of the links which tie work to London is important. London is the capital. Apart from being the seat of Parliament and of central Government, it is also the chosen location for the headquarters of numerous business organisations, of local government associations and of such other organised bodies as the trades unions; it is the centre of the country's economic life, being the chief location for banking and insurance; it is the main centre of the country's cultural life; and it is also by far the most convenient place from which to travel to and from different parts of the country. Government work is accordingly only one part of the complex network of communication to be found in London and which constitutes a major part of London's character as the capital. The juxtaposition of different communities of interest in the capital has come about for their mutual convenience and for ease of despatching business; there is no difficulty in Ministers and officials on the one hand and the bodies which do business with Government on the other seeing each other, whether at short notice or not.

3. In order to explore the strength of these links and the consequences of breaking them, two things were necessary. First, a method of discriminating between the more and less important claims for a London base, so that the least damaging candidates for dispersal could be identified. Second, a method of setting against these disadvantages any advantages which might accrue from dispersal, so that the consequences might be thoroughly explored. The first of these is dealt with in this Appendix and the second in Appendix 6.

4. It is through communications of one sort or another that Government business is carried out efficiently. It may be expected, therefore, that changes in the effectiveness of different modes of communication will affect the efficiency of despatch of Government business. Communication may be over the telephone, on paper, through signals or telex apparatus or other telecommunications device or at a meeting face to face. Officials will themselves decide from day to day which forms of communication are most appropriate to the efficient conduct of their business. The chief component of efficiency in the context of dispersal is the ability of Ministers, officials and others to meet each other face to face. Face-to-face communication is the essential ingredient of Government work in the processes of consultation, briefing, negotiation and decision-making which constitute a substantial part of administration (in any organisation, but especially so in Government)—and it is important not just at the most senior levels, but well down into Departments, certainly at Higher Executive Officer

49

level and sometimes down to Executive Officer and Clerical Officer level. It often occurs at very short notice and is substantially impaired if the staff involved are separated. Communication on the telephone or on paper is much less important, because it need not be substantially impaired by further dispersal.

5. It is worth emphasising the importance of informal contacts also. These contribute a lot to effective working relationships and so make a significant contribution to the despatch of policy work and to relations between colleagues and between Departments and their non-Government contacts.

6. It was decided, therefore, to conduct a study in all Government Departments (and in those other bodies covered by the Location Review) of their patterns of face-to-face communications. In some, additional studies were carried out if the Department felt that there was an aspect of its pattern of communication which required separate analysis, for example of the implications of the annual Budget cycle in the Board of Inland Revenue and HM Customs and Excise and of signals traffic in the Ministry of Defence. The main constituents of each study were:]

(a) An examination of the pattern of contacts at the most senior levels of the Department (including Ministers, the Permanent Secretary and his immediate subordinates).

(b) An examination of patterns of face-to-face communication between the "blocks of work" of which the Department is composed (usually Under Secretary commands) and between them and other Departments and the "outside world".

(c) An examination of the implications of the Department's Parliamentary business (legislation, debates and Questions) for patterns of face-to-face contact.

7. Before the studies are described in detail, it is necessary to draw attention to some features in order to explain how the studies were conducted and the philosophy underlying them. First, the studies were designed to provide an objective data base across all Departments by using a common approach. This would then allow subjective judgment to be applied to the subsequent analysis of the data, which would be free of any element of value judgment about the "importance" of particular links. Second, the studies were designed to ensure that the objective part of the data collected was realistic and also to collect separately any other factors bearing on the relative importance of parts of the data. This was achieved partly by using teams drawn from the Departments; partly by involving each member of a Department down to Higher Executive Officer (and sometimes below that level) in providing information; and partly by explaining fully to all senior staff, both orally and on paper, the importance of the part they had to play in checking the validity of the information at different stages. Finally, it was recognised that present patterns of communication may well reflect inhibitions due to the fragmentation of Departments in buildings throughout London; the study was, therefore, designed to collect data both on the present pattern and on a preferred pattern, assuming that fragmentation had been corrected.

Communications Study Teams and Timetable

8. Because of the large number of Departments to be studied, it was necessary to take them in groups. All studies were completed by autumn 1972. Each Department appointed a small team to conduct the study.

9. Each Departmental team was supported by a "linkman" from a central review team in the Civil Service Department, which also provided a two-day introductory course to explain the whole exercise.

Agreement on Blocks of Work

10. Each Department was divided into "blocks of work". These are essentially groups of staff with an identifiable responsibility and who are in day-to-day contact with each other to such an extent that they should be considered indivisible for the purposes of a dispersal exercise. The most usual grouping for a block of work was that of an Under Secretary command, but there were variations on this common pattern. Agreement on the division of each Department was reached only after consulting all senior staff involved. Ministers and their private offices, Permanent Secretaries and Deputy Secretaries were each treated as separate blocks of work. So also were those heads of Divisions or Branches who had agreed to divide their commands into two or more blocks.

11. Over 1,500 blocks of work were covered by the communications studies. Reference numbers and names for each were incorporated in a comprehensive index used by all Departmental teams for the purpose of identifying contacts between blocks of work. A further 6,000 entries were added to this index, as they arose, to cover contacts with those parts of Government not covered by the Review and others outside Government altogether.

Presentations to Staff

12. An important element in the study was the need to explain its methods and purpose to the senior staff of each Department (down to at least Under Secretary level) and to Staff Side representatives. This was done at a series of presentations. In some Departments it was necessary to hold several, for example twelve in the Ministry of Defence.

Collection of Information

13. Information was collected on the following:
   (i) Patterns of contact of blocks of work.
   (ii) Patterns of contact of the most senior staff and of Ministers.
   (iii) The impact of Parliamentary business.
   (iv) Any other special features.

14. In each block of work questionnaires were completed by all staff down to Higher Executive Officer level (and sometimes lower if there was significant face-to-face contact at these levels). Departmental teams first briefed and then worked through liaison officers in order to reduce the burden of answering queries and progress chasing and to enable them to complete their studies in the time allowed. In order to simplify the

completion of questionnaires, liaison officers first identified likely contacts for their own block of work and lists of these were printed as part of the questionnaire. Staff were then asked to do the following:

(*a*) Identify contacts from the printed list whom they *typically* met *face to face* at least once a month. Add other contacts not on that list. (It was stressed that these contacts could be at formal meetings or informal or by chance, provided that they were relevant to the conduct of business.) A number of rules was established for dealing with, for example, contacts with senior staff; or contacts with common services staff, such as messengers; or for staff recording contacts with clients during the course of short term assignments (*e.g.* Management Services Divisions); or for staff whose contacts are of a cyclical nature (*e.g.* Inspectors); or for contacts with others in the course of attending Committees, etc.; or for contacts having a geographical reference. The contacts identified could, of course, be with other blocks of work within their own Department or with blocks in other Departments or with bodies outside Government altogether. (*Note.* In the first group of Departments studied, contacts at a frequency of once a quarter or more were recorded, but in subsequent groups this was changed to monthly, which reduced by about one-third the number of individual contacts recorded without affecting the total strength of that block's links by more than about 5%.)

(*b*) To record against each contact identified the typical frequency, using a scale varying from daily to once a month.

(*c*) To record against any contacts for which there were significant periods of peak contact the revised frequency, using the same scale.

(*d*) To record against any contacts whose frequency was inhibited by the fragmentation of Departments throughout London a revised frequency, assuming a preferred pattern.

(*e*) To indicate the extent to which the current pattern was likely to remain unaltered in about a year's time. (This question was seeking to establish if the work was basically of a stable pattern, rather than obtain information on impending changes, of which more junior staff would probably be unaware anyway.)

(*f*) To add any other relevant comments.

From the results of the questionnaires a number of analyses was produced to enable the Departmental team to prepare a report for each block of work.

15. The collection of information on the patterns of contact of the most senior staff (Permanent and Deputy Secretaries and the equivalent) and of Ministers was not done by questionnaire, because pilot studies indicated that their contacts were so varied that it was difficult to recall them easily and also because the urgency of meetings was sufficiently important to warrant it being included. It was decided, therefore, to keep a diary log of actual contacts over a four-week period and to use that as a basis for agreeing with the person concerned a pattern representative of typical circumstances. In addition to noting contacts during the chosen period information was also collected about:

(*a*) Notice at which the meeting was arranged, from "immediate", "2 hours" . . . to "2 days or more".

(*b*) Papers sent or received which were reckoned incapable of easy transmission over existing facsimile transmission equipment and, therefore, represented a constraint on separating the recipient and sender.

16. The results were presented to the person concerned in the form of a draft report to enable such changes as necessary to represent typical circumstances to be made. (Many have made the point that at that level there is real difficulty in defining typical circumstances.) Eventually, data on the agreed patterns of contact were submitted for computer processing in similar format to that for ordinary blocks of work.

17. Information on Parliamentary business was usually collected through each Department's Parliamentary Section. Eventually a report was agreed with the Parliamentary Clerk and others as necessary. The object was, first, to understand the Department's style of handling this business and, second, to measure the involvement of particular parts of the Department in the whole process. Parliamentary Questions, debates and legislation were covered.

18. The numbers of Parliamentary Questions arising for oral or written reply each week during the previous three years were ascertained and, over a recent four-week period, the involvement of particular blocks of work was measured. The time constraints and sizes of files involved were also covered.

19. For debates and legislation a similar analysis over three years was made. For all of these types of Parliamentary business the implications for officials were discussed.

20. Special studies were mounted, as necessary, to take account of aspects of communication felt to be relevant to particular Departments and not covered adequately by the communications study proposed. Each study resulted in an agreed report, which would be an adjunct to the main data and for consideration subsequently should those parts of the Department affected be, *prima facie*, candidates for dispersal.

Block of Work Reports

21. The Departmental teams prepared draft reports for each block of work and submitted them to the head of block. This was for two reasons. First, to obtain agreement or suggestions for changes to the pattern of contact presented and, second, to enable points to be incorporated which added to an understanding of aspects of the pattern requiring elaboration. These usually related to the importance of particular contacts (for a wide variety of reasons) or to impending changes, foreseeable or otherwise, which were likely to affect the pattern. The agreed reports then served as basic reference documents for the Review team.

22. Because of the large number of reports to be prepared, and used, a standard style was adopted. Each contained:

(*a*) Description of the functions of the block.

(*b*) Staffing and accommodation details.

(*c*) Analysis of questionnaires

(*d*) Other factors.

(*e*) Two tabulations showing details of typical monthly frequencies of contact with each contact block identified. (These are described below.)

23. The analysis of questionnaires in each report summarised the contact pattern found in terms of the block's contacts within its own Department, particularly with Ministers and senior staff; with other Departments; with bodies outside Government, but within London; and with bodies outside London. The nature of the contact was given, where relevant. This analysis was in terms of percentage " link strength " of contact. The " link strength " of contact with another block is arrived at by multiplying each officer's preferred monthly frequency of contact with that block by a weighting factor proportional to his salary scale. All staff's contacts with that block are then added together to arrive at the " link strength " of contact. This measure is thus a reflection of the value of the hours wasted should these staff decide to travel in order to maintain that contact. Appendix 6 explains how " link strengths " are used to arrive at a " communications damage " measure.

24. The tabulations included in the report do not concentrate only on " link strength ", however, but also show for each equivalent staff grade the total monthly typical frequency of contact with each individual contact block identified. Comparisons of the total typical, peak and preferred frequencies of contact are also shown in summary form.

Departmental Composite Report

25. The results of the communications study for each Department were brought together in one Composite Report. The Composite Report covers the following:

Introduction—origins and reason for the study.

Collection of Information.

Frequency of Communications—analysis of results, with supporting table showing average " link strengths " between each block of work and between them and groups of contacts outside the Department.

Internal Contacts.

Contact with other Departments.

Other London Contacts.

Other Contacts.

Parliamentary Business.

(Other Studies).

Other Relevant Factors

plus the two tables mentioned above, a diagrammatic representation of links within and without the Department and an organisation chart.

26. The Composite Report does not attempt to draw any conclusions on the dispersability of parts of the Department.

27. The Composite Reports were submitted simultaneously to the Review Co-ordinator and to the head of the Department. That marked the end of the communications study and the start of the analysis leading to the formulation of proposals for relocation and to discussions with the Department on their feasibility.

APPENDIX 5

RECEIVING LOCATIONS

General considerations

1. The Government indicated in Cmnd. 4506 that its choice of locations would be influenced by two main considerations, efficiency of operation and regional policy.

Efficiency of operation

2. The " efficiency " consideration consists of the following elements:

(a) Distance from London: What effect would increasing distance from London have on the conduct of business which required the presence of dispersed staff in London?

(b) Capacity: What is the capacity of the location in relation to existing or potential office accommodation and to the ability of the Government to get and keep staff for the local recruitment posts (see below)?

(c) Attractiveness to staff: What is the likely effect on staff dispersed from London in relation to such amenities as housing and educational facilities, the general environment (including the journey to work) and job opportunities for dependants?

Regional policy

3. Dispersal is relevant to regional policy primarily because it is a potential source of new employment in those areas which suffer from chronic unemployment and of varied employment where the main problem is imbalance in job opportunities. Secondarily, it will tend to relieve pressure on resources in the London area.

4. It is not necessary to rehearse the causes of the economic decline of those areas whose problems gave rise to a conscious regional policy or to restate at length their evident needs for injections of new work. Although office employment is a growth sector, there is an imbalance in the distribution of clerical and office work opportunities and in the relative proportions of those employed in such work in different regions. Although there are good reasons for such differences—chiefly that London is the principal office centre and that, while there are some other major centres (e.g. Bristol and Manchester), the economy of many areas is dominated by other types of work—the imbalance is regarded as damaging because, in some areas, the decline in their traditional industries has not been offset by a corresponding growth in office and service employment. A higher proportion of workers has been unemployed in assisted areas than in the rest of the country and in some sub-Regions it is difficult for school-leavers to find work matching their ability levels. There are, accordingly, manpower resources which are out of use altogether or under used (although this pattern of under-employment does not extend uniformly to all locations in an assisted area). Dispersal of civil service work would probably be of most benefit to women, whether actually in employment or potential employees (as two-thirds of all clerical jobs were held by women at the time of the 1966 Census and over half of

all clerical work in the civil service is done by women (see paragraphs 6 and 11 below)), so it is relevant to consider variations in the opportunities available to women, before considering, more generally, differences in the availability of clerical work. The sources used for this are the 1966 Sample Census, the Advance Analysis of the 1971 Census, and Civil Service Statistics 1972.

5. Data from the 1966 Sample Census on office employment (Orders XXI (clerical workers) and XXIV (administrators and managers))—data from the 1971 Census are not yet available—show that over two-fifths (42·8 per cent) of all office workers were then in the South East Region, although it had just under a third of all workers (33·2 per cent). Full details are given in Table 5 (1) at the end of this Appendix. In the country as a whole, 17 in every 100 workers were employed in offices, but in Greater London the number was as high as 25·4. In several regions there was a rough balance between their proportions (or " shares ") of all clerical workers and of all work (e.g. North West Region 12·2 : 12·7, West Midlands 8·9 : 10·0) but this conceals differences within regions and more telling indicators are the distribution of opportunities for women and the proportion of all work in each region which is clerical. (The existing distribution of civil service work is set out in Appendix 1.)

(a) Employment opportunities for women

6. Two-thirds (67·4 per cent) of the jobs in Order XXI (which totalled 3·4 million jobs in 1966) were held by women (as against 7·5 per cent of work in Order XXIV, which totalled 0·765 million jobs). Over half (56·5 per cent) of all jobs in Orders XXI and XXIV taken together were held by women (2·346 million). A large proportion of these opportunities (42·5 per cent) was in the South East, with over a quarter (25·2 per cent) in Greater London. Again, this is in part a reflection of the total population of working women to be found in the South East (over a third, 34·4 per cent), but there is a major difference between this and the overall pattern. In the country as a whole, women employed in Orders XXI and XXIV accounted for 27·3 per cent of all women in employment. In the South East, however, over a third of all women in employment (33·6 per cent) were in office employment, while in the assisted areas proportions were usually less than average:

Region	Percentage of working women in office employment	Difference from average
Scotland	24·0	−3·3
Clydeside Conurbation	27·3	—
Wales	22·8	−4·5
South East Wales	23·9	−3·4
Northern Region	22·7	−4·6
Tyneside Conurbation	27·6	+0·3
Yorkshire/Humberside	22·1	−5·2
West Yorkshire Conurbation	21·9	−5·4
North West Region	25·0	−2·3
Merseyside Conurbation	29·4	+2·1
South East Lancashire Conurbation ...	26·4	−0·9
South West Region	24·7	−2·6
South East Region	33·6	+6·3
Greater London	37·7	+10·4
Outer Metropolitan Area	31·9	+4·6

7. A somewhat similar pattern may be perceived in the Advanced Analysis of Census 1971 statistics (see Table 5 (2) at the end of this Appendix) relating to the economic position of women, large numbers of whom, as indicated above, are employed in clerical and office occupations, including the local recruitment grades of the civil service. The average proportion of women in employment in Great Britain at the Census date was 37·3 per cent, the largest being in Greater London (43·6 per cent) and the least in Wales (30·6 per cent). Above average proportions were to be found, as to be expected, in the major conurbations of West Yorkshire (40·0 per cent), South East Lancashire (40·7 per cent), and the West Midlands (41·2 per cent), while below average proportions were to be found in, among other places, the Northern Region (30·4 per cent), East Anglia (33·5 per cent), the Outer South East (33·3 per cent) and the South West Region (33·0 per cent).

(b) Regional proportions of work in Orders XXI and XXIV

8. Second, while 17 in each 100 workers (17·2 per cent) were employed in offices in 1966, there were wide differences between the South East Region on the one hand, and other regions (including the South West) on the other, on a spectrum ranging from 25·4 per cent in Greater London to 13·1 per cent in Wales (other than South East Wales), as the following list shows:

Region	Percentage of all workers employed in offices	Difference from average
(a) Regions containing assisted areas		
Scotland	14·4	−2·8
Central Clydeside Conurbation	16·7	−0·5
Wales	13·1	−4·1
South East Wales	13·8	−3·4
Northern Region	13·4	−3·8
Tyneside Conurbation	17·0	−0·2
Yorkshire/Humberside Region	14·2	−3·0
West Yorkshire Conurbation	15·2	−2·0
North West Region	16·5	−0·7
Merseyside Conurbation	18·6	+1·4
South East Lancashire Conurbation ...	17·5	+0·3
South West Region	15·0	−2·2
(b) Other Regions		
South East Region	22·1	+4·9
Greater London	25·4	+8·2
Outer Metropolitan Area	21·4	+4·2
East Midlands	13·9	−3·3
East Anglia	13·3	−3·9
West Midlands	15·4	−1·8
West Midlands Conurbation	16·5	−0·7

9. This list has three interesting features. First, only two locations outside the South East Region have above average opportunities, the Merseyside and South East Lancashire conurbations. Second, two of the three least favourable proportions are not to be found in assisted areas, but in the East Midlands and East Anglia. Third, two major locations in assisted areas are better off than the regional average and are near the national average (Central Clydeside and Tyneside); the North West Region, traditionally a focus of office work, was also near the average. However, since 1966, there

has been a down turn in the economy of many areas, at the same time as there has been a general increase in the output of school leavers with improved educational qualifications, and the 1966 pattern is not necessarily a reliable guide to relative needs. And while there are several major office centres outside London—the fact that such locations as Bristol, Cardiff, Liverpool and Manchester already have substantial concentrations of office work affects their ability to take more—it remains the case that some sub-Regions, for example Teesside, are well behind in the office growth stakes.

10. To some extent then, civil service dispersal might alleviate local problems but there are several points to be borne in mind in arriving at a balanced judgment. These are set out in the following paragraphs but should also be read in conjunction with the economic analysis of Appendix 3.

11. The first is simply that dispersal could not be expected *on its own* to make a really substantial contribution to the economic health of any city or region. Its main contribution lies in the jobs to be filled in such a place through local recruitment. Half the non-industrial civil service consists of staff in grades which are filled in this way (Civil Service Statistics 1972). The bulk of these are clerical staff (Clerical Officers and Clerical Assistants), the rest being such staff as typists, machine and duplicator operators, paper-keepers and messengers. The terms of employment of such staff do not require them to serve anywhere other than the area in which they have been recruited. The entry requirement for clerical staff is at GCE " O " level; such appointments are of interest to both school-leavers and older women, but the bulk of the two grades consists of women and girls (65 per cent), as does the annual entry (68 per cent). The remaining—and senior—grades of the Service are filled by internal promotion and by means of national competitions, with entry requirements from GCE " A " level upwards; such staff therefore are not usually recruited locally and, unlike clerical and other staff, are required to serve in any part of the country. As already indicated (in Appendix 2 and the main Report), some 86,000 posts were reviewed, of which some 31,000 are proposed for dispersal. On the basis of the blocks of work covered by the recommendations for dispersal, roughly half the jobs to be dispersed would be in the local recruitment grades; the proposal is therefore that some 15,000 jobs should be made available in new locations (although it is probable that some of the present job holders would move with their work).

12. The numbers involved therefore are simply not large enough to make a major impact unless entirely concentrated in a very few locations, which would not be practicable except, perhaps, on a very long timescale. Thus the argument may turn to the possibility of induced dispersal on the part of private companies. The private sector has not in fact been unwilling to move out of London, but has almost invariably (despite a fair amount of long-range dispersal by the civil service) come to the conclusion that it can gain virtually all the economic benefits of dispersal by relatively short-range moves, and that further movement into assisted areas proper would yield little if any further benefits. Table 5 (3) illustrates this, showing that no less than 91 per cent of the firms moving with assistance from the Location of Offices Bureau and 85 per cent of the jobs concerned are going less than

58

80 miles from London. A similar conclusion can be reached on Government dispersal, even though the Government interprets costs and benefits more widely than the private sector needs to.

13. Second, it has usually been accepted that regional policy carries real costs as well as achieving real benefits and that the organisations to encourage to relocate themselves are ideally those with the weakest links (of any kind) with London and non-assisted areas. This was formalised in the "mobile industry" concept. It will however be obvious that much of the headquarters civil service now in London, with its strong London orientation, hardly fits comfortably into this category nor has the review thrown up many results to confound this expectation.

14. Third, although dispersal has a real contribution to make, it is clearly not tailored to the needs of many areas in the way which, say, companies needing male manual workers tend to be. It is probably much better geared to the correction of an imbalance of employment (where office jobs are seriously lacking) than to the raising of a generally low level of activity. But it is the latter situation which is normally felt to have prior claim to assistance.

The locations studied

15. Ministers directed that a study should be made of a shortened list of places in the light of the broad criteria of efficiency and regional policy, the case for each being considered against a series of standard questions. As Ministers wished to avoid raising expectations prematurely, these locations (listed in paragraph 18) have not so far been made public officially. No local authority has been approached. Some (including Glasgow, Merseyside authorities, Plymouth and Teesside) have themselves approached either Ministers or senior officials. The studies carried out have accordingly been almost entirely within the resources of central Government (the Scottish and Welsh Offices, the English Economic Planning Boards and Departments with major offices in the provinces).

16. Two types of place were identified under the "efficiency" criterion, major centres of communication (in some cases already the location of such Government work as regional administration offices) and places in which certain Headquarters Departments either have a specific interest or already have dispersed work and which are, *prima facie* at least, worthy of consideration as "preferred" locations for further dispersal from those Departments. The places so identified were Basingstoke (Civil Service Department), Coventry (Ministry of Agriculture, Fisheries and Food), Darlington (Department of Education and Science), Norwich (Her Majesty's Stationery Office), Runcorn (Department of Employment), Southend (Her Majesty's Customs and Excise) and Swindon (Ministry of Defence). Croydon was also included as representative of locations at a short distance from London, should relocation over such a distance, but no further, seem warranted.*

---

* Subsequently, DHSS asked that Blackpool be considered as the preferred receiving location for some of its further dispersed work since the Department already has a substantial amount of dispersed work there.

17. The capacity of locations was considered in the light of certain points, including the Government's wish to disperse work to a few major locations, rather than scattering small units over many places. In the case of locations other than most of those which are associated with a particular Department (see paragraph 16), it has accordingly been considered whether they could sustain a dispersal amounting to a few thousand posts.

18. The results of interdepartmental studies, now confirmed by the composition of the blocks of work recommended for dispersal, suggested that, as a working guide, half the posts dispersed from London would be in the local recruitment grades and the questions asked derive from the " efficiency " considerations noted above, in paragraph 2. Conclusions on potential capacity in respect of accommodation and staffing—leaving aside any questions of distance—are set out below.

Region	Location	Capacity*
Scotland	Glasgow	5,000
Wales	Cardiff ... ...⎫	5,000
	Newport ... ...⎭	
Northern	Darlington	500
	Tyneside	2,000
	Teesside	5,000
North Western ...	Central Lancashire New Town ...	3,000
	(Preston-Leyland-Chorley)	
	Manchester	3,000
	Merseyside	3,000
	Runcorn	500
Yorkshire/Humberside	Leeds or	3,000
	Greater Bradford	2,000
East Anglia	Norwich	500
West Midlands ...	Coventry	1,500
South Western ...	Bristol	1,000 or 2,500(†)
	Plymouth	5,000
	Swindon	1,000
South Eastern ...	Basingstoke	500
	Croydon	—
	Milton Keynes	5,000(‡)
	Southend	500

Notes:

   * This is in terms of the total number of posts which could efficiently be absorbed, that is both posts in Civil Service grades where mobility is a condition of service which will be filled mostly by staff moving from London, and posts where there is no mobility requirement and most of which will be filled by local recruitment.

   (†) Over longer term.

   (‡) Could be more over longer term.

19. The capacity figures have been taken as one of the bases in working out proposals as to the number of posts which could be dispersed to particular locations. (The method of doing this is described in Appendix 6.) The capacity figures are in terms of the number of posts removed, whether these posts are to be filled by officers transferring with their work or by local recruitment. They are necessarily subject to considerable limitations, of which perhaps the main ones are as follows:

   (a) The capacity figures had to be related to the information which is now available about receiving locations. This includes the scope for building or leasing offices, recruiting staff and general amenities. There must obviously be substantial uncertainty in speculating about the future, but calculations must of course use the best information available at the time. Perhaps more important, past evidence does not suggest violent changes in such figures as the comparative rates of unemployment between different areas. Thus while the Government's current policies for helping the assisted areas may have major effects on them, nevertheless they are unlikely to affect materially the relative position as between those and other areas. The conclusion from this is that present information is the best guide, however imperfect, for making assessments as between different areas.

(b) The second feature is more difficult. Present figures may be the best guide as between different areas over the next 5 or even 5–10 years. In terms of longer timescales other features come into operation, however. Thus an area chosen as a deliberate growth area will have a higher capacity over a longer timescale than another area which is not receiving the same degree of investment in infrastructure. Obvious examples are new towns, which in their early stages necessarily cannot absorb large numbers of dispersed staff quickly. But new towns on the list of receiving locations can, over a longer period, say up to 20 years, absorb much larger numbers of staff if the expansion of their infrastructure is maintained. So for a longer period than this exercise assumes as the time in which the Government will wish to implement a dispersal programme (that is for longer periods than 10 years) higher figures for capacity could legitimately be taken for such receiving locations as Milton Keynes and Central Lancashire New Town. Exactly the same applies to the Bristol area, if that is defined as including Severnside, but depending on Government decisions about the future of Severnside as a growth area and on exactly where that growth will be allowed to occur in planning terms.

Table 5 (I) : Sample Census 1966, Part I, Table 13 : Occupation

Region	A All in employment 000s			B A as percentage of GB total			C Order XXI 000s			D Order XXIV 000s			E Orders XXI and XXIV 000s			F E as percentage of A			G E as percentage of GB total for orders XXI and XXIV		
	M	W	Total	M	W	Total	M	W	Total	M	W	Total	M	W	Total	M	W	Total	M	W	Total
GREAT BRITAIN	15,574	8,594	24,168	100	100	100	1,112	2,289	3,401	708	57	765	1,820	2,346	4,166	11·7	27·3	17·2	100	100	100
ENGLAND AND WALES	14,137	7,788	21,925	90·7	90·6	90·7	1,027	2,097	3,124	662	53	715	1,689	2,150	3,839	11·9	27·6	17·5	92·7	91·5	92·0
SCOTLAND	1,437·0	805·7	2,242·7	9·2	9·4	9·3	84·5	191·5	276·0	45·9	3·2	49·1	130·4	194·7	325·1	9·1	24·0	14·4	7·1	8·3	7·8
Central Clydeside Conurbation	485·2	286·8	772·0	3·1	3·3	3·2	34·2	77·0	111·2	16·6	0·9	17·5	50·8	77·9	128·7	10·5	27·3	16·7	2·8	3·3	3·1
WALES	759·1	339·7	1,098·8	4·9	3·9	4·6	42·4	75·9	118·3	23·8	1·6	25·4	66·2	77·5	143·7	8·7	22·8	13·1	3·6	3·3	3·4
South East Wales	547·3	248·5	795·8	3·5	2·9	3·3	32·5	58·5	91·0	17·9	1·1	19·0	50·4	59·6	110·0	9·2	23·9	13·8	2·8	2·5	2·6
Rest of Wales	211·7	91·2	302·9	1·4	1·0	1·3	9·9	17·4	27·3	5·9	0·5	6·4	15·8	17·9	33·7	7·5	19·7	11·1	0·9	0·8	0·8
NORTHERN REGION	937·4	467·1	1,404·5	6·0	5·4	5·8	53·2	104·6	157·8	28·9	1·7	30·6	82·1	106·3	188·4	8·7	22·7	13·4	4·5	4·5	4·5
Tyneside Conurbation	236·1	131·5	367·6	1·5	1·5	1·5	17·6	35·8	53·4	8·3	0·4	8·7	25·9	36·2	62·1	10·9	27·6	17·0	1·4	1·5	1·5
YORKSHIRE AND HUMBERSIDE	1,400·7	748·7	2,149·4	9·0	8·7	8·9	81·9	161·8	243·7	58·1	4·0	62·1	140·0	165·8	305·8	9·9	22·1	14·2	7·7	7·0	7·3

West Yorkshire Conurbation	512·5	316·2	828·7	3·3	3·7	3·4	32·7	67·6	100·3	24·5	1·7	26·2	57·2	69·3	126·5	11·0	21·9	15·2	3·1	2·9	3·0
NORTH WEST REGION	1,929·4	1,151·4	3,080·8	12·4	13·4	12·7	136·7	283·4	420·1	83·4	6·5	89·9	220·1	289·9	510·0	11·4	25·0	16·5	12·1	12·3	12·2
Merseyside Conurbation	372·5	219·6	592·1	2·4	2·5	2·5	31·9	63·1	95·0	13·9	1·3	15·2	45·8	64·4	110·2	12·2	29·4	18·6	2·5	2·7	2·6
South East Lancashire Conurbation	721·5	450·2	1,171·7	4·6	5·2	4·8	52·9	116·4	169·3	33·7	2·5	36·2	86·6	118·9	205·5	11·9	26·4	17·5	4·7	5·1	4·9
EAST MIDLANDS	1,013·7	533·0	1,546·7	6·5	6·2	6·4	57·2	115·0	172·2	41·1	2·5	43·6	98·3	117·5	215·8	9·7	22·0	13·9	5·4	5·0	5·2
WEST MIDLANDS	1,555·8	852·1	2,407·9	10·0	9·9	10·0	82·9	213·4	296·3	70·9	4·8	75·7	153·8	218·2	372·0	9·9	25·7	15·4	8·4	9·3	8·9
West Midlands Conurbation	763·6	437·4	1,201·0	4·9	5·1	5·0	42·4	117·6	160·0	35·8	2·4	38·2	78·2	120·0	198·2	10·2	27·5	16·5	4·3	5·1	4·7
EAST ANGLIA	464·7	217·8	682·5	2·9	2·5	2·8	24·8	49·5	74·3	15·6	1·1	16·7	40·4	50·6	91·0	8·7	23·2	13·3	2·2	2·2	2·2
SOUTH EAST REGION	5,049·7	2,958·6	8,008·3	32·4	34·4	33·2	483·4	967·9	1,451·3	301·9	28·9	330·8	785·3	995·8	1,781·1	15·5	33·6	22·1	43·0	42·5	42·8
Greater London	2,410·4	1,568·2	3,978·6	15·4	18·2	16·4	279·5	574·9	854·4	140·8	17·6	158·4	420·3	592·5	1,012·8	17·4	37·7	25·4	23·0	25·2	24·3
Outer Metropolitan Area	1,496·5	789·3	2,285·8	9·5	9·2	9·5	128·4	244·2	372·6	110·3	7·2	117·5	238·7	251·4	490·1	15·9	31·9	21·4	13·1	10·7	11·8
SOUTH WEST REGION	1,026·3	519·9	1,546·2	6·6	6·0	6·4	65·1	126·0	191·1	38·7	2·4	41·1	103·8	128·4	232·2	10·1	24·7	15·0	5·7	5·5	5·6

TABLE 5 (2)   ECONOMIC POSITION OF WOMEN

Region and sub-Region	Population of working age*	In employment†	Percentage
GREAT BRITAIN	23·208m.	8·660m.	37·3
ENGLAND AND WALES	20·961m.	7·847m.	37·4
SCOTLAND	2·247m.	813,200	36·2
Central Clydeside Conurbation ...	735,700	275,525	37·4
Rest of Scotland	1·511m.	537,675	35·5
WALES	1·177m.	360,110	30·6
NORTHERN REGION	1·414m.	486,505	34·6
Tyneside Conurbation	351,535	127,875	36·4
Rest of Region	1·062m.	358,635	33·9
YORKSHIRE/HUMBERSIDE	2·049m.	750,610	36·7
West Yorkshire Conurbation... ...	745,270	299,295	40·0
Rest of Region	1·300m.	451,315	34·6
NORTH WEST REGION	2·898m.	1·114m.	38·5
Merseyside Conurbation	546,560	200,670	36·7
South East Lancashire Conurbation...	1·026m.	418,380	40·7
Rest of Region	1·325m.	495,150	37·5
EAST MIDLANDS	1·424m.	543,395	38·0
WEST MIDLANDS	2·128m.	845,695	39·8
West Midlands Conurbation ...	992,015	409,125	41·2
Rest of Region	1·136m.	463,510	40·7
EAST ANGLIA	719,185	241,415	34·0
SOUTH EAST REGION	7·513m.	2·959m.	39·3
Greater London	3·293m.	1·439m.	43·6
Outer Metropolitan Area	2·240m.	860,415	38·4
Outer South East	1·979m.	659,615	33·3
SOUTH WEST REGION	1·652m.	546,330	33·0

Source: Census 1971 Great Britain Advance Analysis (HMSO, 1972), Table 2.

* Total population, all age groups, minus those born in the year groups 1961–65 and 1966–71.   (Some of those born in the year group 1956–60 are at work, although the majority —not separately identified in Table 2—are still in full-time education.)

† Those who were in a job at some time during the week before the Census and classified as " Economically active persons in employment ".

TABLE 5 (3) DISTANCE THAT CLIENTS OF THE LOCATION OF OFFICES BUREAU HAVE MOVED OR ARE MOVING

Distance from central London	No. of firms	Percentage of firms	No. of jobs	Percentage of jobs
Inside GLC area	535	45	35,884	37
Beyond GLC area—				
19 miles	140	12	7,853	8
20–39 miles	269	22	20,368	21
40–59 miles	67	6	5,731	6
60–79 miles	73	6	12,588	13
Over 80 miles...	114	9	15,260	15
Total...	1,198	100	97,684	100

Source: Location of Offices Bureau, Annual Report 1971–72 Table 10, page 37

305375

C

APPENDIX 6

THE COMPUTER ANALYSIS AND THE CALCULATION OF MARGINAL TRADE-OFF

Introduction

1. Appendix 4 described "link strength" as a measure of face-to-face contact. This Appendix describes how damage to efficiency may be measured. It then shows how, with the aid of computer models, a first choice of dispersal proposals may be made on the basis of numerical criteria and composite measures, particularly marginal trade-off. Finally, it discusses the numerical aspects of choosing receiving locations for work which is considered dispersable.

Communications damage

2. If the would-be participants in a meeting are separated as the result of dispersal, some damage to efficiency will result. The courses of action open are:

(a) to abandon the meeting

(b) for one or more participants to travel

(c) to substitute current forms of telecommunication like the post or telephone for the meeting

(d) to make use of some novel and perhaps better means of telecommunication as a substitute for the meeting.

The last of these is the subject of the investigation into telecommunications whose methods and findings are described in Appendix 7. It is assumed that the post and telephone could contribute little to the avoidance of damage because they are already used in such a way as to avoid unnecessary meetings. It is the first two courses, then, which are taken into account in the measure of damage.

3. If one or more participants travel, some penalty in fares and expenses is incurred. This is taken into account in estimating the overall resource effects of a particular dispersal. It is, however, the absence of participants from their own offices for the period of travel that constitutes the main penalty which must be taken into account in the measure of damage. It seems reasonable to assume that the longer the absence, the greater the damage, and so damage is taken as being pro rata to the time spent in travel (the "separation" time).

4. In order to aggregate the damage incurred by the various individuals in a block of work, some indication of the relative importance of their time is needed. Salary is taken as the indicator on the basis that the Civil Service pays the worth of what it gets in the working time of its staff. Thus, the damage incurred each month in separating a block of work from one of its contacts is obtained by multiplying the preferred frequency of contact of any individual by a salary weighting, adding the results over all individuals in the block, and multiplying the result by the separation. (It will be recalled from Appendix 4 that this is the same as multiplying link strength by separation.) Salary weighting is obtained by taking the ratio

67

of mean salary for a grade to the mean salary of an Executive Officer. Damage is, then, in units of "equivalent Executive Officer hours wasted in travel". An interpretation of a unit of damage is given in the Annex.

5. The effects of abandoning meetings or contacts have been taken into account by observing the discrepancy between preferred frequency and actual frequency of contact in those cases where the parties are already separated. Analysis of questionnaire information shows that in about half the cases meetings are not abandoned however great the separation. For the remaining cases it has been assumed that, when faced with the need to travel, an individual will decide to abandon the meeting if he feels the damage so incurred is less than that caused by travel. (The value of any meeting is therefore equivalent to the damage caused by the travel time at which it would just be abandoned.) Using this assumption and observing how the chance of abandonment increases with the time of separation, it has been possible to calculate the proportions of meetings having a certain value. From this, the damage caused by any given separation has been calculated. It consists of two parts—damage which would result from travelling to a certain proportion of meetings and damage resulting from abandoning the rest. All contacts for all blocks at a given separation yield a total damage of say X units (whether resulting from travel or abandonment). On average, over all these contacts, damage is somewhat less than total link strength multiplied by separation. So it is concluded that if X were divided by the total link strength, the result would be a quantity which is less than the separation. This is called the "effective separation". Damage from either travel or abandonment is, then, link strength multiplied by effective separation. (The idea of effective separation may be illustrated by an example. Consider a group of 100 contacts whose average link strength is L. Say their dispersal involves a separation of 6 hours. Without considering abandonment we would say that the damage is $6 \times 100 \times L$. At this separation, the calculations based on observation of the chance of abandonment might show 45 contacts abandoned. The value of these contacts would vary, but by observation we know that most of the values would be very small; on average they might come to less than one hour of separation, say $\frac{8}{9}$ of an hour. The damage over all 100 contacts is $6 \times 55 \times L + \frac{8}{9} \times 45 \times L = 330 \times L + 40 \times L = 370 \times L$. In other words, a measure of probable damage can be obtained by multiplying $3 \cdot 7 \times 100 \times L$ and the damage is as if the separation had been $3 \cdot 7$. For a separation of 6 hours there is thus an effective separation of $3 \cdot 7$ hours.)

Criteria

6. A dispersal proposal must be judged in the light of many criteria. They include views on the structure and organisation of Departments, special considerations noted during the course of communications surveys, ideas on flexibility in modes of working and so on. It is clear that by no means all criteria can be reduced to numerical form and it would be unwise in many cases to attempt this. However, with some criteria it is possible and where the units of measurement are the same (*e.g.* £ gain or loss of resources) they can be added and subtracted. The result of this process has been to produce three numerical criteria:

68

(*a*) Communications damage, which reflects the effect on the efficiency of the service. The units have been described in the previous paragraphs. The amount of damage is roughly proportional to the distance from London over which work is moved.

(*b*) Resource gain, which combines a variety of effects on national resources. All these effects are expressed in £ and can be totalled. The amount of gain does not vary significantly between the receiving locations under study.

(*c*) Number of jobs dispersed. This quantity reflects the social effects (*i.e.* the creation of employment opportunities), but again does not vary between receiving locations.

7. For any Department of appreciable size, there are many blocks of work, each of which may or may not be proposed for dispersal. The number of possible, but not necessarily sensible, proposals for the Department as a whole can therefore be very large. In order to choose a few proposals for further discussion with the Department, the numerical criteria have been used as indicators. The problem at this point is how to weigh and balance three mutually incommensurate criteria.

8. It turns out that on average the resource gain to be derived from moving jobs to a particular location is roughly proportional to the number moved. This is chiefly because, while there are differences between the gain per "mobile" job, where the incumbent moves with the work, and the gain per "immobile" job, where the incumbent probably does not move, such differences are swamped by factors common to all jobs, especially the cost of accommodation. This means that the total figure for resource gain for a dispersal could alone give a rough guide to the number of jobs it covers and that, conversely, the number of jobs to be moved could give a rough guide to the amount of resource gain to be expected. The benefit attributable to dispersal can, in general, then, be indicated by either resource gain or number of jobs. But, although this principle applies to the average case, there can be some significant variation about this average, because blocks of work differ—they produce more or less resource gain per job moved. It was therefore considered preferable to formulate a weighted sum of resource gain and number of jobs moved as a measure of the benefit due to dispersal and to apply this throughout. As long as each quantity was adequately represented, the precise weight given to each was not considered of great importance. Resource gain and number of jobs to be moved were therefore combined into a single criterion—"benefit" (which was interpreted as resource gain plus a multiple* of the number of jobs to be moved).

---

* The multiple was 7. This was because, at the time it was chosen, it was estimated that about £7,000 of resources would be gained, on average, by dispersing a single job. Because resource gain is measured in units of £1,000, moving one job gives a resource "score" of 7. Multiplying each job by 7 will then give a similar "score" for social effect (or social benefit). (In the actual recommendations, the average resource gain differs somewhat from £7,000, but not so much as to warrant a change in the multiple.) For example, if the dispersal of a block of 100 jobs produces an average resource gain of £7,000 per job, the total resource gain is £700,000 (or 700 units of resource gain); the score for social benefit is taken as $100 \times 7 = 700$, measured in units commensurate with units of resource gain, so that the overall score for benefit is 1,400 units (*i.e.* 700 units of resource gain plus 700 units to represent jobs moved). Equally, if the dispersal of another block of 100 jobs produces an average resource gain of £4,000 per job, the score for benefit is 1,100 units (*i.e* 400 units of resource gain plus 700 units to represent jobs moved).

9. As a result, the balancing of criteria was reduced to a problem involving just two, damage and benefit. These criteria are expressed in mutually incompatible units, the former in terms of equivalent man-hours wasted and the latter in terms of units of benefit. If it were possible to value a unit of damage in benefit terms, one could compare any two dispersal proposals and decide which, on this basis, appeared better. But *a priori* valuations of this kind are not acceptable in the dispersal context because damage to efficiency cannot be repaired by the simple purchase of extra man-hours of effort.

10. It is however feasible to test the effect of a variety of *possible* valuations and find which proposal appears as the best for each. The possible valuations are referred to elsewhere in this report as "link weights", this being the term which has been commonly used in discussion with Departments. When the valuation put on avoiding damage is very low, the best proposal will be that which recommends total dispersal. When the valuation is very high, the best proposal will be that which recommends no dispersal. At intermediate valuations there will be partial dispersals which appear best. A computer model was used to give a series of "best" proposals over the range of valuations of damage.

11. This model was used for each Department individually and for a variety of possible receiving locations for each Department. Two useful features were observed in practice. First, the blocks of work dispersed in a particular "best" proposal nearly always included the blocks dispersed in a less severe "best" proposal. In other words, increased severity of dispersal simply means the addition of some extra blocks rather than a completely different selection. This means that blocks of work can be listed in an order of dispersability. Second, the order of dispersability varies little according to which receiving location is being considered.

Composite measures and marginal trade-off

12. The purpose of using the computer model to produce an order of dispersability was to select, out of the very many possible proposals for a Department, relatively few which are "best" and therefore likely to be sensible. From this set, an even smaller number needed to be chosen for discussion with the Department. Although the discussion was on a fairly detailed basis, including the consideration of individual communication links, the preliminary choice could be made on the basis of slightly aggregated information. This took the form of a number of composite measures:

(*a*) Average damage per job dispersed.

(*b*) Damage for each job suffering broken links on dispersal ("damage per damaged job").

(*c*) Marginal trade-off.

13. In appraising a proposal in detail, the damage incurred in individual cases (by person, grade, block, etc.) will need examination, but as a rough guide the average damage for each job dispersed can be of value. This measure does, however, average over all dispersed jobs, including those—usually in the junior grades—which are themselves unaffected in

70

communications terms. A slightly better approximation to the individual case is, then, the damage as shared between those jobs which *do* incur some sort of damage. This is the " damage per damaged job ".

14. Marginal trade-off has proved to be the most useful composite measure. The principle is simply to see whether, in comparing a " best " proposal with the next most severe one, the added benefit is worth incurring the added damage. If it is judged to be worth having, the more severe proposal is provisionally adopted and the process of looking at the next more severe one is repeated. Arithmetically, the process is fairly simple. For any pair of neighbouring " best " proposals the benefit and damage are found in each case. From these four quantities the difference in benefit and difference in damage are found. By division the amount of benefit per unit of damage is calculated. This is the marginal trade-off.

15. Marginal trade-off is, of course, only a measure, and the desirable value must be a matter of judgment. The measure is particularly useful in arriving at a comparison between Departments. The aim has been to ensure a broad measure of equity by requiring similar marginal trade-offs across Departments, but this principle has not been followed exactly because of the many non-numerical factors and special circumstances which have had to be taken into account. Because the value of marginal trade-off depends on differences in damage and because damage depends on separation, it is evident that marginal trade-off will vary with the remoteness of the receiving location. To compare proposals a single location must be used as a bench-mark. Bristol was chosen for this purpose, as an example of a town some 120 miles from London (although other locations could equally well have been chosen) and all proposals were evaluated for comparison purposes as though Bristol had been the receiving location.

16. It can be shown that there is a very simple relationship between the valuation of damage in benefit terms (mentioned in paragraphs 9 and 10) and marginal trade-off. In fact any " best " proposal remains so for any valuation (" link weight ") which lies between the marginal trade-off to the next most severe proposal and the marginal trade-off to the next less severe proposal. Thus the hypothetical valuations are rough guides to marginal trade-off.

Choice of receiving location

17. It was decided that, for the purpose of discussion with Departments, up to three provisional proposals should normally be suggested. The numerical and other considerations described so far were used to produce up to three proposals of varying severity. Discussion with each Department has led to final versions which might form part of the recommended set of dispersals. These proposals have with a few exceptions (*e.g.* Norwich for HMSO), been independent of the receiving location. The next stage, therefore, was to choose appropriate receiving locations, bearing in mind the demands of efficiency and regional policy and also the possible restrictions on the capacity of locations in terms of the numbers of jobs they could accept.

18. The method used was, first, to treat the smallest dispersal for a Department as a single entity, very much like a block of work. To this

71

was added, for each Department, that group of blocks, considered as another entity, which would yield the next larger dispersal. To this again was added the next group of blocks, again as an entity, which would yield the maximum dispersal suggested. The situation then was that, for each Department, there were up to three " super-blocks " under consideration. The composition of these super-blocks was sometimes varied after discussion with Departments.

19. For each super-block the benefit and damage associated with dispersal to each possible receiving location were calculated. For a given valuation of damage it was then possible to draw up an order of dispersability of all super-blocks.

20. Given the list of receiving locations and their maximum capacities, it then became possible to attempt to allocate work to places so that
  (a) no location received more jobs than its capacity would allow
  (b) there was a reasonable spread of work between regions
  (c) unless otherwise considered, no Department was split between different receiving locations
  (d) the most dispersable super-block was allocated to the most distant location, the next dispersable to the next most distant location and so on, subject to the restrictions in (a), (b) and (c) above.

21. This process was repeated, progressively restricting the choice of numbers and locations for each Department in the light of discussions with them and the other considerations set out above. The complexity of this procedure again necessitated the use of a computer as an aid.

22. The process was repeated with varying numbers for regions to show the results of different degrees of emphasis on regional policy. The report sets out three possible configurations: the recommended one, that involving more than the recommended emphasis on regional policy, and that involving more than the recommended emphasis on efficiency.

ANNEX

NUMERICAL VALUES OF DAMAGE

1. A notional discount factor applied to damage was taken as 10 per cent per annum back to 1971 for the years 1975 to 1995, assuming a constant build-up from 1975 to 1985. The value of this factor is $4 \cdot 5$.

2. Contacts, as surveyed, were in terms of number of contacts per month. To convert to annual terms the surveyed number must be multiplied by 12.

3. In order to avoid large numbers, a scaling reduction of 1,000 was applied.

4. As a result, the damage figures actually quoted are:
(link strength) $\times$ (effective separation) $\times$ $4 \cdot 5$ $\times$ $12 \div 1,000$,
  i.e. (link strength) $\times$ (effective separation) $\times$ $0 \cdot 054$.

72

5. The dispersal of any group of blocks of work to the bench-mark location (Bristol) produces a total figure of communications damage. In order to appreciate what this means in terms of broken communication links (*i.e.* total link strength), the total damage figure is divided by $0 \cdot 054$ and the result of this is in turn divided by the effective separation between London and Bristol. The London–Bristol effective separation is $3 \cdot 7$ hours. Thus, division of the damage figure by $0 \cdot 054 \times 3 \cdot 7 \ (=0 \cdot 2)$ (which in this case is the same as multiplying by 5) will give the total link strength of all the links affected by such a dispersal.

6. For the Bristol bench-mark, then, one unit of damage corresponds to five units of link strength. If this damage were incurred by an Executive Officer it would imply that he or one of his contacts would wish to travel enough to maintain five contacts per month, even after abandoning those contacts considered not worthwhile. Because an Assistant Secretary-hour is worth about three Executive Officer-hours, one unit of damage incurred at the bench-mark by an Assistant Secretary implies that he or one of his contacts would wish to travel enough to maintain one and two-thirds contacts per month.

7. Clearly this provides only a rough aid to subjective judgment. It must be remembered that a contact is defined as between a pair of blocks of work. Thus the number of *meetings* needed will be less than the number of *contacts*. Similarly, people tend to combine meetings so as to avoid unnecessary journeys, so that the number of journeys will be less than the number of meetings. Furthermore, and most important, the number of contacts per month as derived from total damage is a global figure— it applies in some average way to all grades in all blocks whose links are affected by a dispersal. There may be wide variations within any group of jobs so that a more precise appreciation of damage is needed. It is for this reason that individual dispersal proposals as submitted to Departments contain an analysis of what the damage means in terms of contacts for individual blocks.

APPENDIX 7

TELECOMMUNICATIONS

NOTE BY SIR HENRY HARDMAN

1. I have considered the contribution which existing or developing forms of telecommunication might make to overcoming the disadvantages of dispersal and the acceptability of such devices in the context of Government policy work. The nature and results of the studies undertaken so far are described in the Annex.

2. My conclusions are as follows.

3. First, there is a manifest need for an efficient telephone service, making full use of private wires. I would give this priority. Experience, including the time it is taking to introduce the Whitehall CBX system, suggests that if the handicap of the present telephone service could be overcome, it would reduce substantially the burden of dispersal.

4. Second, it follows from the nature of much face-to-face contact in the Government service (see Appendix 4, paragraph 4) that existing or expected telecommunications cannot be considered an effective substitute. Apart from considerations of security, many face-to-face meetings involving the discussion of difficult or contentious issues have a quality which would be impaired by transfer to an audio or television medium. These media are best suited, in my opinion, to such simpler tasks as briefing on non-contentious issues and the transmission of information.

5. Third, where work of the type recommended for dispersal is relocated, the main needs, apart from a reliable telephone service, are for conference facilities and for the display of documents. Some conferences, in the absence of secure methods of communication, cannot be transferred to a telecommunication medium. The same is true of some documents. For conferences which are potentially capable of transfer, television would be the best medium, but the cost studies show that, at present prices, it would be more economic to travel than to use it. On the other hand, the cost of transmitting television signals is expected to fall, by as much, according to some estimates, as 90 per cent over the next ten years and at that point it might be reasonable to provide some dispersed units with access to television systems, if problems of access and security could be overcome. But it is unrealistic to have regard to such hypothetical developments in taking decisions now on numbers which could be dispersed.

6. Fourth, audio-conference facilities, backed up by document transmitters, could make an effective contribution to the despatch of some business. I recommend the use of the device called the Remote Meeting Table (see Annex, paragraph 15). The cost studies show that such conference facilities would be economic alternatives to travel within wide ranges of meeting length, geographical separation and value of staff time. I also recommend the use of document transmitters. At present, these are slow and cumbersome devices, but it is to be expected that they will improve substantially over the next few years.

7. Document transmitters are superior to teleprinters in that they produce exact copies of the papers to be transmitted, but until they are improved more use could be made of teleprinters.

8. However, as in the case of television, these audio-conference facilities are not going to make much difference. Getting telephones which work, including the simple conference facilities of concentrator boards, on a wide scale is what matters.

ANNEX

Introduction

1. In calculating the resource effects of dispersal, some possible effects of changes in telecommunications have been taken into account as part of the economic studies outlined in Appendix 3. These include the increased costs of telephone calls and, in the case of MOD and FCO, the increased costs of signals traffic. Studies concerned specifically with telecommunications have been undertaken with the different intention of discovering the extent to which current and developing communications systems may be used as effective, acceptable and economic substitutes for face-to-face meetings.

2. As a substitute for face-to-face meetings the ordinary telephone has a number of obvious disadvantages. It does not enable participants to see one another. Neither does it enable one participant to see documents held by another. Finally, it allows for only two participants. Devices already exist, and more are likely to become available, which singly, or in combination, can overcome these disadvantages.

3. The range of possible devices is already extensive. Teleprinters are widely used for remote typewritten communication and facsimile machines for document transmission. The Post Office markets loudspeaking telephones which allow for hands-free use and for more than one participant at each end. A device called Confraphone allows for 'phone conversations between two groups of people, but hand switching in the " over to you " style is needed. The Post Office can supply conference systems for attachment to private branch exchanges. These allow for a limited number of internal extension users to be interconnected for conference purposes along with one external user. Provided enough notice is given (of about 24 hours) a local Telephone Manager's office can provide for up to eight conferees at various points to be interconnected. A new device, the Remote Meeting Table, is described separately below.

4. Apart from the audio systems just mentioned, television-based systems are also available. Confravision, a Post Office service, provides ordinary black-and-white television contact between two groups of up to five people each. Participants must go to a Confravision studio and these exist in London, Bristol, Birmingham, Manchester and Glasgow. The need to go to a studio constitutes a major disadvantage as does the cost (the present charge is £120 per hour or £180 per hour according to distance). Other television-like systems are on the market or have been constructed for the

76

private use of some major organisations, for example the Bankers' Trust Company of New York and Massachusetts General Hospital. The Bell Picturephone is a desk-top television system, and the RCA Videovoice a slow-scan television-like transmitter of still pictures.

Specifying needs

5. All the devices and systems so far mentioned may have some useful application in specific circumstances. It cannot be inferred, however, that they are of significant value in alleviating the communications difficulties resulting from dispersal.

6. Three points of major importance can be made at this juncture. First, once dispersal is to be implemented, each communication need must be examined in detail to discover which devices can be of value, how and by whom they should be used, what the cost will be and whether it is warranted, and how economies can be achieved by overall planning rather than piecemeal implementation. Second, in examining general rather than specific applicability of devices, the stress should be not on the devices themselves but rather on the people who will use them and on the tasks for which they are needed. Third, current devices like the telephone are by no means perfectly applied. There should be adequate planning and provision of these commonplace systems in order to provide the service that is really needed of them.

The studies so far undertaken

7. Until the present review, there had been plenty of investigation into the engineering and development of devices but relatively little investigation into their effectiveness in day-to-day use and their acceptability to the user. As part of the review, then, studies of effectiveness, acceptability and cost were undertaken, largely by the Joint Unit for Planning Research of the University of London under joint contract to the Civil Service Department and the Post Office.

8. For the purpose of these studies, the means of communication were classified as:

Telephone

Narrow-band telecommunication

Wide-band telecommunication

Face-to-face.

9. Narrow-band systems are those which require circuits similar to those used for the telephone, but which provide enhanced facilities. The advantages of circuits of this type are that a well-established network exists and that the costs are low. Wide-band systems are those which require the sort of circuits used for television. They have the disadvantage that there is currently no appreciable network and the costs are at present very high. As an example of the comparative prices, a telephone private line over a 200-mile radius costs between about £1,700 and £2,000 per annum according to quality, whereas a television line over the same distance is estimated to cost £81,000 per annum; the ratio is about 40 to 1.

10. Three research methods were used—laboratory experiments, field experiments, and a communications survey. In the laboratory experiments pairs or groups of individuals carried out realistic tasks in a number of alternative ways, *i.e.* face-to-face, over the telephone, using microphones and loudspeakers, or using television. Over 1,000 individuals (drawn mostly from civil servants attending courses at the Civil Service College, Sunningdale) have taken part. The tasks included problem-solving, bargaining and decision-making. The substance of the communications was recorded and analysed statistically for differences in outcome or content which could be attributed to the medium used.

11. The findings from the laboratory experiments take the form of a large list of conclusions relating to specific circumstances. Broadly, the indications are that tasks involving the co-ordination or transmission of fact are not affected by the medium, whereas higher-level tasks which relate to people rather than objects (*e.g.* conflict, formation of opinion, personnel problems) are affected. Where there is an effect, television tends to give results similar to the face-to-face medium.

12. On the question of acceptability, laboratory experiments show television channels to be perceived more favourably than audio channels and to be highly acceptable. However, these conclusions only apply to person-to-person communications and have not yet been demonstrated for group communication. It is already clear, however, that when a number of persons are viewed together on a television screen, very little detail of facial expression can be discriminated.

13. Field experiments consisted of supplying items of equipment for day-to-day use by staff and finding, from interview or questionnaire, the reactions of users. One experiment, involving loud-speaking telephones, facsimile machines and remote writing devices is now complete. Two other experiments using the Remote Meeting Table (see paragraph 15 below) and closed-circuit television are still in progress. The Remote Meeting Table experiment is already producing very encouraging results, but little can be said at present about results from the closed circuit-television trial.

14. In brief, the result of the first field experiment is that reaction cannot be simply related to usefulness for particular tasks. Access to the devices, manner of introduction and support and advice given during initial use are all important. As a simple example, the title " loud-speaking telephone " seems to have obscured in the minds of some the possibility of having " meetings " by grouping people around the instrument.

15. Apart from the Remote Meeting Table (RMT), the audio devices mentioned in paragraph 3 all suffer from a defect when used for multi-person conversations—the speaker cannot be identified unless his voice is recognised or unless he announces himself. The RMT was developed by the Joint Unit for Planning Research as a means of overcoming this defect. Whilst a narrow-band (telephone-like) system, it provides for remote conferences by two groups of participants in which speakers at the remote location are continuously and automatically identified. As a field trial an RMT link was set up in the Scottish Office between Dover House, Whitehall, and St. Andrew's House, Edinburgh. After a year of use, it is clear that it meets a

practical need and is quite acceptable, at least to a certain set of users, including Ministers. Furthermore, it has appeared so acceptable to some that, following demonstrations, two Departments are having systems installed for their own use (as well as a source of further field-trial information). Present plans for the Remote Meeting Table are to increase its penetration by issuing it on a trial basis to those Departments which can provide sufficient traffic. The purpose is to see whether wider availability brings about a relatively sharp increase in acceptability and frequency of use and also to provide more experience of using novel devices of this kind.

16. A communications survey involving some 6,400 respondents was mounted in the Home Office, DHSS, DES and MOD. The questionnaire (" Contact Record Sheet ") asked respondents to report in some detail on a specific meeting in which they had taken part. In particular they were asked whether the business could have been conducted by telephone and, if not, why not. Analysis of the survey results (necessarily involving the skill, judgment and laboratory and field experience of the analysts at the Joint Unit for Planning Research) yielded estimates of the extent to which face-to-face meetings could be substituted by telecommunications media. Because of alternative judgmental views, the results involve ranges rather than single figures. They are:

    (a) 3 per cent of meetings could have used the telephone instead

    (b) between 31 per cent and 49 per cent of meetings could have used a narrow-band system instead

    (c) between 7 per cent and 40 per cent of meetings could have used a wide-band system instead

    (d) between 26 per cent and 41 per cent of meetings would in any case have to be conducted face-to-face.

The small percentage for meetings which could have used the telephone is not surprising, since the telephone is already commonly used as a means of avoiding inconvenient face-to-face meetings.

17. The economics of using a certain medium in those cases where it *could* be used depends on a variety of factors including the distance between participants, the degree of utilisation of a system once installed, and, of course, the capital and running costs of systems, fares, allowances and time wasted in travel. Generalised costings exercises have been performed. These were based on a wide variety of possible separations.

18. On the fairly conservative assumption that a narrow-band system costs four times as much as a telephone in terms of telephone lines, costings show that a group of 400 to 500 people at any one spot would nearly always justify between them the installation of narrow-band systems which provide for hands-free, audio conference and facsimile telecommunication links. Such costings do of course involve a number of reasonable assumptions and, in particular, valuations of staff time. In the present case, ranges of valuation corresponding to those implied by possible link weights (see Appendix 6) in the review decision process were used. Despite some reliance on assumptions, it can be stated with fair confidence that narrow-band systems are effective, acceptable and economic for certain contacts and that dispersals of any reasonable size provide enough of these contacts to warrant installation of the system.

19.   In the case of wide-band no such statement can be made. Currently, the transmission costs of wide-band systems can be as much as 16 to 48 times those of the telephone. For costing purposes it has been assumed that the lower of these figures will apply fairly consistently in the not too distant future. Even so, the result is that there is no obvious general cost justification for systems like closed-circuit television. The best that can be said is that they may be useful for rather special cases, *e.g.* when staff time is valued very highly and where the contact is such as to make some visual element essential.

20.   It has been concluded that any benefits which might be obtained from the use of these systems should be regarded as a means of alleviating some of the communications difficulties imposed by dispersal rather than as a justification for even greater dispersal. As a consequence, the impact of telecommunications on the choice of recommendation has been minimal, but the conclusions reached should be of considerable value in aiding the implementation of a dispersal programme. It is, however, suggested that once a dispersal programme reaches the stage of planning for implementation, each communication need, including ordinary post and telephone needs, should be investigated in detail and become an element in an overall communications plan.

THE HUMAN ASPECTS OF DISPERSAL

1. The Government commissioned the Tavistock Institute of Human Relations to undertake a study of

(a) past dispersal

(b) the attitudes of staff who might be dispersed as a result of the present exercise

(c) experience of the terms and conditions under which dispersed staff are moved.

2. The object of this study, the principal results and recommendations of which are summarised at the end of this appendix, was to provide information relevant to three broad areas of concern—the effective planning and implementation of dispersal moves (what might be characterised as the " welfare " aspects), the financial implications of dispersal for the individual and such general issues as the obligation of staff at and above Executive Officer grade and equivalent level to serve anywhere in the country and the choice of the receiving location.

3. The most important issues may be seen as that:

(a) Dispersal, especially for staff serving in Departments without a large local and regional structure, is a major upheaval in the life of a Civil Servant and his family. It is often much more severe for his wife and children than it is for him as, while he takes a good deal of his " environment " with him in the form of his work and his colleagues, they have to make a completely new start. If the wife is at work in the London area, the change is especially upsetting. Generally speaking, less than one man in five would welcome a move, although up to 85 per cent would disperse with varying degrees of reluctance if transfer to another Department were not possible. Women are more reluctant to move than men, but in the executive grades about 70 per cent would do so if they had to. Clerical staff (who are no longer liable to serve anywhere in the country) show more resistance to dispersal than executive staff and, if transfer is not possible, those unwilling to move are equally likely to resign or accept redundancy terms.

(b) Dispersal can be accompanied by personal financial loss, but against this, officers selling houses in London and the South East and buying elsewhere may be expected to profit from the transaction. By contrast, of course, staff returning to London from the provinces suffer heavy penalties in house purchase and it is increasingly difficult to get staff to return, even on promotion.

(c) The problems of staff who are dispersed are sometimes exacerbated by inadequate information and inadequate management support.

(d) The choice of location is of particular interest and importance to staff. It is difficult to justify the choice of places which appear manifestly less atttractive than those they are leaving, especially if

81

there are problems over job opportunities for dependants; staff would not choose to work and live in a place which they judged to be unattractive in terms of environment, amenities and climate; and many would resent being used as instruments of the Government's regional policy.

(e) Staff have definite regional preferences and over 60 per cent would, given the choice, opt for the Outer South East and the South West rather than for areas with greater capability for population expansion.

(f) Although the posts which civil servants hold are public appointments and may reasonably be regarded as a public resource to be deployed as the Government thinks best in the public interest, it would be unwise to overlook the fact that staff themselves are a major resource. If the Government decides to send work to places which, as the Tavistock Report has shown (see Part 2), staff think unattractive, it must be at pains to explain why it has selected them and what advantages it believes they have. There should, in the Government's attitude, be a careful balance between, on the one hand, a reasonable insistence on the fact that staff have responsibilities as well as rights and, on the other, an intention to do all in its power to make the move out of London (and the later return, should this be necessary) as painless as possible.

(g) Experience shows that, where staff can be offered a real choice of possible dispersal locations, the whole operation goes more smoothly and that the opposite occurs where an unpopular location is imposed. If a choice can be offered, it should be; if there is no real choice, none should be offered.

Recommendations

4. On the planning and implementation of dispersal moves, I recommend that:

(a) The Civil Service Department and individual Departments should mount an exercise, along the lines indicated by the Tavistock Report, to provide co-ordinated information and support services for the staff.

(b) The Civil Service Department should co-ordinate arrangements under which any staff unable or unwilling to disperse could be transferred to work or Departments remaining in London (see also paragraph 6 (a) below).

(c) There should be a thorough programme of information, both Service-wide and Departmental as necessary, to explain the dispersal exercise to staff and the case for individual locations.

(d) If a choice of location can be offered, it should be; if not, and against the background of this report a choice seems unlikely, then it should be made clear at once that there is no choice.

(e) Staff should be made aware of entitlements and of the services available on dispersal.

(f) There should be improved arrangements for staff and their families to familiarise themselves with new locations and the leave allowed for finding and purchasing or renting a new home should be increased.

(g) The arrangements for staff serving in new locations to visit families remaining behind (*e.g.* to allow children to complete school courses) should be improved.

(h) The local authorities concerned should be invited to mount an information exercise on their towns and areas and to co-operate closely with dispersing Departments.

(i) As long a period as possible should be allowed for the implementation of the dispersal programme.

5. On the financial implications of dispersal for the individual, I recommend that the attitude of the Government should be that no-one required to move in the interests of the Service should be expected to lose by it. Other than the points which I have identified in (*f*) and (*g*) above, I make no specific recommendations on this, as I understand that the Civil Service Department and the National Staff Side are in continuous consultation on transfer terms and allowances and that the Department has already expressed its aim as being to ensure that terms and allowances are both fair and easily understood and that they help the course of dispersal (as well as the many staff who already transfer in the course of Departmental business). I should add, however, that in my view the inflated price of houses in London and the South East is going to present a continuing and growing disincentive to dispersed and other provincial staff to move to London and that ways of overcoming this, *e.g.* in aid for the purchase of houses, must be provided.

6. On general issues, my recommendations are as follows:

(a) *The mobility rule.* This applies to all staff at and above Executive Officer and equivalent level and requires them to serve anywhere in the United Kingdom or overseas, if the needs of the Service so dictate. It is a necessary regulation for any large organisation with a regional and foreign substructure. Consequently I endorse the attitude which the Civil Service Department has already taken with the National Staff Side. This is that the need to conduct Government business efficiently must have first priority and that, in some cases, staff will be required to move with their work. But I also fully accept that there will be cases in which transfer will involve real hardship and I accordingly endorse the view of the Department that the best arrangements will be those which make the greatest possible use of volunteers. Moreover I would emphasise the importance of the point I have already made on timing; the more time that can be allowed the better, as this will permit the movement of staff within and, if necessary, between Departments into the posts to be dispersed in good time for the move.

(b) *Transfer arrangements.* I have already touched on transfer arrangements in London, whether within the Department of origin or between that Department and another. I believe that transfer arrangements may also be necessary at dispersal locations, in order to promote the development of careers *in situ* or in the area and to reduce to a minimum the need to return to London either for promotion or for variety of experience. Interdepartmental transfer, whether on initial dispersal or within the dispersal area, is a complex

83

issue—all Departments obviously have promotion and movement arrangements agreed with their own Staff Side—and, as the Civil Service Department has already indicated to the National Staff Side, it is difficult to be precise about it before it has been thoroughly explored with Departments and staff. There would clearly be differing views and interests. However, I recommend that the case for local interdepartmental transfer arrangements should be explored.

(c) *Number of dispersal locations.* Small dispersed units sited in many different locations are very vulnerable in personnel management terms. First, the organisation to which they belong may be wound up and the mobile staff made redundant will need to be placed elsewhere in the Service. Second, the units are usually too small to provide a good range of opportunities either for local promotion or for extending officers' experience by serving in different posts. These two considerations make for considerable difficulty in staffing such units and in moving staff about the country. It is therefore advisable to settle for a few rather than many locations and each should have enough work to provide a good range of career prospects, either within a single Department or between several Departments. As far as a Department is concerned, the dispersal it undertakes should be of such a proportion of its work and staff as to promote good career oportunities at the dispersal location and it should not (although there may need to be some exceptions) divide its Headquarters between more than two locations, London and one other. There is no value in dispersing a handful of posts for dispersal's sake. Indeed, such dispersals should be avoided unless they are of genuinely self-contained blocks of work.

(d) *Career management.* It is important that the pattern of career moves between London and the dispersal locations should be considered carefully by Departmental management. It would be unfortunate if staff outside London had the impression that they were " out of sight and out of mind " and if a feeling grew up that both dispersed work and dispersed staff were of a lower order of importance than work and staff in London. This means that the facilities for reporting on and monitoring the progress of staff serving at dispersal centres are of particular importance.

PART 2

Summary of the Tavistock Report

Introduction

1. The Tavistock Report is based on information about private sector experience of dispersal and similar experience in Government Departments and upon a comprehensive survey by questionnaire and interview carried out in the Home Office, Department of Health and Social Security, Department of Education and Science and Ministry of Defence. Representative samples of staff from all levels were asked their views on how dispersal, if it were to take place, would affect them. Sections I to VI of the report are a detailed analysis of the many factors affecting willingness to disperse and do not give rise to specific recommendations. They are, however, a directly relevant source of information for those concerned with implementing recommendations arising out of Sections VII and VIII.

2. The Tavistock findings are complex and vary in detail within Departments and by grade of staff concerned. This summary can offer only broad conclusions; full details are given in the Tavistock Report and its Appendices.

Factors affecting willingness to disperse

Section 1 : **Provisional intention : willingness to disperse**

3. This Section covers the stated willingness of staff to disperse by grade, occupational group and sex.

4. The report shows that in the Home Office, Department of Health and Social Security and Department of Education and Science only one-fifth of male officers at the grades of Executive Officer (EO) and equivalent level and above would welcome a move, although up to 85 per cent would disperse if transfer to another Department was not possible, over half of them without reluctance. At Clerical Officer (CO) and equivalent level 69 per cent of men would move. Transfer is the preference of one-half of the male COs and, if this was not possible, about one-half would move and most of the rest would accept redundancy.

5. If transfer were not possible, some 70 per cent of single women in grades EO level and above would disperse, but with marked reluctance. Single women at the CO level are less prepared to disperse than Executives, but much the same proportion as at the Executive level would disperse if unable to transfer. Those unwilling to move and unable to transfer are equally likely either to resign or accept redundancy terms. Married women Executives' reluctance to disperse is rare. Married women at the CO level prefer to transfer, but if this were impossible less than one-quarter would move, most of the rest opting for redundancy.

6. Careful interpretation is needed here owing to differences between staff in Departments, such as age, marital status, occupation and so on. In general, however, it can be taken as a broad guide to dispersal intentions since the differences are of only marginal significance in relation to the general overall picture.

85

Departmental similarities and differences

7. For staff at the EO grade level and above there were no significant differences in the distribution of intentions between DHSS, HO and DES. There were, however, significant differences between these Departments as a whole and MOD (Main). The report concludes that the civil/military mix offers different problems from that of a purely civil Department and that this is accentuated in differences between Administration Group staff on the one hand and professional, scientific and technical (PST) and auxiliary specialist grades on the other. In general, the non-Administration Group grades are more prepared to move, less likely to seek transfer to avoid dispersal and more likely to leave the Service if unable to transfer than are the Administration Group grades.

Sex differences

8. Less women than men in the Executive level grades are prepared to disperse and women at the CO level tend to be more reluctant to move than in the Executive. For women, whether they are married or not has a greater bearing than grade, occupation or Department on their intentions towards dispersal.

Differences between grades

9. The distribution in intention of the grades from EO to Senior Principal and above do not differ significantly, but there are some tendencies specific to certain Departments and grades. For example:

(a) Top level Administration Group grades (Senior Principal and above) seem the least prepared to move.

(b) In MOD, HO and DES top level PST men are more prepared to move than their Administration Group equivalents; the reverse is the case in DHSS where top professionals were notably adverse to moving.

(c) With the exception of the DHSS, PST men of Senior Principal level and above are more prepared to move.

Section 2 : Attitudinal factors affecting intention

10. The most important considerations which governed the respondents' replies to other portions of the questionnaire, and in particular their provisional intention, are listed below in order of importance:

Family and personal
Housing and residential
London facilities
Job and career
Situation of new location
Schooling and education
Work environment

Employment of other members of the family

Age

Health

(Family and personal are ranked highest by about 40 per cent and health lowest at 5 per cent. The other factors are more or less evenly distributed between these points.)

11. In particular there was a high relationship between unwillingness to disperse and:

(a) stage of children's education and type of school available

(b) family ties

(c) wish to stay in present work or present Department

(d) job opportunities of spouse

(e) job opportunities for other family members.

These factors thus have considerable implications for the management of dispersal.

Factors leading to application for transfer

12. Family and personal factors are significantly more important considerations for transfer seekers than they are for those who are prepared to move. 71 per cent of the former mentioned these, as compared to 35 per cent of the latter.

13. Concern about job opportunities for husband or wife or family members other than children is also more widespread amongst transfer seekers.

14. Willingness to move is a function of anticipated betterment in a new environment and it is also strongly influenced by the degree of satisfaction with present conditions.

15. The report discusses some of the policy implications of these various incentives and disincentives. When locational factors are set aside for instance, the important considerations differentiating intentions are job and career prospects (which are more important to those more favourably disposed towards dispersal) and family considerations and retirement considerations (which are more important to those less favourably disposed). As already indicated, those more reluctant to move are more concerned about financial implications and the timing of dispersal in relation to the stages of their children's education.

Section 3 : Attitudes towards location

16. This section describes the environmental attributes generally desired of the dispersal location and staff preferences for regions and sub-regions. Likes and dislikes are fairly constant irrespective of Department and grade. Minor differences do exist, however, in higher grade preferences for what can broadly be described as "London culture". This preference is especially marked in the higher grades of DES.

17.   Open spaces come high on the list of desired attributes.   Good communications and London culture both score above the 35 per cent level. Access to coast, airports, clubs, societies, etc., scores below 30 per cent.

18.   On the "dislike side" industrial areas have a high score, at about 37 per cent, traffic density 22 per cent, and then, bunched together at about the 15 per cent level, come urban concentration, difficult travel, pollution, new towns, crowding, bad climate, aircraft noise, etc.

19.   Positive factors include sports and university or historic towns, while negative factors include such factors as unemployment.

20.   The ease with which the new location can be reached from London as a central travel point is also of great importance to those who are preoccupied with family and extended family considerations.

Regional preferences

21.   Table III—1 of the report (reproduced below) gives choice of dispersal location as stated by respondents.   (They did not know which locations (see Appendix 5) were actually under consideration.)   It will be seen that the South West Region is the most popular with 31·6 per cent, closely followed by the Outer South East with 30·1 per cent.   East Anglia comes next with 9·1 per cent and there is then a cluster of regions below the 5 per cent level—North West, Yorkshire and Humberside, Northern, Inner South East, Scotland, Wales, West and East Midlands.

22.   There is some connection between willingness to disperse and stated choice of location.   In general, the more distant the location from London, the more willing to disperse to it are the people who named it, although they are proportionately few.

Choice of dispersal area

Region	Percentage choices of those naming locations who would be prepared to disperse	Percentage choices of those naming locations who would *not* be prepared to disperse	Total
Scotland	3·8	2·0	3·5
Northern	4·0	2·5	3·8
Yorkshire and Humberside	4·3	3·1	4·1
North West	4·4	3·6	4·3
East Midlands	1·6	1·0	1·5
West Midlands	3·0	2·0	2·9
Wales	3·5	1·5	3·2
East Anglia	9·1	5·1	8·6
South West	31·6	27·9	31·2
Outer South East ...	30·1	38·6	31·3
Inner South East ...	4·6	12·7	5·7

Section 4 : Organisational and job linked factors

23. This section discussed the relationship between job satisfaction and related factors which tend to confirm staff in their present working habits and environment and, by contrast, those factors which allow them to see dispersal not as a threat to existing satisfactions but as offering the possibility of potential rewards.

Age

24. Those under 24 are very inclined towards dispersal.

25. There is a considerable drop away from dispersal in the age range 24–29, a rise again for 30–34 and a drop for 34–39. The stable pattern that then follows leads to the expected tail-off at 60 +. Within these age groups the older EO is much less inclined towards dispersal than are the other grades.

Experience of Civil Service life

26. Civil Servants who have spent all of their life in the Service are most prepared to move, particularly those with previous experience of moves. Civil Servants with few years of service are likely to leave if transfer is not possible. Those who have spent 10 years or more in a grade are the most likely to seek transfer.

Job satisfaction

27. Those who are at present satisfied or dissatisfied with their job are the most inclined to disperse, while those who are neither satisfied nor dissatisfied, or who are dissatisfied with future career prospects, are the least inclined to move. This can be interpreted for the former group as seeing their job in a new location either continuing to offer, or offering improved, satisfactions. The latter group see no advantage nor hope of improvement either now or in a new situation.

Section 5 : Personal and family factors

General family factors

28. Single men, married women, officers from small households or with wives who are not working are least inclined to move. Differences in the educational state of children do not appear to play as great a part in an officer's provisional intentions as those of the spouse's occupation.

Physical environment and accommodation

29. The nearer an officer lives to the centre of London and the longer he has lived in his present district, the less inclined he is to move. The nature of an officer's present accommodation does not greatly affect his dispersal intention, but officers who own their property or who rent it are slightly less inclined to disperse than those with mortgages.

30. Over 90 per cent of officers would opt for ownership in a new location, either wholly or with a mortgage. 80 per cent would remain as owners. Thus while the prospect of " owning one's own home " is often given as a strong incentive for moving away from London, it is only likely to apply to 7 per cent. The great majority of officers already own their homes.

Section 6: Special circumstances in dispersal

31. A frequent comment was that there were circumstances about their personal situation that made them atypical as Civil Servants and which would give rise to special problems in dispersal; 38 per cent of respondents indicated that in their view they would have special problems should they be called upon to disperse.

32. Although it could be argued that some of the needs were merely excuses for not wanting to disperse, the figure of 38 per cent gives some indication of the volume of queries (apart from those from other sources) which might be directed towards the personnel management and welfare sections in a dispersal operation. This section therefore will be of special interest to Welfare Officers.

Principal recommendations for Government action

33. The last two sections of the report are taken in reverse order, so that recommendations for the planning and implementation of dispersal may be given first.

Section 8 : The process of dispersal

Recommendation 1—Participation

34. All phases of dispersal demand that the maximum amount of information should be available to those concerned and that management should be in sensitive contact with those who are being dispersed. This required that *a two-way information system be set up* and well used. The demand for concrete information becomes apparent immediately a Department becomes aware that it is a candidate for dispersal. This need could be met through the setting up of the Departmental and central information channels detailed below. The information needs will differ in the three dispersal phases.

Recommendation 2—Consultation

35. The report emphasises that consultation at all stages of dispersal is essential. In the earlier stages of past dispersals it was necessary to generate certain information for planning and decision purposes; to provide information about locations; to assess staff preferences for different locations; to arrange exploratory visits and so on. The readiness of management to invite staff representatives to engage actively in planning and implementation of these activities made a significant contribution to the smooth running of the

operation. Departmental experience indicates that *joint Official Side/Staff Side dispersal committees should be set up* at the earliest possible stage. Both potential dispersers and non-dispersers should feel that those concerned are continuously represented through the whole period of the dispersal process.

Recommendation 3—Central organisation

36. The report advises that *CSD should set up a central organisation* in order to:

(a) secure the provision of data relevant to dispersal management, for example, housing prices, employment trends, changes in staff turnover, etc.;

(b) provide a clearing service for applications from London-based and provincial staff who wish to transfer to dispersing Departments and *vice versa;*

(c) lay down on the basis of accumulating experience, guidelines for hardship committees;

(d) co-ordinate advisory services and as necessary to provide them;

(e) provide a common training for staff employed in Departmental dispersal units (see Recommendations 4 and 7);

(f) set up a forum in which Departmental dispersal officers (see Recommendation 4), can mutually share their experiences.

Recommendation 4—Departmental dispersal officers

37. *A dispersal officer should be appointed* to manage the dispersal process. He should be of rank not less than a Principal, or possibly an Assistant Secretary in larger Departments. He should work with a Dispersal Committee, which should be a Departmental sub-committee of the Whitley Council. Both he and the Committee should have access to professional advice where required. The dispersal officer should have a small staff at his disposal, one of whom should be concerned with liaison with the local authorities in the receiving area and possibly located there to manage that end of the dispersal itself.

Recommendation 5—Dispersal staff training

38. *The dispersal officer and his staff should receive training* in the process and problems of dispersal. If the advisory service for staff (see Recommendation 7) is part of the dispersal unit, then staff of the advisory service should be specially trained in interviewing and welfare matters. It would clearly be of advantage if this training were organised centrally by CSD in conjunction with the Civil Service College and relevant outside advisers (see Recommendation 3).

Recommendation 6—Information to all staff

39. *A Departmental "Dispersal Bulletin" should be brought into being* as soon as a decision to disperse has been taken. It should be attractive

and non-official and serve as the principal medium for regular communications about progress, information about the location, dispersal terms, advisory services and so on. It should be issued to every member of staff involved.

Recommendation 7—Advisory service

40. *An advisory service should be set up* under Departmental dispersal officers. The reliability of indications of intentions to disperse or not is considerably governed by the accuracy of the information that can be provided to individual officers. The report suggests that the information below is essential and that personal interviews should be freely available to members of staff who require clarification. At such an interview cases of hardship can be identified. Each individual should

(a) know whether or not he will be called upon or allowed to disperse (mobility and age considerations)

(b) know the options open to him if he does not wish to move

(c) be well informed about the dispersal location

(d) know the approximate date his present work is expected to move

(e) be familiar with the dispersal terms etc., as they affect him

(f) be offered (*e.g.* through the Dispersal Bulletin) a general and comprehensive framework within which he can make his own appreciation of the problems which he may have to face when making a move

(g) have direct access, on a strictly confidential basis, to professional advisory services should he desire them.

Recommendation 8—Transfer services

41. The report recommends that *inter-Departmental transfers of staff should be co-ordinated centrally* so that service-wide consideration of transfer problems can take place. Officers seeking transfer should have information about the nature of the work available, new training which may be given and whether or not the job may be affected later by dispersal. Opportunities to visit the new Department should be freely available and long periods of delay and uncertainty should be avoided.

Recommendation 9—Redundancy and retirement services

42. The report suggests that *internal offices of the Department of Employment should be set up in each Department* to deal with officers who are redundant and those who retire early but wish to continue in other employment. (It may, however, prove more efficient to set up such an office as part of CSD's central machinery.)

Recommendation 10—Other employment services

43. *Machinery should be set up to ascertain the employment needs of others* (especially spouses) and help given to secure alternative employment in the new location where this is necessary. The evidence suggests that overcoming this problem plays a large part in willingness to disperse.

Recommendation 11—Career considerations

44. The report suggests that it is a task for the career development system to develop appropriate policy for handling officers' anxieties about the effect of dispersal on careers. This points to *the need to examine the likely career consequences for each Department affected,* both at the dispersed and non-dispersed locations.

Recommendation 12—Choice of location

45. *It should be made clear at an early stage whether a genuine choice of location is or is not possible.* If a choice can be offered it should be; if there is no real choice for staff, none should be offered.

Recommendation 13—The chosen location

46. The report suggests that *exhibition/information offices should be arranged covering each location.* The maximum amount of information should be provided both on the spot and through the Dispersal Bulletin and staff and families should have an opportunity to visit it before they are asked to give a formal indication of their readiness to disperse. Close relations should be maintained with local authorities throughout the whole of the dispersal operation.

Section 7: Conditions of dispersal and dispersal allowances

47. The Tavistock Institute approached the survey from the viewpoint that conditions and allowances should be seen as a lubricant to the dispersal process and not merely as recompense for expenses incurred.

Recommendation 14—Preliminary visits

48. *The number of preliminary visits allowed should be reviewed.* At least three seemed to be necessary and they should also include dependent relatives and possibly children.

Recommendation 15—Reconnaissance visits

49. *Reconnaissance visits should be extended and be more flexible.* The reconnaissance is usually made by a party from the London office. The staff are a little suspicious of local authorities who do their best to " sell " the new location and the staff have little opportunity for personal exploration of the new neighbourhood.

Recommendation 16—House buying

50. *The leave allowance for moving and settling in should be reviewed.* The majority of staff take from three to five days' annual leave for this purpose over and above the regulation allowance. The report finds that the allowances and regulations associated with the costs of house buying are considered inadequate. Legal expenses have in the past not been adequately met. Bridging loans are often hard to obtain and the interest on them is not borne by the Department. The procedures for obtaining salary advances for mortgage deposits are untrusting and cumbersome.

Recommendation 17—Bridging visits

51. For single people these are about adequate. For married men separated from their families, they are inadequate. Most go home every weekend, distance permitting, at their own expense. The report suggests that *a more generous allowance geared to distance should prevail.*

Recommendation 18—Transfer grant

52. *The scope and size of these allowances should be reviewed.* They are regarded by staff as a general fund to cover all items not included in other claimable sources. It is inevitable that it should be seen as inadequate by more than half of the staff concerned. Curtains, carpets, appliances and school uniforms appear to be the major expenses for which staff use this grant.

Recommendation 19—Claims procedures

53. The great majority find the regulations difficult to comprehend and in many cases not easily accessible. The report recommends that *a basic " do-it-yourself " system is needed* augmented by the advice of an expert. *The claims procedure* is regarded as cumbersome and often slow and *should be overhauled.* Delays cause additional problems since ready cash is often in short supply during the dispersal moves. Interpretation of the regulations and the claims procedure was usually sought from official sources or failing these from an " office lawyer ". Staff left behind once the main office had moved often felt bereft of information and support in these matters.

Recommendation 20—Disturbance allowance

54. Staff views on whether or not there should be some direct compensation for the disturbance caused by dispersal were mixed, 61 per cent believing that this should be so, but not being clear about what form it should take. Retention of London Weighting (although originally given in order to avoid salary drop) was seen by many as providing such a disturbance compensation. It was also regarded as inequitable by those not entitled to receive it. The report suggests that there is no way for making such a compensation and, therefore, *no action should be taken.*

DETAILS OF THE RECOMMENDATIONS AND
ALTERNATIVE PROPOSALS

1. As the Report indicated (paragraph 17), the review team discussed with most Departments proposals for varying degrees of dispersal. In the case of small Departments there was usually a single proposal, for the dispersal of the whole organisation; for larger Departments, the proposals usually involved three levels of possible dispersal.

2. In assessing the dispersability of Departments, their communications and other data were considered in the light of notional dispersals to each of a number of possible locations, at different distances from London. In order to facilitate a comparative interdepartmental assessment of the effects of dispersal, it was decided to include one particular location in all the analyses, which would be neither near to nor far from London. Bristol, which is 120 miles from London, was selected for the purposes of this overall illustration and has accordingly served throughout as a bench-mark in the analyses of communications data and the assessment of dispersability.

3. This Appendix consists of notes on each Department, giving details of the proposals put to it, of the issues then considered and of the recommendation which has resulted. The summary of *proposals* contains details of the number of posts affected, the communications damage and resource gain associated with their dispersal and of the link weight at which these proposals were found in the computer analysis (these details normally being derived from the notional dispersal to Bristol). As explained in Appendix 6, this link weight provided a useful approximation to the " marginal trade-off " also used in discussion with some Departments, at a stage when neither the location nor the final level of dispersal to be recommended was known.

4. The summary of the *recommendations* also contains details of communications damage, resource gain and number of posts to be moved. These are based on the actual dispersal location proposed for the Department in the Report (paragraph 30). In addition, the " average trade-off " is shown (see paragraph 5, below).

5. As an introduction to the notes on each Department reviewed, Part 1 of this Appendix sets out in greater detail the recommendation and alternatives put forward for consideration in the main Report. The measures used to describe *proposals* originally put to Departments, and summarised in the notes given in Part 2, are communications damage, resource gain and link weight. The measures used to describe the *recommendations* now put to Ministers and summarised below are communications damage, resource gain and average trade-off. All these terms, except average trade-off, are described in Appendix 3 and Appendix 6, but it may be useful to recapitulate them here:

Communications damage is a measure of the loss of efficiency likely to be caused by the proposal. It is based on units which represent an aggregate over all the posts affected of the time taken to travel

95

from the dispersal location to London to enable a meeting to be held, or a contact to be maintained, which would present no difficulty if all those concerned were in London. The further the dispersal location is from London the higher the damage has been found to be. The greater the number of meetings or contacts, the higher the damage will be. A unit of communications damage is not directly comparable to a unit of resource gain.

Resource gain is a measure of the effect of dispersal on national resources. It is in terms of thousands of pounds sterling, discounted to present value.

Link weight is approximate to marginal trade-off (see Appendix 6, paras. 12–16). It represents the amount of additional benefit for each extra unit of damage incurred in going from one possible level of dispersal to the next most severe level. It is thus an indication of the relative severity of each proposal. The process of trade-off is a form of cost-benefit analysis in which the communications damage and resource gain associated with proposals are offset against each other. Marginal trade-off is an indication whether the resource gain to be derived from a proposal is worth having in terms of the damage the proposal would cause to efficiency. The lower the trade-off (that is, the nearer it is to 1), the lower the gain for each unit of damage; the higher the trade-off (that is, the nearer it is to 50 (or more)), the higher the gain for each unit of damage.

Average trade-off represents the benefit per unit of damage to be derived from dispersing the whole Department or a part of it (*i.e.* a group of blocks of work) to the proposed location. Since it is related to a specific recommendation for a specified location, this figure is more useful now than marginal trade-off (link weight) used at the earlier stage of developing proposals for discussion with Departments. (*Benefit* is resource gain, plus a multiple of the number of posts moved (see Appendix 6, paragraph 8).)

6. It should be emphasised that the figures given for average trade-off in the following tables are *averaged* across all the posts contained in the proposal. This conceals the probability that senior officers in the blocks of work proposed for dispersal will be much more seriously affected than their subordinates. It underlines the need for Ministers in charge of Departments for which dispersal is proposed to consider whether it is tolerable in terms of lost efficiency.

The recommended course

7. This is put forward as a starting point for Ministerial consideration. It pays attention both to avoiding excessive loss of effectiveness and to securing new employment opportunities for the regions, attempting a compromise between them. The characteristics are as follows:

Recommended Dispersal

Department	Location	No. of posts	Damage(¹)	Resource gain(²)	Average trade-off(³)
Ministry of Agriculture, Fisheries and Food	Manchester	1,250	978	3,521	12·55
Agricultural Research Council	Manchester	140	214	927	8·90
Civil Service Department ...	Basingstoke	300	} 387	4,500	24·36
	Norwich	357			
	Sunningdale	50			
Her Majesty's Customs and Excise	Southend	500	59	3,660	120·50
Ministry of Defence	Milton Keynes	10,890	4,917	59,354	27·57
Department of Employment ...	Liverpool	1,400	} 970	8,240	19·60
	Plymouth (with Home Office)	140			
Department of the Environment	Bristol	1,248	960	7,039	16·42
DOE—Property Services Agency	Cardiff	4,100	3,575	14,880	12·17
Foreign and Commonwealth Office	Central Lancashire New Town	986	943	4,975	12·60
FCO—Overseas Development Administration	Glasgow	1,177	1,031	3,589	11·47
Department of Health and Social Security	Central Lancashire New Town	980	} 1,162	8,910	16·50
	Newcastle	500			
Home Office	Plymouth	1,437	533	8,310	34·41
Criminal Injuries Compensation Board	Plymouth	83	15	426	63·23
Board of Inland Revenue ...	Teesside	1,610	785	9,725	26·73
Natural Environment Research Council	Swindon	191	182	1,300	14·45
Office of Population Censuses and Surveys	Central Lancashire New Town	920	500	7,404	27·64
Science Research Council ...	Swindon	388	245	2,471	21·16
Her Majesty's Stationery Office	Norwich	380	481	2,695	11·10
Department of Trade and Industry	Cardiff/Newport	1,442	} 791	15,182	35·10
	Teddington	358			
Export Credits Guarantee Department	Liverpool	600	323	3,296	23·18
Totals		31,427	19,051	170,404	

(¹) Units of damage (for definition, see Appendix 6).

(²) £000.

(³) For definition, see paragraph 5.

305375

D

8.   Under this option, some 31,400 posts would be dispersed to a variety of locations, including "regional policy" candidates and places at which Departments already have dispersed work.   The analysis is:

Region	Location		Total
Scotland	Glasgow	1,177	1,177
Wales	Cardiff/Newport	5,542	5,542
Northern	Newcastle	500	2,110
	Teesside	1,610	
North West	CLNT	2,886	6,276
	Liverpool	2,000	
	Manchester	1,390	
Yorkshire/Humberside	—	—	—
East Anglia	Norwich	737	737
South East	Milton Keynes	10,890	12,098
	Basingstoke	300	
	Southend	500	
	Teddington	358	
	Sunningdale	50	
South West	Bristol	1,248	3,487
	Swindon	579	
	Plymouth	1,660	
		31,427	31,427

9.   Some Departments are made to go to regional policy locations.   But certain Departments (*e.g.* CSD, C & E, SRC and HMSO) are allocated to locations in which they have an interest on the basis that it would be bad management to make them go elsewhere.   The fact that other Departments are distributed without regard to the points they have made on locations does not mean that their arguments can be set aside: the purpose of this option is to present a balance between the claims of efficiency and regional policy. It will be observed that the distant locations (Glasgow, Newcastle, Plymouth and Teesside), although featuring in the allocation, receive rather less than a sixth of the total, while the more accessible "regional policy" candidates (Cardiff/Newport, Liverpool and Milton Keynes) receive almost three-fifths.

10.   The analysis used to suggest possible allocations of work to places is described in Appendix 6 (paragraphs 17–22).   In brief, observation of the data leading to the preparation of proposals for discussion with Departments had suggested that a reasonable balance could be struck between the claims of efficiency and of regional policy if dispersal was contemplated which would occur at a link weight of 15.   Similarly, in beginning the process of allocating work regarded as dispersable to possible places, it was necessary to use a valuation of the relative acceptability of damage compared with resource gain, so as to minimise overall damage to the efficiency of the Departments affected by the proposals.   In the light of the criteria prescribed for the review and of the discussions with Departments, this emerged as an average trade-off of 15, although it was recognised that this could not be regarded or treated as an absolute boundary ; in some cases, special

circumstances suggested a different treatment. In the event, there were a few allocations which occurred at an average trade-off of less than 15. These are the Agricultural Research Council (8·90), HMSO (11·1), the Overseas Development Administration (11·47), the Property Services Agency (12·17), the Ministry of Agriculture, Fisheries and Food (12·55), the Foreign and Commonwealth Office (12·6) and the Natural Environment Research Council (14·45). There are management reasons why dispersal to Norwich, which is already its dispersal location, should be acceptable for HMSO, on the understanding that some liaison unit will be maintained in London. In the case of MAFF, there is a choice to be made between the Department's preference for a central location and the Government's general policy of securing new employment opportunities in more distant areas. The pattern of the ARC's communications will be changing in the wake of changes in the pattern of Government-financed research and development and will be heavily influenced by the build-up of the research competence of the Ministry of Agriculture; it is generally recognised that there would be great advantage if the Ministry and the Council were co-located. Similarly, there could be management and professional advantages in bringing the PSA together, on an acceptable timetable, which should somewhat offset the disadvantages of stretched communication links. The FCO and ODA work, however, is recommended for CLNT and Glasgow by its relative dispersability; this too illustrates the chief dilemma presented by this exercise, namely the choice between keeping damage to a minimum and achieving benefits for assisted areas. The Natural Environment Research Council is proposed for co-location with the Science Research Council in Swindon. The economies of scale and the advantages to each Council likely to accrue from this mitigate the disadvantages to the NERC, but it will have to be considered whether each will need to retain some sort of base in London.

11. A second comment on the recommendations is that, while work is allocated to Newcastle, Plymouth and Teesside, it is at average trade-offs which are better than the threshold I think it reasonable to set at 15·0. Again, however, the Ministers concerned will need to consider whether the damage involved is acceptable, bearing in mind that it is averaged over all the staff dispersed and that its incidence will be uneven, with the most senior staff being the worst affected.

First Alternative (the " efficient " solution)
12. This is the course in which the most emphasis is laid on reducing damage to a minimum, while still aiming for a substantial dispersal. Its characteristics as compared with the recommended course are set out below:

	Efficient solution					Recommended solution				
Department	Location	No. of posts	Damage (¹)	Resource gain(²)	Average trade-off(³)	Location	No. of posts	Damage (¹)	Resource gain(²)	Average trade-off(³)
Ministry of Agriculture, Fisheries and Food*	Coventry	1,250	550	4,164	23·47	Manchester	1,250	978	3,521	12·55
Agricultural Research Council*	Coventry	140	120	1,005	16·47	Manchester	140	214	927	8·90
Civil Service Department	Basingstoke Norwich Sunningdale	300 357 50	387	4,500	24·36	Basingstoke Norwich Sunningdale	300 357 50	387	4,500	24·36
Her Majesty's Customs and Excise	Southend	500	59	3,660	120·50	Southend	500	59	3,660	120·50
Ministry of Defence	Milton Keynes	10,890	4,917	59,354	27·57	Milton Keynes	10,890	4,917	59,354	27·57
Department of Employment	Liverpool	1,540	950	8,225	20·00	Liverpool Plymouth	1,400 140	970	8,240	19·60
Department of the Environment	Bristol	1,248	960	7,039	16·42	Bristol	1,248	960	7,039	16·42
DOE—Property Services Agency	Cardiff	4,100	3,575	14,880	12·17	Cardiff	4,100	3,575	14,880	12·17
Foreign and Commonwealth Office*	Bristol	986	634	5,075	18·90	Central Lancashire New Town	986	943	4,975	12·60
FCO—Overseas Development Administration*	Manchester	1,177	717	3,445	16·29	Glasgow	1,177	1,031	3,589	11·47
Department of Health and Social Security	Newcastle Central Lancashire New Town	500 980	1,162	8,910	16·50	Newcastle Central Lancashire New Town	500 980	1,162	8,910	16·50
Home Office*	Liverpool	1,437	435	7,660	40·62	Plymouth	1,437	533	8,310	34·41
Criminal Injuries Compensation Board*	Liverpool	83	13	400	75·39	Plymouth	83	15	426	63·23
Board of Inland Revenue*	Leeds	1,610	643	9,000	31·45	Teesside	1,610	785	9,725	26·73
Natural Environment Research Council	Swindon	191	182	1,300	14·45	Swindon	191	182	1,300	14·45
Office of Population Censuses and Surveys*	Titchfield	920	273	7,406	50·67	Central Lancashire New Town	920	500	7,404	27·64
Science Research Council	Swindon	388	245	2,471	21·16	Swindon	388	245	2,471	21·16
Her Majesty's Stationery Office	Norwich	380	481	2,695	11·10	Norwich	380	481	2,695	11·10
Department of Trade and Industry	Cardiff/Newport Teddington	1,442 358	791	15,182	35·10	Cardiff/Newport Teddington	1,442 358	791	15,182	35·10
Export Credits Guarantee Department*	Cardiff	600	277	3,404	27·43	Liverpool	600	323	3,296	23·18
Totals		31,427	17,371	169,775			31,427	19,051	170,404	

* Locations changed in efficient solution.

(¹) Units of damage (for definition, see Appendix 6).

(²) £000.

(³) For definition, see paragraph 5.

13. Here, certain Departments are allocated to their existing or preferred dispersal locations; damage is reduced by 8½ per cent but resource gain drops by 0·4 per cent. The 31,400 posts are dispersed to a variety of locations; the analysis is:

Region	Location		Total
Scotland	—	—	—
Wales	Cardiff/Newport	6,142	6,142
Northern	Newcastle	500	500
North West	Liverpool	3,060	5,217
	Manchester	1,177	
	Central Lancashire New Town	980	
Yorkshire/Humberside	Leeds	1,610	1,610
East Anglia	Norwich	737	737
South East	Milton Keynes	10,890	13,018
	Basingstoke	300	
	Southend	500	
	Sunningdale	50	
	Teddington	358	
	Titchfield	920	
South West	Bristol	2,234	2,813
	Swindon	579	
West Midlands	Coventry	1,390	1,390
Totals		31,427	31,427

14. Under this option, most of the more distant locations (Glasgow, Plymouth and Teesside) receive nothing: the DHSS work going to Newcastle is associated with work already there. These locations are omitted, not by design, but because the analysis rejects them in consequence of the excessive damage associated with such distances.

Second Alternative (the " regional " solution)

15. This option is presented in order to explore the implications of a dispersal programme which provides long-distance relocation at the expense of efficiency, so that its advantages and disadvantages can be explored. Its characteristics, in comparison with the recommended solution, are as follows:

	Regional solution					Recommended solution				
Department	Location	No. of posts	Damage(1)	Resource gain(2)	Average trade-off(3)	Location	No. of posts	Damage(1)	Resource gain(2)	Average trade-off(3)
Ministry of Agriculture, Fisheries and Food*	Liverpool	1,250	999	3,776	12·55	Manchester	1,250	978	3,521	12·55
Agricultural Research Council*	Liverpool	140	218	953	8·84	Manchester	140	214	927	8·90
Civil Service Department	Basingstoke Norwich Sunningdale	300 357 50	387	4,500	24·36	Basingstoke Norwich Sunningdale	300 357 50	387	4,500	24·36
Her Majesty's Customs and Excise	Southend	500	59	3,660	120·50	Southend	500	59	3,660	120·50
Ministry of Defence*	Cardiff Milton Keynes	6,218 4,672	7,237	60,163	18·85	Milton Keynes	10,890	4,917	59,354	27·57
Department of Employment	Liverpool Plymouth	1,400 140	970	8,240	19·60	Liverpool Plymouth	1,400 140	970	8,240	19·60
Department of the Environment	Bristol	1,248	960	7,039	16·42	Bristol	1,248	960	7,039	16·42
DOE—Property Services Agency*	Teesside	4,100	5,200	15,950	8·59	Cardiff	4,100	3,575	14,880	12·17
Foreign and Commonwealth Office*	Liverpool	986	840	4,800	13·90	Central Lancashire New Town	986	943	4,975	12·60
FCO—Overseas Development Administration	Glasgow	1,177	1,031	3,589	11·47	Glasgow	1,177	1,031	3,589	11·47
Department of Health and Social Security	Newcastle Central Lancashire New Town	500 980	1,162	8,910	16·50	Newcastle Central Lancashire New Town	500 980	1,162	8,910	16·50
Home Office	Plymouth	1,437	533	8,310	34·41	Plymouth	1,437	533	8,310	34·41
Criminal Injuries Compensation Board*	Plymouth	83	15	426	63·23	Plymouth	83	15	426	63·23
Board of Inland Revenue*	Plymouth	1,610	772	9,650	27·04	Teesside	1,610	785	9,725	26·73
Natural Environment Research Council	Swindon	191	182	1,300	14·45	Swindon	191	182	1,300	14·45
Office of Population Censuses and Surveys	Central Lancashire New Town	920	500	7,404	27·64	Central Lancashire New Town	920	500	7,404	27·64
Science Research Council	Swindon	388	245	2,471	21·16	Swindon	388	245	2,471	21·16
Her Majesty's Stationery Office	Norwich	380	481	2,695	11·10	Norwich	380	481	2,695	11·10
Department of Trade and Industry*	Newcastle Newport Teddington	1,142 300 358	1,095	15,655	25·40	Cardiff/Newport Teddington	1,442 358	791	15,182	35·10
Export Credits Guarantee Department*	Glasgow	600	455	3,282	16·43	Liverpool	600	323	3,296	23·18
Totals		31,427	23,341	172,773			31,427	19,051	170,404	

* Locations changed in regional solution.
(1) Units of damage (for definition, see Appendix 6).
(2) £000.
(3) For definition, see paragraph 5.

102

16. The number of posts dispersed is again the same as that under the recommended solution, but the number forced to go to the more distant locations is increased. It will be noticed that this is usually achieved at the price of a big increase in damage and that the level of damage associated with the regional solution is some 22 per cent higher than that associated with the recommended solution, while the resource gain has increased by less than 2 per cent. Equally, some Departments with a preference for particular locations are not permitted to take them up. Departments are allocated to the distant locations because, in terms of the measures used, they could go there with relatively less damage than other Departments. But this does not mean that such allocations (for example, of the PSA to Teesside or of the ECGD to Glasgow) are anywhere near making the best locational sense for the Departments concerned. On the one hand, damage is increased because of the greater distance involved while, on the other, such an allocation disregards arguments made by the Departments concerned about their case for a location which is readily accessible not only to London but also to other parts of the country.

17. The one merit of this option is that it does favour the regional policy candidates, other than Yorkshire/Humberside. The analysis is as follows:

Region	Location		Total
Scotland	Glasgow	1,777	1,777
Wales	Cardiff/Newport	6,518	6,518
Northern	Newcastle	1,642	5,742
	Teesside	4,100	
North West	Liverpool	3,776	5,676
	CLNT	1,900	
Yorkshire/Humberside	—	—	—
East Anglia	Norwich	737	737
South East	Milton Keynes	4,672	5,880
	Basingstoke	300	
	Sunningdale	50	
	Teddington	358	
	Southend	500	
South West	Bristol	1,248	5,097
	Plymouth	3,270	
	Swindon	579	
Totals		31,427	31,427

103

NOTES ON THE RESULT OF THE REVIEW FOR THE DEPARTMENTS AND ORGANISATIONS COVERED

CENTRAL COUNCIL FOR AGRICULTURAL AND HORTICULTURAL CO-OPERATION

(32 posts in one building)

1. The Council was not formally covered by the communications study. Whether or not it should be dispersed was left for MAFF to consider once their own communications study was completed and proposals had been put to them.

2. The MAFF study showed that five blocks have contact with the Council; but two of these—the Permanent Secretary and the Under-Secretary of the Horticulture Group—have contact only at peak times. Of the remaining three blocks, only one—ADAS Headquarters—is recommended for dispersal. The contact here is a once-monthly frequency by a Principal and an SEO. The Assistant Secretary of the Co-operation and Labour Division and two of his staff in Branches A and B each have weekly contact with the Council. One other officer in these branches has once-monthly contact. Thus the major contacts are with MAFF blocks not recommended for dispersal.

3. I therefore recommend that the CCAHC should not be dispersed.

AGRICULTURAL RESEARCH COUNCIL
(140 posts in one building)

1. The communications study showed that 17·9 per cent of the Council's total link strength represented contact within the Council and that dispersal could be obtained at a comparatively acceptable trade-off between gains and damage to communications. The total dispersal of the Council was therefore proposed for discussion.

Communications Damage	Resource Gain	Link Weight
165	1,005	11·9

2. In discussion it was recognised that the White Paper on Research and Development (Cmnd. 5046) would lead to changes in the Council's methods of operation and patterns of contact. In particular, some 55 per cent of the Council's funds will come from the Ministry of Agriculture in about three years' time; it is therefore expected that contact with that Department will greatly increase. Separation from the relevant parts of MAFF would accordingly be likely to cause damage to efficiency greater than that suggested by the data on communications collected during the study. However, it is likely that the damage could be reduced to an acceptable degree if dispersal of the Council were to the same location as the principal client divisions of MAFF.

3. The Council also emphasised that damage to efficiency would be reduced if facilities were retained in London for meetings of the Council and its Committees, whose members are recruited from universities and other bodies throughout the United Kingdom. Such recruitment would prove very difficult if the Council's meetings were held outside London because of the inconvenience this would cause.

4. On location, the Council was faced with something of a dilemma. On the one hand, as mentioned in paragraph 2, contact with the Ministry of Agriculture is likely to increase in the near future, particularly the close working contact with the Chief Scientist's organisation. This argues for the Council being dispersed to Manchester with those parts of MAFF being recommended for dispersal there. On the other hand, the great majority of the research institutes and units for which the Council is responsible are concentrated in Southern England, East Anglia and round Edinburgh. It would therefore be difficult for the Scientific Advisers and senior administrators at the Council's headquarters to maintain their essential regular and frequent contact with the work of the institutes on the ground from such a location as Manchester. On balance, however, I feel the most sensible course would be for the Council to be co-located with the dispersed parts of MAFF from whom it will shortly be receiving the majority of its funds.

5. I recommend, therefore, that the ARC should be dispersed to Manchester with those parts of the Ministry of Agriculture, Fisheries and Food dispersed there, but that facilities, including an adequate secretariat, to serve meetings of the Council and its Committees be provided in London.

Communications Damage	Resource Gain	Average Trade-off
214	927	8·90

MINISTRY OF AGRICULTURE, FISHERIES AND FOOD

(3,285 posts in 10 buildings)

1. The communications study showed that 76 per cent of the total link strength of those parts of the Department covered by the study is internal to the Headquarters office in London. The analysis of communication patterns suggested that dispersal by the Department could be explored in three broad areas which were related both in communications and functional terms. The Department was invited to discuss the implications of three levels of dispersal where the trade-off between damage and gain appeared attractive:

(1) Dispersal of the entire Department other than Ministers, Permanent Secretary, the Legal Adviser, Parliamentary Branch, and the Appointments Section, a total of 2,441 posts and a further 400 or so supporting staff.

Communications Damage	Resource Gain	Link Weight
1,927	12,272	12·47

(2) Dispersal of 1,496 posts leaving in London, in addition to those excluded from Proposal 1, all the Deputy Secretaries and the major policy Divisions including those concerned with the major EEC issues.

Communications Damage	Resource Gain	Link Weight
953	6,948	14·67

(3) Dispersal of 588 posts, principally in non-policy blocks, such as those concerned with financial, statistical and economic work, in the outer London area. (This proposal included the Home-Grown Cereals Authority, a report on which is submitted separately.)

Communications Damage	Resource Gain	Link Weight
302	2,835	16·96

2. Each proposal included an allowance for office service staffs but excluded the common service element in several blocks which were set aside for later consideration.

3. In response, MAFF argued that Proposal 1 was unacceptable in management and organisation terms, principally because of the inclusion of the economic policy groups, which would be the most heavily involved in advising Ministers on EEC agricultural policies. The Department further argued that, given the interrelation of the major policy-making areas, there could be no effective splitting of these groups in order to provide some dispersal by them. In general, MAFF considered that the groups dealing with policy on commodities, general food and agricultural policy and other international affairs, as well as EEC, could not function effectively away from London. A prerequisite to maintaining an effective service to senior

officials and Ministers was the retention of these groups in London in order to preserve essential contacts with Ministers, with other central economic departments in Whitehall and with the business, commercial and embassy world. Given this, it was also essential to retain the bulk of the Economic/Statistics Group which provides a professional service to the economic policy Divisions.

4. It was therefore agreed that dispersal on the basis of Proposal 1 could only be obtained at a price in damage to efficiency which was unacceptable.

5. In the context of a consistently applied policy of dispersal of some policy work and subject to certain modifications which largely follow from the argumentation in paragraph 3, MAFF should be able to accept dispersal on the basis of Proposal 2, to the extent of some 1,250 jobs to a suitable location. The principal modifications allow retention in London of most of the Economic and Statistics Group, staff engaged on horticulture, fertilisers and feedingstuffs (in Defence/Emergencies and Crop Improvement Division), and Branches A and B of Defence/Emergencies Division. Against this MAFF may be able to afford less priority for the retention in London of posts concerned with administrative work on farm safety and of two Under-Secretaries, and the related Deputy Secretary, posts on the agricultural side. The modified proposal would disperse the following posts:

	*Number of Posts**
Deputy Secretary	6
Plant Variety Rights Office and Seeds	39†
Livestock Improvement and Forestry A/S	3
Branch A (Livestock Improvement)	22
Branch B (Forestry and Metrication)	4
U/S Lands Group	3
Land Improvement	35
Land Use and Tenure	57
Land Drainage	69
U/S Animal Health	3
Animal Health Divisions	195
Information Branch B (Publications)	40
Information Branch C (Visual Aids)	35
U/S Safety, Pesticides and Infestation Control (SPIC)	3
A/S SPIC	3
SPIC Branch A	23
U/S Regional Administration	3
Regional Administration Division	122
Research and Development Requirements	48
Statistics IIA (Pinner)	15
Statistics IIB (Pinner)	13
Audit and Costings (Pinner)	20
Investigation Division (Pinner)	22
Staff Training (Pinner)	36
Office Services Division (Kew)	13

	Number of Posts*
Director-General Agricultural Development and Advisory Service (ADAS)	3
Deputy Director-General ADAS	7
HQ ADAS	140
Vet Staff	77
Other Office Services and Specialist Support Staff	191
Total	1,250†

* Figures include allocations of common service staff.

† Consideration is being given to resiting PVRO and Seeds Division separately, and to the inclusion of the recently appointed Chief Scientist and some scientific staff in the Headquarters units to be dispersed; these adjustments would not however significantly affect the total of posts proposed for the new dispersal site.

6. On location, MAFF feels that it must be reasonably accessible to its regional offices as well as affording access to Brussels. With the establishment of the National Agriculture Centre at Stoneleigh, near Coventry, the West Midlands is becoming the focus of agricultural interest which would be enhanced by the presence in that area of a dispersed headquarters office. MAFF's preference would be for a location in the Midlands in or near Coventry. Apart from the above considerations, such a location would facilitate travel on official business to and from London.

7. I recommend that MAFF should disperse 1,250 posts on the basis of Proposal 2 with the modifications described in paragraph 5. I have much sympathy with the Department's preference for a location in the Midlands and Ministers will wish to consider this carefully. Again there is a choice to be made between the interests of efficiency and those of regional policy. Should Ministers wish to press for a more distant dispersal from MAFF, I feel that the jobs concerned could be dispersed further, particularly if the location were a good national and international communications centre, without causing unacceptable damage to efficiency. I therefore recommend dispersal to Manchester.

Communications Damage	Resource Gain	Average Trade-off
978	3,521	12·55

Against this recommendation Ministers will wish to consider the greater advantages of a Midlands location, which, apart from the considerations put forward by the Department, would result in less damage to efficiency and in a geographical sense would appear more practicable both for MAFF and for the Agricultural Research Council, for which I am recommending the same location.

ARTS COUNCIL OF GREAT BRITAIN

(134 posts in one building in London)

1. The communications study showed that over 80 per cent of the contacts of the Council are with organisations and individuals in London; on average the frequency of these contacts was reported as high. In addition, the Council claimed, there were many informal contacts maintained in London that were of importance, owing to the position of London as a centre for the arts.

2. I recommend that this argumentation be accepted, and that, as analysis of the communications pattern suggested, the benefits of dispersal of the Council could only be achieved at an extremely high cost in terms of damage.

Communications Damage	Resource Gain	Link Weight
770	842	2·3

3. I therefore recommend that the Council should not be dispersed.

BRITISH COUNCIL

(1,420 posts in 10 buildings in London)

1. The communications study showed that almost two-thirds of the total link strength was between blocks within the Council. Analysis of communication patterns suggested that most of the blocks of work were sufficiently inter-linked to make it desirable for them to be located together and that there were only two blocks where the trade-off between damage and gain appeared more attractive than for the remainder. The Department was invited to consider the implications of two proposals:

(1) Dispersal of entire British Council, involving 1,420 posts.

Communications Damage	Resource Gain	Link Weight
1,830	8,900	10·3

(2) Dispersal of Books " A " and Home " A " involving 260 posts.

Communications Damage	Resource Gain	Link Weight
290	1,500	11·5

Each number of posts included a *pro rata* allocation of common service staff.

2. In connection with the first proposal, the Council pointed out that about 90 per cent of its external contacts are with London, largely because London is both the major centre in Britain for its activities and the main centre for overseas visitors. The volume of its work is growing because of increased demands in a number of areas, including Europe. The Council indicated that it would have considerable difficulty in fulfilling its responsibilities in a location other than the centre of London.

3. On the second proposal, the Council argued that the computer analysis made Home " A " appear more suitable for dispersal than is the case. This was because the considerable number of contacts made by staff at Grade G (EO) and below had not been included in the communications study; 88 per cent of the total staff of Home "A" were at Grade G or below. The addition of these contacts would heavily increase the strength of the link with overseas visitors to London. The majority of overseas visitors are students who go initially to London; subsequently about half of them are placed in London colleges because it is these which hold many of the courses most suited to the needs of the visitors. For Books "A", the other block involved in the second proposal, regular contacts with publishers and major libraries are an essential part of its professional work. There are some 90 posts which seem to be dispersable (the bulk of them from Books " A ") and these are connected with the technical processing, supply and despatch of publications. The Council recognise that there is a case for relocating these posts, but would prefer a location within the free delivery zone of their commercial suppliers in London to anything more distant from the rest of the organisation.

4.   At present the staff of the Council are scattered over a large number of buildings but the situation will be very much improved when they are able to occupy their new office in Carlton House Terrace, which is in the course of erection.   All the evidence suggests that the levels of dispersal envisaged in the two proposals could be achieved only at a very high cost. Neither is it possible, in the context of this review, to justify recommendations for the dispersal of some 90 posts, representing less than 7 per cent of the total complement of the Council.   It would make little sense in organisation or management terms to recommend the relocation of such a small part of the Council to a centre that was distant from London, while a recommendation which involved moving posts from central London only as far as the suburbs of London would contribute little to dispersal policy.

5.   My general recommendation is that the British Council should not be dispersed.   However, I would like to qualify this by saying that there is a case for moving some 90 posts from central London to a new location within the free delivery zone of their commercial suppliers based in London (paragraph 3).

BRITISH FILM INSTITUTE

(173 staff in 4 buildings)

1. The communications study showed that the Institute has a high level of contact with organisations and individuals located in London. These include, in particular, members of the public, television, film and theatre bodies, commercial organisations, the National Film Theatre, students and authors. In all, links with London amount to 75 per cent of all contacts. Analysis of communications patterns suggested that the benefits of dispersal could be obtained only at an extremely high cost in terms of damage compared with benefits.

Communications Damage	Resource Gain	Link Weight
689	1,451	3·9

2. No proposal for dispersal was put to the Institute and I recommend that it should not be dispersed.

THE CHARITY COMMISSION

(200 posts in 2 buildings in London)

1. For the purposes of the communications study, the Commission was divided into two parts, the Official Custodian's Division whose 55 staff had very strong links with the rest of the Commission in London and who expressed the desire for strong links with the Commission's dispersed office in Liverpool, and the remainder of the Commission with 145 staff.

2. The contacts of the remainder of the Commission with the Official Custodian represent 17 per cent of all its contacts, and it had a preference for links with the Liverpool office which amount to 10 per cent of all contacts.

3. Liverpool seemed the more suitable location on organisation and management grounds and a proposal for a dispersal there of the entire London office was made to the Commission. Data for Liverpool were:

*Communications Damage	Resource Gain	Link Weight
201	1,352	13·7

4. In response, the Commission pointed out that the advisory and quasi-judicial nature of its work made it important for representatives of charities to take the initiative in coming to the Commission's Headquarters for personal interviews; most of these representatives live in the South of England and many of them are volunteers. The London Headquarters is responsible for charities located in the southern half of England and it would be difficult to establish and keep the close relations with trustees of charities, that the Nathan Committee on Charitable Trusts recommended, if the Commission were relocated in Liverpool.

5. Another point made by the Commission was that the Charities Act 1960 requires the Commission to maintain a Central Register of Charities which must be open to the public, and it was considered that relocation would make the Register less accessible to users; it would be impracticable to maintain the Register in London while the rest of the office were located elsewhere because some of its files are required for day-to-day work in the Department.

6. In addition to these points, the Commission emphasised the importance of a secure system of immediate two-way transmission of original documents between the Official Custodian for Charities and the City; delay could lead to financial loss to the charities concerned. In fulfilling his responsibilities, the Official Custodian comes in contact with nearly all the 169 member firms of the London Stock Exchange as well as every merchant bank.

7. Against this background I recommend that the Commission should not be dispersed.

---

* Because of the strong ties with Liverpool, an illustration based on Bristol would be misleading for the Department.

CIVIL SERVICE DEPARTMENT

1. The Department already has substantial dispersal at Basingstoke (Civil Service Commission, 544 posts); the Civil Service College has wings in Edinburgh and Sunningdale; and, in addition to Chessington, there are 381 computer/statistics staff at Norwich.

2. The review covered 1,948 posts, a few of which were in three small bodies which, though not part of the CSD proper, are staffed from it. They were the Government Hospitality Fund, the Civil Service Sports Council, and the Civil Service Council for Further Education. The staff are presently housed in 13 buildings, including the Chessington Computer Centre.

3. The communications study showed that 50 per cent of the total link strength was internal to the blocks of work under review and that contacts with other Departments in London accounted for half of the remaining links, a reflection of the Department's central management function. Less than 4 per cent of link strength was with the Basingstoke divisions.

4. The Department's preferred location for the bulk of dispersal would be Basingstoke, and the analysis was conducted on this basis. The Department was invited to consider three possible levels of dispersal:

(1) Dispersal of 29 blocks of work, the largest being the Chessington Computer Centre, the London wing of the Civil Service College, Statistics Division, Conditions, Welfare and Training Divisions, Pay Divisions, Manpower Divisions, Personnel Services, Management Personnel, Superannuation Divisions, Behavioural Sciences Research Division, and the Civil Service Selection Board (CSSB): a total of 1,293 posts including *pro rata* allocation of common services staff.

Communications Damage	Resource Gain	Link Weight
656	8,500	13·8

(2) Dispersal as under Proposal 1 but excluding Pay, Manpower, and Conditions and Welfare Divisions: a total of 1,030 posts.

Communications Damage	Resource Gain	Link Weight
444	7,000	17·7

(3) Dispersal of the Chessington Centre, the College, Statistics Divisions, and the Civil Service Selection Board: a total of 678 posts.

Communications Damage	Resource Gain	Link Weight
203	4,800	22·4

(In this case all figures are based on dispersal to Basingstoke since notional dispersal to Bristol would not generate the same proposals for comparison. The resulting impression that the CSD is relatively easy to disperse is therefore misleading, as damage would be higher and marginal trade-off lower if the same proposals *were* for a Bristol location.)

5. The Department argued strongly against dispersal on the basis of Proposals 1 and 2. The principal arguments rested on the following points.

117

The Department had an important central management function for the entire civil service and it was essential that the policy divisions as a whole should be in close touch with the top personnel management of all Departments, with senior staff and Ministers in CSD, and with the National Staff Side. The Pay Divisions, in particular, had an important role in advising Ministers on Public Sector Pay, an area of work which had assumed great political sensitivity in recent years. Most policy branches were liable to frequent meetings with establishment staff in other Departments, with the headquarters of all Civil Service Staff Associations and the Staff Side in the course of considering and implementing a wide range of issues on recruitment, central management, pay, superannuation and other issues arising, for example, from the Fulton Report. It was observed that in many senses the senior staff and principal policy divisions were the " Personnel Division " for the whole civil service. As such, they required close contact with Departments and Staff Associations which could not be efficiently maintained away from London and the National Staff Side have made strong representations to this effect.

6. Although in communication terms the Civil Service Selection Board and the Civil Service College appear highly dispersable, the analysis on which dispersal was proposed did not allow for the costs of travelling by course members, candidates, lecturers and board members in attending sessions at a dispersed location. Although a cost-benefit analysis showed that there would be a net gain in terms of benefits, there are disadvantages arising from dispersal which cannot be quantified. In the case of the College, a number of longer-term courses would need to become residential. Apart from the very hostile reaction by the young people involved which would almost certainly follow such a move, the whole College programme would need to be revised and with the loss of ease of access which London affords could result in difficulties in recruiting lecturers (many of whom are not civil servants). In the case of CSSB, the selection boards for graduate recruitment would also need to be residential, since the bulk of candidates come from the London area and the rest of the country. In both cases the Department is opposed to dispersal.

7. The Department's preference on location for the major part of dispersal is Basingstoke. The recruitment areas of CSD have already been dispersed there and there is a common staffing policy for the London and Basingstoke offices. Because of changes in working patterns arising from mechanisation of procedures and the Fulton Report there has been contraction of work at Basingstoke, with a resulting imbalance in career prospects for staff there. There are, therefore, good management reasons for preferring Basingstoke as the main dispersal location. There are, however, two exceptions to this. The principal exception is the Chessington Computer Centre. If the Department is required to disperse the Centre, it would prefer to locate it in Norwich because the Central Computer Agency (which is part of the CSD) already has a computer installation there which could probably be suitably expanded. Indeed, a feasibility study in this connection has already been started. Second, if the London office of the Civil Service College is to be dispersed, the most natural location would be Sunningdale, where its headquarters is located.

Recommendation

8. I accept the force of the Department's arguments against the dispersal of its central management divisions. However, in my view, there is a number of divisions in the Department which it should be easier to disperse from London. These are the divisions whose functions are less concerned with policy and it should be possible to disperse them at an acceptable price in damage to efficiency. The blocks concerned are:

	Posts (approx.)
Statistics Divisions	100
Behavioural Sciences Research Division . . .	30
Superannuation Division	60
Personnel Services (part) and Organisation Division . .	40
Civil Service Catering Organisation	40
Associated Ancillary Services	30
Total	300

I also believe that the Chessington Computer Centre should be dispersed, together with some parts of the Civil Service College dealing with shorter courses.

9. I recommend, therefore, that the Department should disperse all those jobs listed in paragraph 8 and that they should be relocated as proposed in paragraph 7. The total numbers for each location would be:

	Posts
Basingstoke	300
Norwich	357
Sunningdale	50

Communications Damage	Resource Gain	Average Trade-off
387	4,500	24·36

CIVIL SERVICE PAY RESEARCH UNIT
(46 posts in 1 building)

1. This Department was not subjected to the full communications study, but submitted a statement of communication needs which formed the basis of consideration. In the light of this, dispersal appeared possible at a cost in loss of efficiency which appeared acceptable. It was assumed unrealistic to split the Unit and a proposal for total dispersal was put to the Office.

2. The two main objections to dispersal advanced by the Unit were, first, the difficulties in obtaining staff (who come on secondment for periods of three to five years) in locations with far fewer civil servants than the London area and, second, the importance of proximity to the CSD's Pay Divisions which are not recommended for dispersal and to Staff Side representatives.

3. Against this background, I recommend that the CSPRU should not be dispersed.

COMMUNITY RELATIONS COMMISSION
(54 posts in one building in London)

1.   About 80 per cent of the Commission's high level of contacts are with a large number of organisations and individuals in London, including voluntary organisations, members of the public, overseas visitors and the Commission's own Regional Development Officers.   The benefits of dispersal could be obtained only at an extremely high cost:

Communications Damage	*Resource Gain*	*Link Weight*
168	286	4·0

2.   I recommend that the Commission should not be dispersed.

CRIMINAL INJURIES COMPENSATION BOARD

(83 posts in one building)

1. The communications study showed fairly low levels of contact outside the Department. Most contacts are with the general public at hearings which are held in a number of locations in England, Wales and Scotland. In the event of dispersal, special arrangements will be required for hearings in London, where they take place about once a week, in the same way as hearings are currently arranged outside London.

2. The result of the analysis was:

Communications Damage	Resource Gain	Link Weight
12	418	83

3. A proposal was made to the Board for the dispersal of the entire staff of the Department.

4. In discussion with the CICB, the Board drew attention to the forthcoming review of the Scheme they administered and pointed out that the Secretary was to be a member of the review body and that the Chairman and others would be called upon to provide information and give evidence. This would be difficult if the move were in train. Further, the review might lead to changes in the Board's structure and difficulty could be caused if the office were moved before those changes took effect. They thought, therefore, that the move should not take place until the process of review was completed and any changes had been implemented. However, significant changes in their current communications pattern were not expected. They also expected recruitment of seconded legal staff to become more difficult from a location outside London where they would not have so many Departments with legal staff to draw upon. Although the Board has no particular affinity to any location, the staff require access to reasonable travelling facilities for attendance at hearings as they occur. The Board took the view that it was vital to the continued efficiency and well-being of the staff that career development (which it could not provide standing alone) should not be impeded. They therefore considered that the Board should not be moved to a location which did not also receive a substantial and suitable part of the Home Office, or if present difficulties could be overcome, some other suitable Department.

5. In my view, the Criminal Injuries Compensation Board should be dispersed. I therefore recommend the Board should disperse to Plymouth, the location which I have recommended for the dispersal by the Home Office.

Communications Damage	Resource Gain	Average Trade-off
15	426	63·23

HER MAJESTY'S CUSTOMS AND EXCISE

(some 2,000 posts in 10 buildings)

1. Out of a total staff of 24,000, the Department of Customs and Excise has only 2,000 Headquarters staff in London. The remaining 3,000 Headquarters staff, including the VAT Control Unit, are in Southend, the Department's dispersal location under Flemming and earlier schemes.

2. The study of communications showed that 69 per cent of the Department's total link strength represents contact within London Headquarters, 3·2 per cent with Customs Headquarters blocks already at Southend and 0·2 per cent with Treasury Ministers. The remaining 27·4 per cent covers contact, mostly in London, with other Government Departments, trade associations, commercial organisations, etc. Contact with Treasury Ministers is mainly at Chairman and Deputy Chairman level but there are in addition important contacts with Treasury officials and Parliamentary Counsel at Under-Secretary, Assisant Secretary and Principal levels.

3. Following analysis of the communication patterns (in which the links of the Chief Inspector and his Office as well as those of Management Services Division A were disregarded because in the event of dispersal these three blocks would require reorganisation by Customs), three proposals were submitted for discussion with the Department. The proposals were as follows:

(1) Dispersal of the entire Department including the Chairman *i.e.* 1,777 posts. In this case the three blocks mentioned above would follow the rest of the Department. This would bring the total proposal figure to 1,960.

Communications Damage	Resource Gain	Link Weight
1,834	11,446	1·7

(2) Dispersal of 1,306 posts, leaving in London all Commissioners, other than the Commissioner for General Customs, and the blocks concerned with Revenue Duties and VAT (other than those at Southend). In addition the Solicitor's Office and the Investigation Division would stay in London.

Communications Damage	Resource Gain	Link Weight
945	8,414	13·0

(3) Dispersal of 513 posts, made up of three blocks, Stores Branch, Valuation Division and Accountant and Comptroller General's Office (London).

Communications Damage	Resource Gain	Link Weight
160	4,059	16·3

4. The Department argued that it could not function efficiently if there were total dispersal from London. The principal disadvantages would be the serious adverse effect on the way in which senior staff, principally the Chairman and Deputy Chairman, provided a service to Treasury

Ministers; this could be particularly damaging during the Budget period, but in modern conditions the service is needed throughout the year. Closely allied to this was the Department's wider involvement in fiscal matters, requiring urgent consultation between senior staff in the Department and Treasury officials and Parliamentary Counsel, both on Taxation proposals and accompanying legislation. More generally, there was a need for continuing discussions with other Departments, principally Treasury, DTI and MAFF in considering policies and subordinate legislation concerned with import duties and general Customs issues. This form of consultation has increased since the signing of the Treaty of Accession to the EEC and will remain a significant workload in the foreseeable future. Furthermore, the numbers and frequency of meetings with EEC officials in Brussels have increased sharply, with more than 400 meetings anticipated during 1973 needing Customs representation at a senior level. This scale of meetings is expected to continue unabated and is essential if the Department is to maintain necessary contacts and properly fulfil its European commitments. It was the Department's view that if it were totally dispersed the price to be paid in damage from all aspects would be unacceptable.

5. Customs felt that a number of these arguments also applied to a large extent to Proposal 2, but there was as well a number of additional constraints that would apply. The main ones are as follows. Since the study of locations has demonstrated that Southend could not absorb this number of posts, a dispersal on this basis would result in a three-way split of the Department's Headquarters—between London, Southend and another location—with serious implications for staffing and management. The Department also felt that the split was unacceptable on organisational grounds as it would separate two Commissioners (the Director of Establishments and Commissioner for Import Duties, etc.) from their operational divisions and from other senior staff and that they could not function efficiently in this way. A number of blocks in the proposal were concerned with subordinate legislative work and separation would seriously damage essential communication with other Departments and with other Customs blocks. Finally, the Department attached importance to the implications for adequate career development of staff and stressed that further dispersal would seriously impede the flexible deployment of staff between different areas of Headquarters work, and would impair efficiency and morale.

6. Subject to the need to retain in London a staff of about 20 in the Accountant and Comptroller General's Office to provide facilities for the Bank of England and the Joint Stock Banks the Department should be able to disperse on the basis of Proposal 3. This number could be accommodated within the Department's existing dispersal location at Southend.

7. I therefore recommend that Customs and Excise should disperse some 500 posts to Southend. This figure is based on the agreed modification to Proposal 3, as mentioned in paragraph 6, and also includes a proportion of staff from the three reorganised blocks.

Communications Damage	Resource Gain	Average Trade-off
59	3,660	120·50

124

8. Because of the previous interest in the siting of VAT Headquarters and the claims of regional policy, I have given serious consideration to the possibility of a much more substantial dispersal by Customs. An obvious solution would be for the Department to attempt to disperse more staff to Southend where it already has a large Headquarters element, but it has been established that there is only accommodation for a further 500 staff.

9. In view of the accommodation constraints at Southend I have, therefore, looked at the possibility of moving a significant proportion of the Department's London Headquarters to a more distant location. If more emphasis has to be given to regional policy then the most appropriate solution would be to disperse some 1,370 posts, *i.e.* the level of Proposal 2 plus a proportion of posts from the three reorganised blocks, to Central Lancashire New Town, for which the measures are:

Communications Damage	*Resource Gain*	*Average Trade-off*
1,474	8,817	12·49

But this increases the damage by almost 26 times more than the recommended solution, while it only doubles the resource gain. It also splits the Department's Headquarters between three locations, the objections to which are already summarised in paragraph 5.

10. Moreover, I am bound to add that I was much impressed by the Department's argument that entry into the European Economic Community had fundamentally changed the character of its work and its communication needs. Between now and 1980 systems of administration and control covering import duties and reliefs, quantitative and qualitative import controls, and the taxation of tobacco, wines, spirits and beer, as well as VAT, will have to be harmonised on whatever common arrangements may eventually be agreed. This will require changes not only in policy and legislation but also in a multiplicity of detailed administrative procedures. Close and efficient communications with Brussels, with Ministers and other interested Departments, particularly, Treasury, DTI and MAFF, and within Customs and Excise itself will be essential.

11. For all these reasons I advise against the course explained in paragraph 9 and have not included it in my alternative "regional" solution.

MINISTRY OF DEFENCE

1. The Ministry of Defence is the largest employing Department in Central Government, with responsibilities for Service, research, development and production establishments spread throughout the United Kingdom as well as Armed Service units in various parts of the world. It is also the largest Department in the London area, with a total of 23,400 Headquarters staff under review, including about 5,000 staff in various establishments outside the centre and some 3,000 Armed Service personnel. Prior to 1963, when Sir Gilbert Flemming made the last report on the dispersal of Government Headquarters work, the Departments now comprising the MOD had dispersed some 7,400 Headquarters posts from London, mainly from the Admiralty to Bath and from the Air Ministry to Harrogate. Sir Gilbert Flemming himself, whilst making a number of specific recommendations for the dispersal of certain blocks of work from the " Defence Group ", also raised the possibility of " major surgery " being carried out on the Group with large blocks of staff being removed from London (Report, paragraph 48).

2. However, since 1963 what is now the MOD has undergone a number of major reorganisations in bringing together four separate Departments into one unified Ministry. Most recent of all is the establishment of the Procurement Executive in 1971. Since 1963 some 1,300 Headquarters posts have been dispersed from London and a further 375 are planned to go, the major receiving areas being Bath and Harrogate once more, plus Taunton and Worcester (see Appendix 2). Several of the moves recommended by Sir Gilbert Flemming have not been implemented, including that of the Master-General of the Ordnance (MGO), whose Department Sir Gilbert Flemming thought could be moved from London if really substantial dispersal were contemplated (Report, paragraph 52), as there proved to be strong organisational objections to them. The previous Administration decided that MGO and his staff (some 1,500 posts) should move to Cardiff, but this decision was set aside whilst Mr. Derek Rayner undertook his study of the whole Defence procurement organisation in 1970–71. In fact, only 300 or so staff of the MGO's Department were included in my two middle proposals (6,218 posts and 10,890 posts) for the MOD.

3. The communications study was complicated by the formation of the Procurement Executive, which necessitated a novel approach to take account of the reorganisation then in train; by the size of the Department; by the inherent complexity of the MOD both in organisational terms and because it deals both collectively and separately with the three fighting Services; and by the need to mount additional studies to take account of other factors bearing on patterns of contact, including the necessity to remain in a state of operational readiness for civil and military emergencies. A further factor is the historical accident of wartime dispersal which tends to have created different patterns of work and communications in different areas of activity.

4. The analysis of the data reflected two main features, the very high level of contact inside the Department for large numbers of staff and the extensive links of many others with MOD establishments and with

manufacturers throughout the country, but particularly in the South and South West. For these reasons, the analysis pointed on paper at least to dispersal of the whole Department to one location rather than dividing it between several, and the Department argued that this location should be on or near the London–Bath axis. The order of dispersability for such a single receiving location as Bristol suggested two levels of dispersal, one at 3,993 posts and the other the whole Department, save about 1,000, including Ministers and their staff who had been regarded as fixed in London from the outset. There was virtually no change, however, in the value of the trade-off between these two levels (about $15 \cdot 7$). This order of dispersability did undergo minor changes when other single receiving locations were considered, because of the influence of the contacts of some parts of the Department with each other and with different parts of the country.

5. Because there was only one location capable of accommodating really large numbers of staff, other analyses were done assuming four receiving locations, each capable of receiving a part of a large dispersal. This pointed to two intermediate proposals of 6,218 and 10,890 jobs. The receiving locations used were on a south-westerly axis from London, but chosen as representative of distance rather than as specific candidates.

6. Four proposals were put to the Department for discussion, therefore:

Proposal A—3,993 posts in 54 blocks of work to one location. This involved 3,206 Central posts, 591 Army posts and 196 Procurement Executive posts, but none from the Air or Navy Departments. Most of the jobs involved were from the DUS (Civilian Management)'s command, the DUS (Finance)'s command and the Chief of Personnel and Logistics' command.

Communications Damage	Resource Gain	Link Weight
2,206	25,408	$15 \cdot 7$

Proposal B—6,218 posts in 83 blocks of work to two locations such as Basingstoke (2,788) and Swindon (3,430). This involved 4,173 Central posts, including those in Proposal A plus 967 Defence Intelligence Staff, 796 Army posts, 1,235 Air posts and 14 Procurement Executive posts, but none from the Navy Department. The posts from the Air Department included the whole of the Air Member for Personnel's command.

Communications Damage	Resource Gain	Link Weight
2,946	37,504	$19 \cdot 1$

Proposal C—10,890 posts in 124 blocks of work to three locations such as Cardiff (3,430), Basingstoke (3,864) and Swindon (3,596). This involved the same 4,173 Central posts and 796 Army posts as in Proposal B, 2,180 Air posts and 3,741 Procurement Executive posts, but none from the Navy Department. The Air Department posts were as in Proposal B, plus almost all staff in the Air Member for Supply and Organisation's command. The Procurement Executive work comprised

127

the whole of the Controller of Aircraft's command and almost all of the Controller of Guided Weapons and Electronics' command, plus contracts, costs and accountancy branches in the Controller Policy's command.

Communications Damage	Resource Gain	Link Weight
6,872	64,535	14·7

Proposal D—22,400 posts to Milton Keynes. This involved the whole Department except 1,000 posts, including Ministers and their staff fixed in London, and the 3,193 posts in the Quality Assurance Directorates at Woolwich, Bromley and Harefield. These had been considered fixed in the analyses, but with dispersal at this level it was felt necessary to discuss the possible relocation of this work also.

Communications Damage	Resource Gain	Link Weight
8,000	104,000	28

7. The proposal papers recognised the radical nature of the last proposal and acknowledged the many problems it raised, but felt that it needed to be explored because the analysis showed its effect on efficiency, as measured by the communications data above, to be broadly acceptable. In addition, the average number of contacts per person affected by this proposal was actually less than in other proposals.

8. The Department decided to concentrate on Proposals B and D. It chose Proposal B because it thought it might be required to make a more substantial contribution to dispersal than was contained in Proposal A; moreover, because of its greater size, Proposal B had the advantage of allowing a body of staff to be dispersed which would be reasonably self-contained for management purposes. In the Department's view, Proposal C had no such advantage over Proposal B and would, in addition, involve a much greater degree of disruption to its work and organisation. Proposal D was also reviewed because it offered the most radical approach and because it was in keeping with one of the main objectives of the exercise.

9. After examination by the separate single-Service Boards, the Defence and Central Staffs and the Procurement Executive, the Department argued that Proposal D was unacceptable for the following main reasons:

(*a*) It would destroy the unification of policy with management which was one of the main aims of the 1964 reorganisation. A pattern similar to the pre-1964 organisation would emerge, with all the inefficiencies that that entailed, made worse by the tendency for two distinct groups of staff to develop, a policy-making group in London and a management group at the dispersed location. This could only harm the morale and efficient working of the Department and pose insuperable difficulties in proper career development.

(*b*) It would seriously, perhaps dangerously, reduce the Department's speed of reaction to emergencies. New methods of communications were unlikely to be of much help in this respect.

(c) It would produce grave staffing, security and sociological problems. Of the possible receiving locations, only Milton Keynes appeared to be a candidate to absorb a dispersal of this size, but the MOD would soon so dominate such an environment that it would take on the character of a " company town ".

(d) There were in any case grave doubts whether Milton Keynes could absorb such a large dispersal, even over a long timescale. The review team had assessed Milton Keynes' capacity at 5,000 posts by the early 1980s, with the possibility of more in the longer term.

10. Although the Department did not examine Proposal C (10,890 posts) in any detail, it argued that this proposal offered the worst of all worlds. The damage to the efficiency and organisation of the Department would be unacceptably high, especially since such a dispersal would probably have to be spread over at least two, or even three, locations, thus adding to the management and organisational problems which this proposal would cause.

11. The Department recognised that, if it must disperse, there were advantages in dispersing a large body of staff to one location in order to provide a self-contained management unit. On this basis, dispersal along the lines of Proposal B (6,218 posts), which did not appear to involve a totally unacceptable degree of damage to the efficiency of the Department, might be tolerable. Such a solution, the Department stressed, would be subject to further consideration being given to such factors as the absorption capacities of locations and timing, and to its undertaking an organisational review of the blocks of work to be dispersed. On this last point, the Department suggested that the communications study had produced misleading results since it had taken insufficient account of the importance, as opposed to the frequency, of contacts between various parts of the organisation. The Department emphasised that, because it was an amalgamation of five Departments and was still in the process of absorbing the Ministry of Aviation Supply, it was presented with quite different problems from other Departments in centralising control of policy, centralising arrangements for achieving economies of scale in administration and decentralising executive responsibilities. A large number of staff had dual lines of reporting. The Department argued, therefore, that to disperse certain blocks of work contained within some of the proposals did not make good management or organisational sense. The impact of dispersal on the Department as a whole would need to be assessed to ensure that the correct balance of control in the Department was maintained. In considering the dispersal proposals, the Department argued that it had not had sufficient time to carry out this assessment and that, when it had eventually been decided how many MOD posts should disperse and to which location, it would need to undertake an exercise of its own to decide which posts should go. This organisational review was likely to take some months.

12. On location, the Department argued strongly for dispersal along the London–Bath axis. Many of its major Service and research establishments were concentrated in the south and south west, and dispersal along the axis should reduce substantially the damage to efficiency which dispersal would entail. Dispersal over a somewhat greater distance, for example to Cardiff,

129

might be acceptable if a smaller number of posts were dispersed. However, dispersal over a much greater distance was, in the Department's view, not acceptable. The Department has already dispersed those areas of work which could be located at some distance from London. Any additional dispersal would need to provide for the most effective possible communications, both for personnel and for information, principally with London but also, and still important, with other centres (such as research establishments) which had hitherto been dealt with from London.

Recommendations

13. In terms of the number of posts to be dispersed from MOD, it appears that a dispersal of the order of 6,218 posts could be satisfactorily implemented without lowering efficiency unacceptably. It is argued that greater numbers would present severe organisational difficulties, touching in particular upon the Department's ability to respond effectively to sudden emergencies. I should have wished to have explored these arguments with the Department in greater detail, but, since this has not been possible, I must record my own judgment, as a basis for Ministerial discussion. This is that the 10,890 posts in Proposal C are not those which would normally be seriously involved in these emergencies, and that the effect on efficiency of dispersing them would prove as tolerable as in Proposal B. I am not unsympathetic with the Department's wish to carry out its own internal study to determine which posts should be dispersed, and I fully accept that such an analysis, which would bring the experience and judgment of all parts of the Department to bear on the issues, would be a valuable supplement to the study of communication patterns which has formed the basis of my proposals and which itself provides basic evidence to support the case for dispersal. I would, indeed, have been happier in making recommendations if we had had more discussions and made greater progress during the three months at our disposal but, equally, from my own experience of the Department, I am sure that my proposals in general provide a sound basis for considering its dispersability.

14. I recognise that the management of such a large dispersal will present considerable problems and I therefore recommend that it should be spread over a long period. I also recommend that, to reduce the management and organisational difficulties involved, dispersal should be to a single location quite near to London. Milton Keynes is the obvious choice since, over the lengthy timescale I have mentioned, it should be able to absorb this number of posts and it is a location not very far removed from the Department's own preference for the London–Bath axis. Further, Milton Keynes is only 45 miles from London and such a location should keep damage to communications and disturbance of staff to a minimum.

15. I recommend that those blocks of work in my Proposal B, possibly subject, with the approval of Ministers, to revision as to composition in the light of MOD's further studies, but numbering not less than 6,218 posts, should be dispersed from MOD to Milton Keynes in a first phase, which might be implemented by about 1980. I also recommend that the MOD should disperse a further 4,672 posts to Milton Keynes in a second phase, bringing the total number dispersed to the level of my Proposal C. The

separation into two phases would allow revised estimates to be made nearer the time of the receiving capacity of Milton Keynes, which must depend on the continued development of that new town. Doubts about Milton Keynes's capacity do not arise in my recommendation for MOD in the alternative " regional " solution which comprises the dispersal of 6,218 posts to Cardiff and 4,672 to Milton Keynes.

Communications Damage	Resource Gain	Average Trade-off
4,917	59,354	27·57

DEPARTMENT OF EDUCATION AND SCIENCE

(1,361 posts, of which all but 90 are in one building; the remainder are in 3 small detached groups concerned with Arts, Libraries and Training)

1. The Department has a sizeable dispersed unit of work at Darlington (664 posts), and certain other staff (Her Majesty's Inspectorate of Schools and supporting staff) distributed throughout England.

2. The communications study, and subsequent analysis, showed DES to be a very tightly knit Department, with few, if any, truly " self-contained " portions of work whose dispersal would create no major problems. Although it was clear from analysis that even small-scale dispersal would cause a high degree of communications damage in relation to resource gain, two proposals were prepared for discussion in order to explore the difficulties:

(1) Dispersal of the entire Department excluding Ministers, Permanent Secretary, the Deputy Secretaries for Arts and Science, the Office of Scientific and Technical Information, Science Branch and the Arts and Libraries Branch, a total dispersal of 1,270 posts.

Communications Damage	Resource Gain	Link Weight
1,600	8,000	9

(2) Dispersal of 180 posts, consisting of Universities Branch, Awards Division, Teachers II Branch, Youth Services Division and Head-quarters and Associated Inspectors of Teacher Training.

Communications Damage	Resource Gain	Link Weight
210	1,200	11·0

3. The Department argued that dispersal under Proposal 1 would place a very serious limitation on the effectiveness of the Department's operations in its main role as an " extended secretariat ". DES is a relatively small Department with few direct executive powers and is almost wholly concerned with policy issues. It relies a great deal on the extent to which it can influence others. The principal difficulties would arise from the separation of operational divisions from senior officials and Ministers. The need for co-ordination of policy creation between groups, for frequent discussions with the top of the office and Parliamentary business was likely to increase even more as education policy received more attention in Parliament and amongst the general public.

4. In the Department's view, contact with other social policy Departments, likely to increase, would also be impaired by dispersal. The Department attached particular importance to contact with local education authorities and other educational, cultural and scientific interests. A central location in London was most desirable for maintaining contacts with the independent educational institutions throughout the country, with the local authorities and with numerous other organisations and associations, with

132

whom there was continuous consultation. Under the local government reorganisation recently enacted there will be 96 English (and 8 Welsh) authorities and the headquarters of 34 of these will be within a 60-mile radius of central London. Apart from local education authorities, 75 per cent of all bodies and organisations concerned with education and allied matters were within the London area. Total dispersal of all but senior staff would damage these contacts to a degree which Ministers were likely to find unacceptable.

5. Even on Proposal 2, the Department considered that the specific blocks suggested for dispersal were so closely concerned with the co-ordinated development of educational policy that it would cause unacceptable disruption of the organisation and management of total operations if they were detached from the main headquarters of the Department.

6. In general, the Department's case against dispersal, largely confirmed by the quantitative assessment of its dispersability, rests on the following points:
 (a) It is a homogeneous unit and any further splitting of the Department would be arbitrary.
 (b) The Department consists largely of comparatively small policy support groups without whose immediate availability Ministers and senior officials could not operate effectively.
 (c) The load of Parliamentary business is comparatively heavy.
 (d) The degree of contact with educational and cultural authorities and other organisations is high, and many of these are either in the London area or find London the most convenient point of reference.

7. In the light of the above arguments, I recommend that DES should not be dispersed, either in whole or in part.

DEPARTMENT OF EMPLOYMENT

(2,788 posts of whom 500 are located in Watford and the remainder in 15 buildings in Central London)

1. The Department has a dispersed unit, consisting of some 700 posts, at Runcorn. Other Headquarters work has also been resited at Watford (500 posts).

2. The communications study for DE was completed in March 1972 and reflected the organisation then existing. The study showed that 69 per cent of link strength reflected contact within the Headquarters part of the Department. Analysis of the data suggested that substantial dispersal could be obtained at a trade-off between communications damage and gains which appeared acceptable. The proposals put to the Department were as follows:

(1) Dispersal of 2,645 posts, leaving in London Ministers, the Permanent Secretary, the Deputy Secretaries concerned with incomes and economic policy and industrial relations, the Solicitor and his staff, Information Branch, Industrial Relations Branch and most of the Incomes and Economic Policy Branches.

Communications Damage	Resource Gain	Link Weight
1,219	12,739	13·57

(2) Dispersal of 2,016 posts. In addition to the blocks above this proposal would retain in London the Deputy Secretary for training matters, Training Divisions, Research and Planning and Statistics Divisions and the Overseas Divisions.

Communications Damage	Resource Gain	Link Weight
769	9,224	21·26

3. In discussion with the Department towards the end of 1972, it was recognised that some reorganisation had already taken place since the time of the communications study and that radical changes would be made within the next two to three years. These latter changes, in particular, must largely invalidate the results of the communications study. It was accepted, therefore, that dispersal could not be considered on the basis of the proposals and the Department was invited to consider the possibility of a counter-proposal which took account of expected needs under the reorganisation.

4. Proposed changes in the functions of the Department will lead to the creation of a Manpower Services Commission, Employment Services Agency, Training Services Agency and possibly of a Safety and Health Authority. A large proportion of DE posts, including Headquarters posts, will be absorbed in these new organisations. It is expected that they will be largely self-supporting for establishments and finance purposes and that their Headquarters need not be in London. Posts at present in DE Headquarters which

will be subsumed in the new organisations could, therefore, be dispersed. The areas of work concerned are:

Training Divisions (including Under-Secretary)	.		355 posts in London
			60 posts in Watford
Directorate of Safety and Health	.	.	491 posts
Employment Services Division II	.	.	118 posts in London
			54 posts in Watford
Total	.	.	.	.	1,078

(Numbers include an allowance for common service staff and other supporting services.)

A further 300 or so staff, mainly from Establishments and Finance Divisions, could be added to these, giving a total of about 1,400 staff.

5. As regards the much reduced number of posts which would remain in London after reorganisation, the Department argued that dispersal of any of these in addition would impose an unacceptable burden on management. An exception to this was a unit of 27 staff dealing with unemployment benefit administration; but since this unit is likely to be transferred to DHSS in a few years it was accepted that a decision on location should be deferred until then. Other exceptions were the Central Office of Industrial Tribunals (COIT) (41 posts) and the part of the Employment General Division dealing with work permits for immigrants (140 posts), which could probably be relocated.

6. The arguments against dispersing remaining Headquarters posts rest mainly on the following points: the co-ordination required between the operational divisions, between them and senior officials and between senior officials and Ministers; the volume of Parliamentary business; the degree to which the policy areas of the Department need to react to such urgent business as strikes, pay disputes and other industrial relations problems; and the location in London of the headquarters of many of the trades unions and employers' associations. In order to maintain an efficient service to meet these needs, the Department regarded London as an essential location for Headquarters staff. In other respects DE was concerned that further dispersal would impose too great a burden on the staff at a time of extensive reorganisation. It stressed the considerable dispersal which has already taken place to Watford and Runcorn and that all Headquarters work which could be regionalised already has been. (At present, out of a total staff of some 35,000, only about 3,500 are Headquarters posts. Only 2,300 of these are in central London. If the dispersal proposed is implemented, the London Headquarters will reduce to around 1,000 posts.)

7. On location, the Department argued that the Employment and Training Agencies must be together and that there would be advantages (though not overwhelming ones) in having any Safety Agency in the same place. All these agencies would be controlling area organisations with large numbers of local offices. For this purpose a reasonably central site with good communications to all parts of the country would be necessary. The

critical problems in relation to location would arise from the creation of the Manpower Services Commission and any Safety and Health Authority. These bodies, which would be responsible for the management of the Agencies, would consist of representatives of the CBI, the TUC and local authorities, serving part-time, and most of these people would be London-based. The representatives themselves would rely heavily on back-up services from the staff of their organisations in London. If the Manpower Services Commission and the Safety Authority were to be able to develop effective control of their Agencies, the Department considered it essential that the Headquarters of the Agencies should be sufficiently near London to permit reasonably frequent visits by Members without necessarily involving a whole-day visit. To achieve this, a dispersal location would have to be within $1\frac{1}{2}$ to 2 hours' travelling time of London. The Department therefore considered it essential that the dispersal location should be in the area bounded by the North of London, Leicester, Birmingham and Bristol. In the Department's view, any location further away from London (e.g. Liverpool) would seriously endanger the chances of making the new and delicate arrangements to associate the CBI and TUC with the management of the Manpower Services develop effectively. If the additional posts referred to in paragraph 5 were to be dispersed, the Department felt that the COIT should be in a location where there was an existing Industrial Tribunal Office and that the 140 posts dealing with work permits for immigrants should be co-located with the Immigration and Nationality Department of the Home Office.

Recommendation

8. I recommend the dispersal of the 1,400 posts made up as proposed, of the COIT and of the two sections of the Employment General Division dealing with work permits for immigrants. I have sympathy with the Department's preference for dispersal area, the arguments on which once again illustrate the character of London as outlined in the main report and in Appendices 4 and 10. If Ministers were to place the main emphasis on efficiency, they might wish to accede to the Department's arguments, but if it is to be placed more on regional policy, the work could go to a further location without too much additional loss of efficiency. Taking account of the criteria prescribed for the review, and of the list of locations approved by Ministers, I recommend that the Agencies should be dispersed to Liverpool, such a location also being suitable for the Central Office of Industrial Tribunals. I also recommend that the 140 posts dealing with work permits for immigrants should be co-located with the Immigration and Nationality Department of the Home Office.

Communications Damage	Resource Gain	Average Trade-off
970	8,240	19·60

DEPARTMENT OF THE ENVIRONMENT

(12,833 posts in 43 buildings)

1. The study of communication patterns showed that 69 per cent of the total link strengths recorded were between DOE blocks in London. The remainder were with other Government bodies in London (9·5 per cent), other bodies in London (11 per cent), fringe bodies (1 per cent) and other bodies outside London, including DOE regional offices (9·5 per cent).

2. Two months after the completion of the communications study the Property Services Agency was formed. This involved about one-third of the total number of posts reviewed but the data were still considered to be broadly representative of the communication needs of the Department. By dividing the Department initially into a relatively large number of blocks of work it was hoped that problems with the data caused by subsequent reorganisation would be minimised. Further analysis on this basis suggested that the Department could be treated for the purposes of the exercise as several groups of larger blocks of work which were related in communications and functional terms and that dispersal might be possible in three broad areas where the trade-off between damage and gains appeared attractive. The Department was therefore invited to consider three proposals:

Proposal	No. of posts	Communications Damage	Resource Gain	Link Weight
1	5,994	4,623	56,806	12·05
2	3,615	2,225	43,590	14·63
3	1,897	655	31,456	17·16

Each number of posts included a *pro rata* allocation of staff from those blocks concerned with the provision of office services.

3. In the course of discussion, the possibilities were narrowed down to
   (a) the relocation of most of the Property Services Agency (up to 4,100 posts);
   (b) the relocation of some 1,250 other posts, described in paragraph 11.

4. Among the issues considered in identifying these possibilities were the evidence provided by the communications study about the strength of the links binding the major policy areas of the Department to London and the fact that one of the principal objectives at which the formation of the Department in 1970 was aimed was to bring together in a single organisation related policy areas (*e.g.* planning and highways). It was not felt that either the communications data or the organisational aims of the Department would justify dispersal in such areas.

Property Services Agency

5. The total headquarters staff of the PSA in London is about 5,200, of whom some 1,100 are concerned with the management of the Government's office estate in London. The potentially dispersable element therefore totals some 4,100 posts, but this figure needs to be qualified so as to take account of the probability that some of the work may be decentralised to regional

137

administration centres. The PSA is now engaged in a study of its long-term organisation, with particular reference to the amount of extra work which could be placed in regional centres; it is difficult to estimate how many posts would be involved, but it could be in the range 500 to 1,000. (Decentralisation may be legitimately regarded as a contribution to dispersal policy, although the reasons for it are more directly administrative.) The number of posts potentially dispersable away from London could therefore be about 3,600 (*i.e.* 5,200—(1,100 + 500)), but it is impossible to set a precise figure on it at this stage.

6. For some years the Department has been relocating work in the area of what has now become the PSA in Croydon. More is due to go under existing plans, some of which the communications study showed could be moved beyond the London area. Most of the remainder, including work already at Croydon, was shown to be firmly tied to London and did not figure in the initial proposals.

7. The Department was prepared to relocate the bulk of PSA Headquarters work to Croydon and so to bring about the major concentration of the PSA in that location.

8. There are however two principal objections to Croydon as a dispersal location. First, it is well within the London area and the relocation of work there is not the sort of dispersal the Government is seeking. Second, it is an area of competition for locally recruited staff and the PSA would be likely to encounter recruitment problems.

9. The possibility was then considered of relocating the whole PSA Headquarters outside London. The managerial advantages of bringing the various Headquarters elements together were reassessed and found to go some way to justify extending the communication links of the elements not proposed for dispersal; this suggested that to disperse them was less damaging than dispersing some of the policy areas included in the initial proposals. It was therefore proposed that the PSA should be relocated beyond London.

10. In responding to this new proposal the Department maintained its view that relocation of the bulk of the PSA in Croydon was the best solution and that it made an adequate contribution to the movement of work out of central London. But, subject to a number of qualifications, it did not exclude completely the possibility of relocating the bulk of the PSA outside London. These qualifications, five in all, must be borne in mind in considering any relocation of PSA. First, the movement of work to Croydon started about 1968 and is still continuing. It would be unreasonable to subject either the organisation or the staff to an early further move, particularly as many staff have now moved their homes to within reasonable access of Croydon. Secondly, as the PSA came into its new form only in September 1972, it would be prudent to allow it some time to settle down as a new management entity and also to enable the staff to adjust before dispersal. Third, the PSA will be deeply involved in the dispersal programme, as the provider of Government accommodation, and it would not be sensible to contemplate moving it until the main stages of the programme are complete. Fourth, it would need a location with

good communications to London and to other parts of the country, as its clients (other Departments), and therefore its operations, are countrywide and will be even more so when the dispersal programme has been completed. Finally, that part of the PSA concerned with the management of the office estate in London must clearly remain in the London area to enable it to discharge this responsibility in an efficient manner.

Other posts

11.   Dispersal could be contemplated somewhat more readily in certain areas of work not directly associated with the Department's main policy areas, but not without reservations.   It was considered possible that dispersal might be feasible in the following areas:

A.   DEPARTMENT OF THE ENVIRONMENT

	No. of posts
Establishments Management Services Divisions . . .	90
Statistics A, B, C and H Divisions	100
Public Sector Superannuation Division	30
Establishments Group	120
PLUP 4 and PUP 6 Divisions	41
Planning Inspectorate	450
Statistics, Data Processing (Hemel Hempstead) . . .	63
Housing 9 Division	70
PLUP 2 Division	72

B.   ASSOCIATED BODIES

	No. of posts
Development Commission	21
COSIRA	100
Countryside Commission	91
Total	1,248

12.   The reservations are that, first, the Statistics, Data Processing work has already been relocated (in Hemel Hempstead).   Second, the Development Commission, COSIRA and the Countryside Commission will need to select their new locations with due regard to their accessibility to both their clients and related authorities.   Third, some of the work (chiefly that of the Planning Inspectorate) might be a better candidate for regionalisation than for dispersal, *en masse*, to a single location.   Fourth, other work in the area covered by A above would best be sited together with DOE work already in a regional centre; from the Department's viewpoint, the best choice would be Bristol.

Recommendations

13.   I recommend that the bulk of the Property Services Agency should be dispersed, at the end of the dispersal programme, to Cardiff, which in my view will give the Agency the accessibility it needs to London and elsewhere.

As already noted, the *potentially* dispersable element of PSA Headquarters amounts to some 4,100 posts. This is the figure I have used in calculating dispersal possibilities, but it should be noted that there is a strong probability that some of this work will be devolved to regional centres, reducing the total of 4,100 by perhaps up to 1,000 posts (which would, as also noted, be a contribution to dispersal policy). The figure of 4,100 should not, therefore, be regarded as an immutable target for a single location dispersal. The characteristics of this would be:

No. of posts	Communications Damage	Resource Gain	Average Trade-off
4,100	3,575	14,880	12·17

14. I should also record that the Department would have much preferred that a location for PSA should not be specified at this early stage in its existence, when its operational organisation might well undergo substantial changes and when the timing of its dispersal was some few years ahead; and that any location suggested for it should be regarded as provisional and subject to review in the light of the operational requirements laid upon it and of its relations to its clients, when their dispersal had taken effect on the present pattern of relations. I am not unsympathetic to these views, but I have specified a location, to provide a firm basis for Ministerial discussion of this in relation to other issues.

15. It should be noted that about 1,100 staff (out of the total of 5,200) concerned with the management of the London Estate will need to be retained in the London area; much of this work might be relocated in Croydon, at the cost of some loss of efficiency.

16. I recommend that 1,248 posts, noted in paragraph 11, should be dispersed with due regard to the points made in paragraph 12. For those posts which have no prior locational requirements I suggest Bristol, since it has a DOE regional administration of a suitable size. The characteristics on the assumption that all the work is located at Bristol of this would be:

No. of posts	Communications Damage	Resource Gain	Average Trade-off
1,248	960	7,039	16·42

17. It will be noted that these recommendations in terms of numbers are very nearly at the level of the most severe Proposal 1 put to the Department.

EXCHEQUER AND AUDIT DEPARTMENT
(418 posts in London)

1. E & AD was considered in two parts, the senior audit staff (27) located in London and the rest of the staff, of whom 59 are at the London Headquarters office, 332 are attached to other departments in London and 159 are attached to other departments outside London.

2. The study of the communications of the senior staff showed that 57 per cent of link strength represented contact within the Headquarters office and analysis suggested that dispersal could be obtained only at a price in trade-off between gains and damage which would be comparatively severe.

3. Against this background and taking account of the small size of the Department, no proposal for dispersal of the Headquarters staff was put to E & AD.

4. The outstationed staff of the Department were not formally studied. Their communication links are in the main with the accounts and contracts staff in the Department to which they are attached. In those cases where dispersal of this work is recommended, there will be clear implications for the E & AD staff concerned. These will follow the decisions taken by Ministers on each Department.

5. I do not recommend dispersal of any of the Headquarters staff of E & AD. The outstationed staff have necessarily to be with the accounting and financial branches of the departments they are auditing and dispersal of such branches will mean that some of the Comptroller and Auditor General's staff will have to follow.

EXECUTIVE SPORTS COUNCIL

(114 posts in one building)

1. The Council (97 posts) and their Regional Office (17 posts) both have high levels of contact with organisations based in London, particularly the National Sports Governing Bodies. The benefits of dispersal could therefore be obtained only at extremely high cost:

	Communications Damage	Resource Gain	Link Weight
ESC . . .	241	485	4·8
Regional Office .	37	89	5·6

2. Against this background I recommend that the Council should not be dispersed.

EXPORT CREDITS GUARANTEE DEPARTMENT

(1,480 posts in three buildings)

1. The communications study endorsed the conclusions of an earlier management report (the Scholey Report) which recommended dispersal of what is now, following a recent reorganisation, the Department's Marketing and Servicing Group. One Under-Secretary is responsible for the whole Group and the various areas are closely linked both organisationally and in terms of communications. The study also confirmed the strength of the remaining Divisions' links with the City and with areas in the Treasury and in DTI not proposed for dispersal.

2. Accordingly a single proposal was put to the Department, for dispersal of the whole Marketing and Servicing Group (comprising the Finance Division (150 posts), Comprehensive Guarantee Division (194), Status Branch (162), Data Processing and Statistics Branch (81), Claims Branch (169) and Regional Organisation Branch (9)), a total of 765 posts including common services.

Communications Damage	Resource Gain	Link Weight
310	4,100	30

3. In discussion with the Department it was accepted that certain work was to be devolved to regional offices under current management plans and that this would remove about 150 posts from the area for dispersal proper. It was also accepted that some reorganisation would be necessary to maintain certain essential links with London and with Divisions not included in the proposals. In round figures, therefore, the posts for dispersal number about 600.

4. In general, the Department did not dissent from the findings of the communications study, nor from dispersal of the Marketing and Servicing Group in principle. But it did point to a number of serious risks and practical difficulties connected with the efficiency and economy of the service offered to exporters stemming from the need to provide a speedy and competent credit insurance and financing support service to exporters on a commercial basis. In particular a high degree of technical versatility is required of middle-grade and senior staff, acquired through the broadest possible experience. If the organisation is to be divided into two parts, transfers of staff for management purposes, career development and staff training will present serious problems. One special factor is that staff trained in the Department are highly valued by the commercial world and some losses especially of senior officers to the private sector must be expected.

5. In view of the proportion of senior staff aged over 50 there would be advantage in any dispersal being deferred for about five years (though this does not apply to Data Processing Branch, where work needs to begin on a new computer unit as soon as possible). Since there might be further changes in organisation before dispersal takes place, the Department should have some flexibility in deciding which posts should be dispersed in the light of the organisational structure at that time.

6. With regard to location, the Department (a small one, with about 1,500 Headquarters staff) argued that in the interests of effective management and the provision of an efficient service to exporters the two Headquarters should be located not more than 100 miles apart, ease of access between the two being the main consideration. Nevertheless, dispersal over a somewhat longer distance from London should be tolerable provided that the receiving location offered very good communications. For the above reasons the Department had been thinking in terms of the London–Bristol axis. Because of the concentration of exporters in the Midlands and the South East they would not in any event want to go north of Manchester/Leeds.

7. In my view Liverpool would be a suitable location from the point both of communications and of proximity to a large commercial centre.

8. I therefore recommend that ECGD should disperse 600 posts to Liverpool.

Communications Damage	Resource Gain	Average Trade-off
323	3,296	23·18

FOREIGN AND COMMONWEALTH OFFICE

(2,395 posts in 13 buildings)

1. The communications study was less illuminating in the case of the FCO's " political " and ancillary Departments than in some other areas of Government because of the necessity of frequent changes in distribution of responsibilities in response to developments in international affairs. Such reorganisations are a regular feature, and it is clearly necessary for the Office to be in a position to respond quickly to crisis situations in any part of the world and to balance its resources accordingly. There are however some areas of comparative stability and it was these which on the whole the study indicated for further examination.

2. Two levels of dispersal were proposed to the Office:

(1) Dispersal of 986 posts in Accommodation and Services Department, Security Department, the Migration and Visa, Nationality and Treaty, Consular and Claims group, the London Passport Office, Training Department and Finance Department.

Communications Damage	Resource Gain	Link Weight
640	5,000	15

(2) Dispersal of 782 posts as for the first proposal but excluding Accommodation and Services and Security.

Communications Damage	Resource Gain	Link Weight
480	3,900	16·5

3. In discussion of the proposals, the Office drew attention to the serious difficulties in both management and operational terms of dispersing FCO work outside London. The FCO's role in responding to emergencies arising without warning could involve any Department in the Office, and this was not able to be fully reflected in the communications study. The FCO was the headquarters of a world-wide Diplomatic Service which could only function effectively if its headquarters organisation remained integrated. Dispersal would mean delay in communications and increased risk. And dispersal was liable to bear more hardly on Diplomatic Service officers than on the average Home civil servant since they relied on having a settled home base in a single location in the intervals between diplomatic postings. Finally, in the Department's view, the concentration of its scattered departments into a single, purpose-built office would produce a greater resource gain than dispersal, without any communications damage, and would permit a substantial reduction, rather than an increase, in the numbers of FCO staff.

4. In particular the Office did not consider it could properly discharge its responsibilities if the Migration, Nationality and Consular areas were removed from headquarters (except that the Visa area might with advantage be located with the Home Office). There were recent examples—*e.g.* the Uganda situation—of the kinds of crisis in which they were liable to be

caught up. Training Department represented a comparatively small number of staff and a substantial part of all the training offered was carried out in short sessions and by staff from other Divisions; dispersal would entail a complete reconsideration of the basis of training. The Security staff needed to be where the majority of FCO staff were located. The Passport Office was in operational terms dispersable but this might not be acceptable to Ministers or to the general public, to whom its location in London was a considerable convenience.

5. However, it appeared that the dispersal of about 280 posts (not including common services), or about 630 if dispersal of the whole Passport Office were required, could be tolerated, though not without loss of efficiency. This number was made up of the Passport Office (32, or 384 for the whole Office and common services), Accommodation and Services and Security concerned with the overseas estate (47), Visa (23), Finance (110), and Library and Records Department (70) (which was not included in the original proposals). The common services factor was calculated at about 25 per cent, excluding communications staff, *i.e.* about 60 additional posts. In discussion of priorities in the event of any further dispersal, the Office made clear that they attached particular importance to keeping in London the Migration, Nationality and Consular areas. The "tolerable" figure therefore approaches, but falls somewhat short of, the lower of the two initial proposals (about 780 posts).

6. It is my view that the blocks of work contained in my first proposal are relatively dispersable and could be dispersed over quite a considerable distance more readily than some of the other blocks proposed for relocation. I accordingly recommend that the FCO disperse 986 posts to the Central Lancashire New Town.

Communications Damage	Resource Gain	Average Trade-off
943	4,975	12·6

FOREIGN AND COMMONWEALTH OFFICE: OVERSEAS DEVELOPMENT ADMINISTRATION

(1,426 posts in two buildings in London, plus 381 posts of the Directorate of Overseas Survey, Tolworth—total 1,807)

1. The communications study showed that about 60 per cent of the total link strength was between blocks of work within the Administration. Analysis of comunication patterns indicated that the Administration could be treated in two parts, one comprising blocks of work with a comparatively low level of communication links with contacts in London, while the second contained blocks which had a higher level of such contacts as well as close links with each other. The analysis also suggested that dispersal might be possible in two broad areas where the trade-off between damage and gains appeared attractive. The Administration, therefore, was invited to consider the implications of two different proposals:

(1) Dispersal of the entire Headquarters, including the Directorate of Overseas Survey, Tolworth (but excluding the Minister, his private office and Parliamentary Clerk) to a location within reasonable travelling distance of London. Also excluded from this proposal were the three fringe bodies, the Centre for Educational Development Overseas, the Inter-University Council and the Council for Technical Education and Training for Overseas Countries, for whom the trade-off was unattractive. Total: 1,807 posts.

Communications Damage	Resource Gain	Link Weight
2,211	7,748	4

(2) Dispersal of Economic Planning-Statistics Division, Overseas Manpower Division, Overseas Services Resettlement Bureau, Accounts Department and the Directorate of Overseas Survey, Tolworth. Total: 1,177 posts.

Communications Damage	Resource Gain	Link Weight
553	3,955	8·26

Each number of posts included a *pro rata* allocation of staff from those blocks concerned with office services.

2. ODA considered the proposal for dispersing the entire Headquarters unworkable. The Department would be divorced from its Ministers and the close working relationships that were felt to be essential between the ODA and FCO staff engaged in their respective Geographical and International Departments would also be affected. ODA would be located further away from the FCO than at present and this would run counter to Government policy by weakening the FCO/ODA links which the 1970 merger of the Departments was intended to strengthen. Other reasons put forward in opposition to this proposal included ODA's important links with the Treasury, DTI and the Bank of England; its position as the UK centre of an international aid business; the importance of London both as a centre for a continuous stream of visitors from similar agencies abroad and for

147

making important contacts with the private sector; and the problem of reconciling the removal of ODA to the periphery of London with the Government's intention to give an increasing lead in the international development field.

3. It was therefore agreed that dispersal of the entire Headquarters could be achieved only at a price which was likely to be unacceptable.

4. If ODA were dispersed on the basis of the second proposal, the Department wished to enter certain reservations. A dozen professional staff from Statistics Division should remain in London with their colleagues in Economic Planning. Up to 25 staff from Overseas Manpower Division should stay to service the interviewing of candidates for overseas appointments. Finally, ODA seriously questioned the desirability of moving the Directorate of Overseas Surveys, which was already located in purpose-built accommodation 15 miles from the centre of London, particularly as staff numbers were to be reduced and the future of the Directorate was due to be reviewed before the dispersal proposals could be implemented. If, in spite of this, it was still decided to recommend that the DOS should be moved, the preferred location was Basingstoke to enable the Directorate to be near its other scientific units which are due to move there shortly. (The communications study showed that the DOS had significantly more contact with these units than with any other block of work.) Common administrative services could be provided at Basingstoke, a town which was suitably placed to give the DOS reasonable access to the Ordnance Survey at Southampton, with which the Directorate has important contacts. ODA considered they would gain no special advantage in locating the DOS in the same place as the Overseas Manpower Division.

5. Should the Overseas Manpower Division be moved, the preferred location would be within reasonable travelling distance of London and Heathrow. This is because in the course of each year some 600 of the approximately 9,500 people working overseas, either directly in the employment of ODA or supplemented from aid funds, call at ODA when on leave to discuss personal affairs with the Manpower Division. They are not UK civil servants and, when in England, need to maintain contact with several different parts of ODA at a minimum of inconvenience to themselves and their employers; locations which are distant from London would be considered unsuitable in this respect.

6. In the light of these arguments, ODA's preferred location for *all* dispersed work was Basingstoke, with Milton Keynes as a second choice for all except the DOS.

7. However, the communications data suggest that dispersal of all the blocks in this second proposal could be over a comparatively long distance, if Ministers are prepared to set aside the strong case made against this by the Department on grounds which I regard as very reasonable. Of the list of potential receiving locations chosen by Ministers, one which gives an appropriate level of communications damage and resource gain is Glasgow. It has an airport with frequent daily flights to and from London, making it possible, even though infinitely less convenient, for the overseas visitors to Britain to maintain their contacts with Overseas Manpower and other ODA Divisions. Dispersal proposals for the DOS might have to be

148

re-examined in the light of any subsequent decisions affecting its future, but in the meantime it does not appear that the Directorate would suffer an unacceptable level of communications damage by being dispersed to Glasgow. Common administrative services could be provided if all the dispersed ODA work was co-located.

8. I therefore recommend that ODA should disperse 1,177 posts, including DOS, to Glasgow, but this is an instance in which Ministers will want to consider very seriously the balance between the claims of regional policy and of efficiency, which would point to a location much nearer London.

Communications Damage	Resource Gain	*Average Trade-off*
1,031	3,589	11·47

REGISTRY OF FRIENDLY SOCIETIES
(102 posts in one building)

1. The analysis of communications data suggested that dispersal of RFS as a whole could be obtained at an acceptable trade-off between gains and damage to communications. The small size of the Registry ruled out consideration of partial dispersal. A proposal for dispersal of RFS as a whole was therefore put to the Registry.

Communications Damage	Resource Gain	Link Weight
99	844	15·6

2. The Registry argued that, although it possessed statutory powers, these were limited and cumbersome. Wherever possible, the Registry used methods of consultation and persuasion to bring registered societies in line with the agreed modes of operation. An essential prerequisite for the effective performance of these functions was ease of informal contact with people who might well be visiting London primarily to attend meetings with bodies other than RFS. In this way advance warning could be obtained of impending financial instability which could endanger investors in registered societies.

3. The RFS also commented on the small size of the Registry, which already made management of staff difficult in the career-planning sense. The RFS thought that such difficulties would be exacerbated by dispersal, even to a location shared with some other Departments.

4. If dispersed, RFS argued that it would find it more difficult (though perhaps not impossible) to satisfy the statutory requirement that its files should be available for public inspection. At present, large numbers of investors in registered societies visited the offices to examine records held there so that there was a danger that dispersal would mean that the public would be inconvenienced more than would the officers.

5. Although in quantitative terms this organisation appears dispersable, I am satisfied that the Registry's arguments should be accepted as indicating that dispersal could only be obtained at a cost in terms of damage to efficient operation which would be unacceptable.

6. I therefore recommend that the RFS should not be dispersed.

THE GAMING BOARD FOR GREAT BRITAIN

(42 posts in one building in London)

1. Three-quarters of the Board's contacts are with organisations and individuals employed in London, which has the highest numbers of casinos, greatest volume of visitors and easily the largest turnover of money for gaming of any city in Great Britain. It is desirable for the Board to remain in close proximity to the gaming areas of the West End and Mayfair and in close contact with the Gaming Trade Associations and the Metropolitan Police. The benefits of dispersal could be obtained only at an extremely high cost:

Communications Damage	Resource Gain	Link Weight
128	222	4·0

2. I recommend that the Board should not be dispersed.

GOVERNMENT ACTUARY'S DEPARTMENT
(56 posts in one building)

1. The study of communications showed that the bulk of the Department's link strength reflected contact within the Department and analysis suggested that dispersal could be obtained only at a marginally acceptable trade-off between damage and gains. However, a proposal for complete dispersal was discussed with the Government Actuary.

Communications Damage	Resource Gain	Link Weight
74	500	11·4

2. In arguing against dispersal, the Department attached greatest importance to the likely staffing difficulties, particularly with highly-trained professional actuaries. The actuarial profession is very heavily concentrated in London and few Fellows would willingly leave the area where the best jobs are available. In the next three years the three most senior men in the Department would be retiring and this would make the five Principal Actuaries (Assistant Secretary level) the key men for ensuring continuity in the Department. During this time, the Government's Bill for a new pension scheme would bring considerable work for actuaries outside as well as inside the Service and make GAD vulnerable to the approaches of private firms who wished to recruit experienced staff. The Department had found it very difficult to recruit experienced staff mainly because of the attractive salaries offered by competitors. The Department feels it is imperative that nothing should be done which might induce the staff to leave for work elsewhere and an announcement that the Department was to move away from London would cause an immediate loss of key staff.

3. Although the fear of recruitment difficulty *out* of London is an almost unique argument against dispersal, I believe that the problems for the Department are real. I recommend, therefore, that GAD should not be dispersed.

DEPARTMENT OF HEALTH AND SOCIAL SECURITY
(5,571 posts in 29 buildings)

1. DHSS already has the great bulk of its staff outside its central London Headquarters. There are two Headquarters offices at Newcastle (10,700 posts) and Blackpool (3,000 posts), and there are also 54,000 staff in some 750 local and regional offices throughout the country. These are for the most part Social Security offices.

2. Because of the extensive reorganisation planned for those areas of the Department concerned with Health and Personal Social Services, DHSS was reviewed in two parts:

(a) The Social Security side (principally the areas dealing with National Insurance, Supplementary Benefits and supported and related blocks), together with several blocks providing services to both parts of the Department. Ministers and Permanent Secretaries were included.

(b) Those areas concerned solely with Health and Personal Social Services and a related fringe body, the Health Education Council.

3. This division proved to be convenient, since the study showed that conclusions could be reached on each side separately, save for one or two areas identified below and subject to some general considerations relating to the effective management of an integrated Department.

DHSS (Social Security) (2,509 posts in 12 buildings)

4. The communications study showed that 69 per cent of the total link strength was between blocks within the whole Department; 57 per cent was within the Social Security side; and 12 per cent was with the Health side. Analysis of communication patterns suggested that the Department could be treated as several groups of blocks, which were related both in communications and functional terms, and that dispersal could be regarded as possible in three broad areas where the trade-off between damage and gains appeared attractive. The Department was therefore invited to consider the implications of three different proposals:

(1) Dispersal of the entire Social Security side other than Ministers, the Permanent Secretary and several blocks which provide services to both parts of the Department. This proposal included the Second Permanent Secretary and involved a total of 1,630 posts.

Communications Damage	Resource Gain	Link Weight
1,002	10,309	21

(2) Dispersal of the Supplementary Benefits Group, Regional Directorate, parts of Insurance Division C and Finance Division, the Office of the Registrar of Non-Participating Employments, the Office of the Chief Insurance Officer and several blocks providing establishment services, a total of 1,215 posts.

Communications Damage	Resource Gain	Link Weight
643	7,681	21

153

(3) Dispersal of all the blocks included in Proposal 2, except the Supplementary Benefits Group and the Regional Directorate, a total of 570 posts.

Communications Damage	Resource Gain	Link Weight
257	3,411	29

Each number of posts included a *pro rata* allocation of staff in those blocks concerned with office services and excluded posts in the Management Services and Statistics and Research Divisions, which were set aside for later consideration.

5. DHSS argued that, notwithstanding the quantitative results of the study, a dispersal greater than the lowest of the three proposals given in paragraph 4 above would not be sensible in relation to the need to maintain an efficient service to Ministers, and would not have sufficient regard for the problems already inherent in the management of an organisation already widely distributed throughout the country (see paragraph 1 above). Less than 4 per cent of Social Security personnel were based in the London Head-quarters. To go much below that small proportion could seriously damage the support required by officers who, in turn, were responsible for advising Ministers. Much importance was attached to maintaining the capacity to advise Ministers in the now too-frequent short-term crises in which Social Security payments, especially Supplementary Benefits, were involved. It was important, too, to maintain a capacity for efficient contingency planning and policy formulation, such as that required for the annual up-rating of Social Security benefits and for studying the implications of proposed Government measures such as tax credits. Substantial dispersal would also jeopardise the concept of developing integrated policies for social and health needs which was implicit in the creation of a unified DHSS. The reorganisation of the Health side, including the creation of client-based divisions, had the concomitant implication that a greater degree of interchange and co-ordination than before would be required between the two sides of the Department. Therefore, to go beyond the smallest of the three dispersal proposals would be against the judgment of the Department of what was essential to its proper functioning. That proposal appeared to provide an equitable balance between the claims of dispersal policy and the duty of DHSS to maintain its efficiency.

6. If, despite these considerations, Ministers were to decide that a larger dispersal was required, DHSS considered that the Department could not function and serve Ministers, even at a lower level of efficiency, without the retention in London of the Second Permanent Secretary, the Deputy Secretaries and adequate staff for an essential policy and operational nucleus. DHSS considered that in such circumstances the quality of decision taking would be affected because of the separation of key posts from supporting posts.

7. Although it was therefore agreed that dispersal on the basis of the more severe of the initial proposals could be achieved only at a price which was likely to be unacceptable, in the light of the Government's wish to disperse as many staff as possible DHSS was asked to consider, as an alternative, which blocks of work could be dispersed in part.

8.   Notwithstanding the objections expressed by DHSS (as in paragraphs 5 and 6 above) a dispersal of about 1,200 posts, *i.e.* of the same order as Proposal 2, could be achieved by adding part blocks to the lowest proposal, as follows:

> *Whole blocks:* Branch A5 of Insurance Division A (Adjudication Arrangements); Family Support Branch FS2; Chief Insurance Officer's Office; Registrar of Non-Participating Employments; Instructions Branch with Printing and Stationery; Establishments Personnel EP2 Hinchley Wood; Staff Training (Social Security).   Total 368.

> *Part blocks:* Insurance Divisions B (Benefits) and C (Contributions); Supplementary Benefits; War Pensions, Industrial Injuries, and Attendance Allowance; Regional Directorate; Finance Division; Establishments Division; Statistics Branches SR3 and 5.   Total 630.

With common service staff and some professional (medical and legal) support the total would be about 1,200.

9.   In view of changes in organisation over the next few years, there should be some flexibility in deciding precisely which posts should be dispersed, *i.e.* decisions should take account of the timing of dispersal and the organisation of the Department at that time.

10.   As regards location, a Social Security dispersal could be over a comparatively long distance.   The Department already has large HQ Offices at Newcastle and Blackpool which would benefit from additional career opportunities.   In both of these offices there is work which fits naturally with some which may be dispersed from London, and it would be sensible to associate the one with the other.   For example, War Pensions and other work on the disabled could go to Blackpool where the main support groups for these categories are located, rather than Tyneside, whereas any further dispersal of National Insurance Contributions work should naturally link up with similar work already at Newcastle.   On these grounds DHSS would favour Blackpool for the bulk of the dispersal, not least because the Department knows that there is a supply of high-quality clerical labour in that area (whereas there are considerable doubts about this on Tyneside, not least owing to the existing level of demand).   Blackpool is not included in the list of receiving locations agreed by Ministers, but DHSS has since asked that its case for Blackpool as a preferred location (and it is a strong one) should be clearly stated in the final report.   On the other hand, the Newcastle area is in greater need of the additional opportunities and it is perhaps more sensible that DHSS should go to Tyneside than another Department.

11.   Against this background, I recommend that DHSS (Social Security) should disperse a total of 1,200 posts; of these 500 should be dispersed to Tyneside.   The best location for the remaining 700 posts is Blackpool but this is not on the approved list of receiving locations.   I recommend that these posts be dispersed to Central Lancashire New Town because this is reasonably nearby.   But I believe that Blackpool would be a preferable centre.   If the 700 posts could be dispersed there, I believe that the Social Security contribution to dispersal would provide a very acceptable balance between ensuring minimum damage to the operations of the units recommended for dispersal and meeting the regional policy criterion.

DHSS (Health and Personal Social Services) (3,062 posts in 20 buildings)

12. The communications study in Health took place at a time when the Department was engaged in large-scale reorganisation plans arising from a major review of the organisation and operation of its work. Blocks of work accounting for almost three-quarters of the posts will be directly involved in this reorganisation and these blocks have very strong external links with London, including important contacts with non-Government bodies. At the time of the communications study there was considerable uncertainty about the likely future shape and operation of the Health Department and its relationship with a reorganised National Health Service; this is likely to have resulted in an under-valuation of the communications damage to these blocks which would result from dispersal. It is clear that to obtain some resource gain from moving jobs from this part of Health away from London would necessitate paying a high price in terms of lost efficiency.

13. Analysis of the communications data suggested that other blocks of work—Supply Division, Accountant General's Division, Statistics and Research SR1 & 2, Management Services MS2 and Staff Training (Health) —totalling 940 posts (including a *pro rata* allocation of office services staff), offered more potential for dispersal. An approach along these lines was made to the Department.

Communications Damage	*Resource Gain*	*Link Weight*
491	2,979	14

14. DHSS argued that much of AGD is organised to enable the Accountant General to function as an adviser on financial policy and on the financial implications of all policy proposals. It was clear that AGD would be affected by reorganisation and this would result in the various sections of the Division becoming more closely bound to their " client " policy divisions. The Division would be required to make a crucial contribution to a comprehensive planning system to be introduced in the Department and extended into the NHS.

15. Part of the expected outcome to the reorganisation proposals for Statistics and Research Division would be the formation of a central unit with a maximum of 170 posts and this would be suitable for dispersal. Under the same proposals, the professional statistical staff would be required to work very closely with the main policy divisions and should not be dispersed.

16. Since the communications study, some reorganisation had taken place in the Department's Management Services, which had affected MS2 in particular. The various Management Services Branches (General, Operational Research and Computers) work on a customer/contractor basis and this makes it necessary for senior MS staff to be in close contact with their customers, the policy divisions. It would be possible, however, to relocate those Management Services people engaged primarily on assignment work (who tend to be the more junior staff), plus those doing work of a technical or advisory nature—about 60 posts in all.

17. The Department made a strong case against a complete dispersal of Supply Division because of the effect this would have on the Division's important London business contacts (at least 25 per cent of its total link strength) which, in the main, could not be replaced at another location. It also had important links with other Divisions which were considered unsuitable for dispersal. In the light of this, it was suggested by the Department that it might be reasonable to disperse no more than 50 posts, unless the receiving location to be recommended was somewhere near London, in which case all, or practically all, the Division could be dispersed, up to 400 posts.

18. Staff Training (Health) would not function satisfactorily if removed too far from the Divisions it serves. The balance of advantage was felt to lie in retaining this small unit (20 posts) in London.

19. The case made by the Department against dispersing AGD, Staff Training (Health) and the professional staff from Statistics and Research Divisions seems a reasonable one. As far as Supply Division is concerned, the Department is prepared for the whole of it to be dispersed provided it is relocated within reasonable distance of London (in order to reduce the damage to business contacts and to links with other Divisions which would result from dispersal to a more distant location). Otherwise it is prepared to disperse only 50 staff. The analysis of communications showed Supply Division to be the least dispersable of the five blocks under consideration; the link weight for the solution which included Supply being no more than $6 \cdot 9$ at the Bristol benchmark. The Department's team which studied the organisation of Supply Division argued effectively that it was necessary for the five branches of the Division to have continued close association. In the light of this, the Department's case seems reasonable.

20. On the question of location, the Department would prefer to send the 170 Statistics and Research staff to Blackpool to join similar work being done at the Central Office. They would like to see the 60 Management Services staff located with up to 400 from Supply Division at a " near London " location. On the evidence, however, it does not seem sensible in organisation and management terms to locate separately such a small number (460) of the total Department; the damage to efficiency would outweigh the resource gain involved. It would seem that the most efficient solution would be to disperse the Statistics and Research posts to Blackpool together with the 50 Supply Division posts (since a part of this Division is already located at Blackpool) and the 60 Management Services posts.

21. The Department's case for having Blackpool added to Ministers' agreed list of receiving locations has already been referred to in paragraph 10; it is strengthened by the fact that posts from Health as well as Social Security would link up with similar work already at Blackpool. As Blackpool, however, is not on the list of receiving locations, the place on the list which is nearest to it (Central Lancashire New Town) is the one shown in the recommendation.

22. I recommend the dispersal of 280 DHSS (Health) posts to Central Lancashire New Town with a rider that, if possible, Blackpool should be added to the approved list of receiving locations and the 280 posts should go there instead.

Summary of recommendations for DHSS

23. I recommend the dispersal of 500 posts to Tyneside and 980 posts to Central Lancashire New Town (unless Blackpool is added to the list of approved receiving locations, in which case the 980 posts should go there instead).

Communications Damage	Resource Gain	Average Trade-off
1,162*	8,910	16·5

---

* Because some of the blocks of work concerned have been suggested by the Department and are different from those included in proposals put to the Department, and because they are of a different structure from those in the communications study, it was not possible to evaluate the damage associated with the recommendation. The figure given, therefore, is proportional to the damage which was incurred in the original proposals. The justification for this is that the Department regarded what is now recommended as less than the damage which would be incurred in the original proposals.

HOME-GROWN CEREALS AUTHORITY
(49 posts in one building)

1. The analysis of communications data suggested that dispersal of the Authority as a whole could be obtained at an acceptable trade-off between gains and damage to communications. The small size of the Authority ruled out consideration of partial dispersal; a proposal for total dispersal was therefore put to the Authority.

2. In considering the dispersal proposal, the Authority argued that its work was likely to change substantially within about a year. In the future it would relate in large measure to the EEC's Common Agricultural Policy and Intervention. Consequently, staff in London would be reduced. But links with the Economic Divisions of the Ministry of Agriculture, Fisheries and Food would be of a very high frequency. It therefore argued that it would be best located with the Economic Divisions of MAFF. Since these Divisions are not proposed for dispersal, dispersal of the Authority could only be achieved at a high cost in terms of damage to efficient operation.

3. I therefore recommend that the Home-Grown Cereals Authority should not be dispersed.

HOME OFFICE

(3,831 posts in 18 buildings)

1. The communications study revealed that the heaviest commitment in terms of face-to-face contacts fell on the more senior staff and that a high proportion (61 per cent) of the Department's link strength represented contacts within the Department. The remainder of the contact, in terms of link strengths, is with bodies outside London, *e.g.* local authorities, police forces, etc. (14 per cent), with other Government Departments in London (8 per cent), other non-Government Departments in London (9·5 per cent) and Home Office fringe bodies (2 per cent).

2. Analysis of these communication patterns suggested that the Department could be treated as several groups of blocks which were related both in communications and functions terms, and that dispersal could be regarded as possible in three broad areas where the trade-off between damage and gains appeared attractive and consistent with proposals placed before other Departments.

3. The Department was therefore invited to consider the implications of three proposals:

(1) The dispersal of 3,231 posts, leaving 600 posts in London together with the most senior staff and the two computer units (which have close links with the Metropolitan Police and are in purpose-built accommodation). The blocks remaining in London included the Deputy Secretaries, Northern Ireland Department,* Public Relations Branch, Community Programmes Department, Legal Adviser and Branch, Criminal Department, General Department, the majority of Police Department and the Chief Scientist.

Communications Damage	Resource Gain	Link Weight
1,850	17,200	15·72

(2) The dispersal of 2,922 posts, leaving in London the majority of Probation and After-Care Department and Fire Department (excluding G 3) in addition to those left by the first proposal.

Communications Damage	Resource Gain	Link Weight
1,510	15,200	17·66

(3) The dispersal of 1,470 posts, leaving in London the majority of the Department. The blocks dispersed would be Immigration and Nationality Department, Warning and Monitoring Branch, Statistical Division, Finance (Grants) and Accounts Branch. All this work, with the exception of the Warning and Monitoring Branch and the Pay Section at Vauxhall, is already located in the Outer London area.

Communications Damage	Resource Gain	Link Weight
331	7,793	35

Each proposal included a *pro rata* allocation of staff concerned with common services.

---

* This was before the formation of the Northern Ireland Office.

4. Although there are important links with blocks outside the Department, the overall pattern of communications showed that the most important links were between blocks *within* the Department and with police forces, fire services, local authorities, prisons, etc., spread around the country. Most existing and preferred communications were internal to each set of blocks of work contained in the three proposals ; in the second proposal, for example, only 35 per cent of all preferred contact was with blocks of work remaining in London, representing on average less than one contact per dispersed member of staff (although clearly a greater load fell on the more senior staff).

5. The Department argued that there was insufficient evidence to demonstrate that dispersal at the levels proposed could be achieved without destroying the effectiveness of the Department's primary role in the maintenance of law and order. Ministers and the Permanent Under-Secretary of State would not be able to meet the day-to-day demands on the Home Office unless all four Deputies were available for consultation and they in turn would, in many cases, be separated by these proposals from their top level advisers and formulators of policy.

6. Senior staff isolated from their Departments would need additional secretariats and facilities involving extra costs and more staff; establishment and office services would need to be duplicated; and there would be serious career management and manning problems. Dispersal on this scale would absorb a large share of planning and initiatory capacity for a number of years.

7. The Department also argued that dispersal would reduce the facility for moving subjects and staff from one part of the office to another and that it would produce two disparate and less easily managed offices of different size.

8. Although other special considerations were emphasised in relation to the rest of the Home Office, attention was necessarily focused on the Prison and Immigration and Nationality Departments as they account for a good part of the posts involved in the proposals.

9. The arguments by the Home Office against the dispersal of the *Prison Department* were of two main kinds, the management of crises, whether in general or in individual cases, and the developing part the Secretary of State wished the Department to play in relation to other policy functions in the Home Office and to the non-Government social service activity focused in London.

10. The *Immigration and Nationality Department* was also shown, quantitatively, to be highly dispersable. IND has moved from High Holborn to Croydon, without prejudice to the main location review. This was in response to severe pressure on the London office estate. But the Home Office has argued that even a move to Croydon results in a loss of effectiveness and public convenience. There has indeed already been adverse comment on this move in the House of Commons. It also argued that relocation of IND implied substantial dispersal.

11. In conclusion, the Home Office was of the opinion that the cost of communications damage seemed far to outweigh resource gains and benefits. But it looked again at those areas of work which appeared

F

peripheral to the main function of maintaining public order and safety and at those which could reasonably be located outside central London. In sum its case is as follows:

(a) The move of Immigration and Nationality Department to Croydon is a form of dispersal.

(b) Warning and Monitoring Branch have independently chosen to be located with or near Royal Observer Corps headquarters at Oxford. This is under discussion.

(c) Tolworth (where some of the work proposed for dispersal has already been located) should be considered as a dispersal location: if this view were accepted 41 per cent of the total headquarters staff could be regarded as already " dispersed ".

(d) There are possibilities for regionalisation of some parts of the Home Office, mainly in Prison Department, involving about 350 posts.

12. Further consideration of the proposals must take account of the following points:

(i) Immigration and Nationality Department appears to be a strong candidate for dispersal because of its high staff numbers, the consequent resource gain and the *comparative* weakness of its links to London. Against this:

(a) The most senior staff should perhaps be kept in London.

(b) In the light of recent developments, it may be that the burden of work for the Department is likely to grow more, rather than less, onerous and politically sensitive.

(c) If the Government decides to disperse this Department, a long timetable should be allowed to overcome the worst effects of a second disruption to management and staff.

(d) If the Department was moved to a less accessible location than London, it would probably be essential to maintain enquiry points at several major cities.

(e) As an alternative to dispersal to a single location, some of the work could be devolved to a regional organisation.

(ii) The Prison Department as a whole also appears comparatively dispersable, but there is a nice balance between the special considerations and damage on the one hand and the benefits on the other.

Recommendations

13. Although the Home Office has advanced powerful arguments against the dispersal of more than a very small number of posts, I am not convinced that dispersal could be achieved only at a price in damage which Ministers would find unacceptable. This is a case in which Ministers must balance their policy goals with great care. The Home Office is especially liable to sudden crises on which Home Office and other Ministers need instant and sustained support from officials. If, however, they accept that some Home Office work should be dispersed, I believe that a basis on which decisions might be reached would be as follows:

162

		No. of posts
Finance (Grants) and Accounts Branch . .		181
Statistical Division		133
Immigration and Nationality Department . .		1,123
Total		1,437

(The staffing figures include *pro rata* allocations of such common service staff as messengers and typists.)

14. In addition, the Prison Department Directorates of Works and of Industries and Supply (some 400 posts) are not inextricably tied to London and, to that extent, are candidates for dispersal. The Department might however prefer this to be substantially regionalised and based on existing regional centres at Birmingham, Bristol, Manchester and Redhill. A Headquarters unit would be left and it would be for consideration whether this should remain in London or be dispersed too. It might also prove possible to devolve more Prison Department casework, on grounds of operational and organisational efficiency, to regional offices.

15. I would regard the work described in paragraph 13 above as, relatively, a candidate for long-range dispersal and I recommend that it be moved to Plymouth.

No. of Posts	Communications Damage	Resource Gain	Average Trade-off
1,437	533	8,310	34·41

16. I should however draw attention to the fact that some of this work has been located in the London suburbs, in some cases as a direct result of Sir Gilbert Flemming's exercise in 1962–63. It is therefore for consideration whether further relocation, whether conducted at a late stage in the exercise or not, may be regarded as either necessary (a substantial part of the resource advantage having already been secured) or fair to the staff concerned. If Ministers decide to accept the risk of damaging morale by dispersing such work again, I would strongly recommend a late rather than an early move.

305375

F 2

IMMIGRATION APPEAL TRIBUNAL

(36 posts in one building)

1.   Because of the very limited field of contact within which the Tribunal operates, it was agreed that a general statement from the Tribunal about its contacts would be more valuable than completion of the communications study questionnaires.

2.   In the report the Tribunal suggested that London was by far the most sensible location for its work. It is essentially a regional office, and, if dispersal were to occur, a London regional office would have to be set up. The essential working contacts of the Tribunal are most frequent with the Treasury Solicitor's Department and Treasury Counsel. It must also work at the centre of a communications network maintained with adjudicators at Dover, Gatwick, Southampton and Norwich. Other regional and sub-regional offices are at Birmingham, London Airport, Leeds and Manchester.

3.   Against this background, I recommend that the Immigration Appeal Tribunal should not be dispersed.

CENTRAL OFFICE OF INFORMATION

(1,298 staff in 9 buildings, 2 in the Whitehall area and the remainder in various locations within 16 miles of central London)

1. The communications study showed that 42 per cent of the link strength was internal to the Department. The substantial amount of external contact, much of which was with other Government Departments in Whitehall and with Press, radio and television in London, reflected the special functions and character of COI.

2. Analysis of the communications data showed that there was a very sharp division between a group of under 200 posts (in Accounts Branch, Tours and Production Services Division (Distribution and Shipping Section), Central Film Library, Hayes Vaults) which appeared highly dispersable by the measures used, and the remainder of the Department for which a very high price would have to be paid for dispersal. The figures were:

Posts Dispersed	Communications Damage	Resource Gain	Link Weight
181	55	4,485	50
307	159	5,153	7

3. A closer examination was made of the data on the four blocks of work which appeared most dispersable. This revealed that, for all four blocks, the low overall frequency of contact suggested a high degree of dispersability; but that the economic arguments for dispersal were weakened by the fact that each block was already some distance from central London (in accommodation with modest rentals), with small numbers of staff and, in the case of the film vaults at Hayes, in purpose-built accommodation.

4. Apart from such small blocks of work as the Hayes Vaults, the only parts of COI which appeared at all readily dispersable were those concerned with Establishments and Organisation, Finance and Accounts. There were strong arguments, particularly in view of the recommendations of the Fulton Report, against considering partial dispersal which would separate the "personnel" divisions from the rest of the Department.

5. Despite the initial quantitative evidence, it became apparent that no satisfactory partial dispersal of COI would be possible, while the price in communications damage for total dispersal would be excessively high. For these reasons, no dispersal proposals were sent to the Department.

6. I recommend that COI should not be dispersed.

305375

F 3

BOARD OF INLAND REVENUE

(3,942 posts in 21 buildings in London)

1. Inland Revenue's contribution to the existing dispersal programme has been substantial. Since May 1963, 5,870 Inland Revenue jobs have been dispersed from London (over 25 per cent of the total dispersed in that period) and plans are currently in hand to disperse 900 more.

2. Analysis of the communications pattern suggested that the Department could be treated as several groups of blocks (69·9 per cent of the total link strength was between blocks within the Department), which were related in both communications and functional terms, and that three levels of dispersal could be envisaged. The Department was therefore invited to consider the implications of three different proposals:

(1) Dispersal of the entire Head Office unit, 3,942 posts.

Communications Damage	Resource Gain	Link Weight
2,332	22,955	1

(2) Dispersal of the Director of Stamping, the Superannuation Funds Office, Establishments MS (ADP), the Estate Duty Office, the Accountant and Comptroller General, the Inspector of Foreign Dividends, the Controller of Stamps, Central Training, Investigation Section, the Chief Inspector's Establishments, Organisation, PAYE/ADP unit and Inspecting Officers, and the Chief Valuer; the proposal involved 2,986 posts.

Communications Damage	Resource Gain	Link Weight
1,610	16,695	16·4

(3) Dispersal of the Director of Stamping, the Superannuation Funds Office, Establishments MS (ADP), the Estate Duty Office, the Accountant and Comptroller General, the Chief Inspector's PAYE/ADP unit and the Inspector of Foreign Dividends, totalling 2,162 posts.

Communications Damage	Resource Gain	Link Weight
638	11,681	17·0

Each number of posts included a *pro rata* allocation of registry staff, typists and messengers.

3. Inland Revenue argued that it would prove an unacceptable burden on the working of the Department for those blocks involved in Budget work to be dispersed from London. Despite the quantitative results of the study, it was maintained that, because of the unpredictability, urgency, frequency and importance of these contacts, given the present timing involved in Budgetary legislation, it would create a burden far above the level established by the quantitative data if Proposal 1, dispersal of the entire Head Office unit, were to be carried out. Also, for management reasons, for which the

quantitative study did not make allowance, the Department would want to suggest alterations to Proposals 2 and 3 (if either of these courses were to be recommended to Ministers), which would, in its view, constitute organisationally less damaging changes.

4. As a result of discussions with Inland Revenue the three proposals set out above were therefore modified to take the following form:

(1) Dispersal of the Accountant and Comptroller General, the Estate Duty Office, the Chief Valuer, the Chief Inspector's PAYE/ADP and Manpower Planning Units, Inspecting Officers London Section, Clerical Establishment Section and Organisation Section, Establishments Management Services (ADP), Personnel and Manpower Organisation groups and Training and Investigation Sections, the Controller of Stamps, the Director of Stamping, the Solicitor's Office (apart from 60 posts), the Inspector of Foreign Dividends and the Superannuation Funds Office*; this proposal involved 3,445 posts.

(2) Dispersal of all posts proposed in 4 (1) above, except the Inspector of Foreign Dividends and the Superannuation Funds Office; this proposal involved 2,960 posts.

(3) Dispersal of all posts in 4 (2) above, except half of Establishments, Investigation Section, all the Solicitor's Office (apart from the Rating Section), A&CG Establishments, Chief Valuer Establishments, Chief Inspector (Inspecting Officers London), Chief Inspector (Clerical Establishment Section) and Establishments Division Personnel and Manpower and Organisation Groups; this proposal involved 2,260 posts.

5. But after these modifications Inland Revenue argued that the quantitative approach of the review had failed to bring out the immediacy and importance of the many contacts relating to Budgetary legislation. In its view, therefore, Proposals 4 (1) and 4 (2) would still produce unacceptable levels of damage. Dispersal on the basis of the revised Proposal 4 (3), however, although causing an unwelcome degree of inefficiency, could be tolerated if certain key officers, including the Chief Valuer and the Accountant General, remained in London so that they would maintain their necessarily close association with the Chairman and the Board.

6. On the question of location, Inland Revenue emphasised that good communications between the dispersal centre and London and also between the centre and some 1,300 local offices of varying sizes were essential. For this reason, dispersal should be to a place along what it called the country's "spinal column", giving reasonable access to both London and all parts of the country. The Department suggested that Leeds might be a suitable location.

7. It is my view that a revised Proposal 4 (3), involving the dispersal of a total of 1,610 posts over a comparatively long distance should not pose insuperable difficulties for Inland Revenue, although a location at a medium

---

* With the introduction of the Government's new occupational pension scheme, the Superannuation Funds Office needs to be co-located with the Occupational Pensions Board of DHSS. It has recently been agreed that these offices should be located on the periphery of London, in the Hinchley Wood/New Malden area, where there is already an Inland Revenue Office (the Surtax Office), running down as a result of taxation changes.

distance would undoubtedly be more convenient. Again, there is a choice to be made between the strong case for a central location, which fits the responsibilities laid upon the Board for managing a widely distributed system, and a more distant location, more in need of new employment opportunities. (I would, however, regard the creation of new work in Leeds as a good contribution to the needs of the Yorkshire/Humberside Region for varied employment.)

8. The revised Proposal 3, involving a total of 1,610 posts, would consist of the following areas of work:

> The Accountant and Comptroller General's Training Section and ADP unit, the Estate Duty Office, the Chief Inspector's ADP and Manpower Planning Units, Establishments MS(ADP) (excluding PRISM unit) and Training Units, Chief Valuer Training, the Controller of Stamps and the Director of Stamping.

9. I recommend, therefore, that Inland Revenue should disperse 1,610 posts to Teesside.

Communications Damage	Resource Gain	Average Trade-off
785*	9,725	26·73

---

* Because some of the blocks of work concerned have been suggested by the Department and are different from those included in proposals put to the Department, and because they are of a different structure from those in the communications study, it was not possible to evaluate the damage associated with the recommendation. The figure given, therefore, is proportional to the damage which was incurred in the original proposals. The justification for this is that the Department regarded what is now recommended as less than the damage which would be incurred in the original proposals.

LORD CHANCELLOR'S DEPARTMENT
(235 staff in four buildings in London)

1. The communications study showed that 26 per cent of link strength was internal to the Department. The subsequent analysis of communications data suggested that dispersal of the Department, in whole or in part, would involve an unacceptable price in terms of damage. The measures obtained for a dispersal of 156 posts, which excluded those posts fixed in London, would be:

Communications Damage	Resource Gain	Link Weight
315	1,379	6·0

2. Only by reducing the number of posts dispersed to well under 100 would the trade-off between gain and damage be made comparable with that envisaged in the more severe proposals sent to other Departments; moreover, partial dispersal of a small Department like LCD would be unlikely to be viable in management terms.

3. Further strong arguments against dispersal of any part of the Lord Chancellor's Department's Headquarters are, first, the Department's central role as a secretariat to the Lord Chancellor, and, second, the need to maintain frequent contact with the Law Courts.

4. Having considered both the quantitative and qualitative evidence, I decided that no dispersal proposal should be sent to LCD and I recommend that LCD should not be dispersed.

MEDICAL RESEARCH COUNCIL
(305 posts in one building)

1. The communications study showed that 55 per cent of the Council's total link strength represented contact within the Council and analysis suggested that dispersal could be obtained only at a relatively poor trade-off between damage and gains. The measures for the dispersal of the whole Council were:

Communications Damage	Resource Gain	Link Weight
510	1,973	7·9

2. The Council has high levels of contact with teaching hospitals and medical schools in London. The majority of its research establishments are all in London and the South East. No dispersal proposal was therefore put to the Council.

3. Against this background, I recommend that the MRC should not be dispersed.

NATIONAL DEBT OFFICE
(58 posts in one building)

1. The communications study showed that 50 per cent of the Office's link strength represented contact within the Department and 25 per cent represented contact with non-Government bodies in London. Analysis suggested that dispersal could be obtained at an acceptable trade-off between damage to communications and gains. A proposal for complete dispersal was therefore put to NDO.

Communications Damage	Resource Gain	Link Weight
52	379	15·0

2. In discussion, the Department maintained that its contacts, although only at a moderately frequent level, were none the less important and would be difficult to maintain or replace if it were relocated. Because of the importance of these contacts, arising from the Office's position as "investment manager of national funds", with Executive Directors and the Chief Cashier at the Bank of England and their Deputies, and with the Government Broker and his Deputy, the benefits of dispersal of the Office would be obtained only at a high cost in damage to efficiency.

3. I agree that the importance of the Office's contacts is not fully brought out by the quantitative data. I therefore recommend that the Office should not be dispersed.

NATIONAL ECONOMIC DEVELOPMENT OFFICE

(215 posts in one building)

1. The communications study showed that 50 per cent of the Office's link strength represented contact with the Director General, and 20 per cent with the Treasury and DTI, and analysis suggested that dispersal could be obtained only at a comparatively severe trade-off between gains and damage to communication. The comparative measures are:

Communications Damage	Resource Gain	Link Weight
738	1,600	4·2

2. The Office would suffer a high degree of damage in dispersal and it could not efficiently fulfil its function as the secretariat for the National Economic Development Council. No dispersal proposal was therefore put to the Office.

3. I recommend that NEDO should not be dispersed.

NATURAL ENVIRONMENT RESEARCH COUNCIL

(191 posts in one building)

1. The communications study and subsequent analysis suggested that the Headquarters staff of the Council could be located outside London at a relatively acceptable trade-off between gains and communications damage. A proposal for the dispersal of the entire Council was therefore put to NERC.

Communications Damage	Resource Gain	Link Weight
250	1,345	11·0

2. After the communications study was carried out, it became apparent that the White Paper, A Framework for Government Research and Development (Cmnd. 5046), would have far-reaching effects on the Council. Much of its funds will, in future, come from MAFF, DTI and DOE, and the contacts between the Council and these Departments are likely to be greatly increased. However, it would not be possible to disperse the Council with these Departments to a common location since the parts of the latter which are concerned with the Council are unlikely to be located in the same place. Whatever dispersal location were chosen, there would inevitably be a need for senior officers to spend a considerable amount of their time away from their offices, both in London and elsewhere.

3. Nevertheless, damage to the Council's efficiency if dispersed could be minimised in several ways. First, the Chairman, whose appointment is a part-time one and who could not operate effectively outside London, would wish to retain an office in London, together with a small secretariat. Second, facilities should be provided in London for meetings of the Council and its Committees, whose members are recruited from universities and other bodies throughout the United Kingdom (recruitment would prove very difficult if the meetings were held outside London, because of the inconvenience this would cause). Finally, the Council could advantageously be co-located at Swindon with the Science Research Council, with whom it has some important contacts. If pressed to disperse, Swindon would be the Council's preferred location.

4. I recommend that NERC should disperse to Swindon with the Science Research Council, facilities, including an adequate secretariat, being provided to serve meetings of the Council and its Committees in London.

Communications Damage	Resource Gain	Average Trade-off
182	1,300	14·45

I have recommended that, because of accommodation difficulties, the SRC should disperse at an early date. Given NERC's preference for co-location, I recommend that NERC should disperse at the same time so far as this is possible.

OFFICE OF POPULATION CENSUSES AND SURVEYS
(920 posts in two buildings)

1. The Office already has about 600 dispersed Headquarters staff at Southport and about 1,000 at Titchfield (Hampshire).

2. The communications study indicated that 50 per cent of the London Office's links were internal, while the main other areas of contact were other London Departments (18 per cent) and the Titchfield branch (11 per cent). Although the Office was divided into only eight blocks of work, the analysis suggested three possible levels of dispersal:

   (1) Dispersal of the entire Office.

Communications Damage	Resource Gain	Link Weight
338	7,500	1

   (2) This involved Social Survey Division, Establishments and Accounts, and Marriage and Registrations Divisions, with a total of 800 posts.

Communications Damage	Resource Gain	Link Weight
275	6,700	25

   (3) This involved only Establishments and Accounts, and Marriage and Registrations Divisions, with a total of 592 posts.

Communications Damage	Resource Gain	Link Weight
169	5,300	29

3. As a Department, OPCS appears unusually easily dispersable, on the basis of these figures. The Office itself feels, however, that although a short-range dispersal of the entire Department might be feasible, a longer range dispersal would cause unacceptable damage. In particular, it is feared that the Social Survey and Medical Statistics Divisions would be badly hit by losses of trained and highly marketable staff—especially since many are married women who are tied to London because of their husbands' jobs—and by the removal of field organisers to a less central location than London. The Office also feels that there would be career disadvantages for its general Statisticians since dispersal would take them out of the swim of the Government Statistical Service. The Office's view that expansion on its present site at Titchfield might not be possible has been borne in mind, as well as the fact that Titchfield is not particularly easy to travel to from the rest of the country. The Office has a centre at Southport and it might be sensible if dispersal were to a location reasonably nearby. Its own preference is for a location in South Hampshire within easy reach of Titchfield.

4. If the Office is dispersed, in order to avoid almost certain loss of many of its trained survey practitioners and of medical statisticians, neither of whom could be replaced quickly, if at all, the Office would probably need

174

to retain a number of such posts in London together with a handful of other senior posts, the public search rooms, a few registration consultants and some limited support staff. The total number which the Office would wish to retain in London would be up to 100 posts.

5. With the exception of the small London office mentioned above, I therefore recommend that the whole of OPCS be dispersed to Central Lancashire New Town since this location is on the list approved by Ministers and is reasonably near to Southport.

Communications Damage	Resource Gain	Average Trade-off
500	7,404	27·64

6. I should however record that the Office is already inconveniently fragmented (between London, Southport and Titchfield). If the London Headquarters were now divided between London and CLNT, this comparatively small Office would be distributed over four locations; this runs counter to the avoidance of unnecessary fragmentation and to the promotion of managerial and organisational efficiency by, so far as possible, concentrating dispersed work in a few locations. It is therefore to be considered whether there would be equal merit from the regional policy viewpoint if the dispersed work joined that already at Southport (which is also in Lancashire). And if, on balance more weight were to be attached in the case of this Office to the " efficient " option in my report, it would be for consideration whether dispersal should be in the Portsmouth-Titchfield area (the Office now at Titchfield moving to a new site to join work removed from London).

MINISTRY OF POSTS AND TELECOMMUNICATIONS
(396 posts in one building)

1. The analysis of the communication data showed that 71 per cent of the Department's link strength related to contact within the Department and suggested that a substantial level of dispersal could be obtained at a poor trade-off between damage to communications and gains.

2. However, two dispersal proposals were put to MPT as a basis for discussion:

(1) Dispersal of 385 posts, leaving in London only the Minister and his Private Office.

Communications Damage	Resource Gain	Link Weight
520	2,192	1

(2) Dispersal of 264 posts, comprising the whole of the Directorate of Radio Technology together with the bulk of the Administration and Radio Department.

Communications Damage	Resource Gain	Link Weight
270	1,890	9

3. The main argument advanced by MPT against Proposal 1 was that dispersal on such a scale would seriously inhibit the Department's services to its Minister. Despite the evidence of the communications study that the *average* level of contact between officers in the blocks proposed for dispersal and the Minister's office was low, it was argued that the contact between the Minister, the Secretary and other senior staff was frequent and important.

4. Partial dispersal as suggested in Proposal 2 would, the Department argued, separate technical advisers (in the Directorate of Radio Technology and the Radio Regulatory Division) from the senior officers whom they advise. By depriving policy-makers of readily accessible technical support, this proposal would reduce efficiency by an unacceptable degree.

5. MPT stressed that the relatively small size of the Department already made staff management and career development difficult; these difficulties would, in the Department's view, be much greater if dispersal (particularly of only part of the Department) took place.

6. More generally, MPT had vital and frequent links with the Post Office Corporation, Cable and Wireless Ltd., the BBC and the IBA. All of these were with London Headquarters offices and would suffer in a dispersal situation.

7. It was accepted than any dispersal of MPT was likely to cause an overall degree of damage to the Department's efficiency which would be greater than the concomitant gains could justify.

8. Against this background, I recommend that MPT should not be dispersed.

POTATO MARKETING BOARD

(46 posts in one building)

1. The Board was not formally covered by the communications study. Whether or not it could be dispersed was left for MAFF to consider once their own communications study was complete and proposals had been put to them.

2. The study showed that 11 MAFF blocks have contact with London-based Agricultural Marketing Boards. None of these 11 blocks is recommended for dispersal.

3. I therefore recommend that the Board should not be dispersed.

PUBLIC WORKS LOAN BOARD

(47 staff in one building)

1. The communications study showed that about 50 per cent of the Board's link strength reflected contact within the Department and about 40 per cent reflected contact with non-Government bodies in London. Analysis suggested that dispersal could be obtained only at a comparatively poor trade-off between damage and gains. However, a proposal for complete dispersal was put to the Department for discussion.

Communications Damage	Resource Gain	Link Weight
81	349	8·4

2. The Department argued strongly against dispersal and felt that it could not carry out its functions efficiently if located away from the City. It stressed in particular the high level of contacts with the Bank of England and with the chief offices of the joint stock banks, which highlight the general work of the Board in its function as part of the central financial complex of the City.

3. Against this background I recommend that the Board should not be dispersed.

RACE RELATIONS BOARD
(31 posts in one building in London)

1. The Board has high levels of contact with persons or organisations in the London area which include, in particular, the Metropolitan Conciliation Committee staff and complainants and respondents from London. The benefits of dispersal could be obtained only at an extremely high cost:

Communications Damage	Resource Gain	Link Weight
149	327	3·6

2. I recommend that the Board should not be dispersed.

OFFICE OF THE REGISTRAR OF RESTRICTIVE TRADING AGREEMENTS

(71 posts in one building)

1. The analysis of the communications study showed that, in comparison with the figures for other Departments, the Office would be relatively severely damaged by dispersal. The measures were:

Communications Damage	Resource Gain	Link Weight
101	516	9·7

2. Moreover, the Office is about to be absorbed into the new Directorate of Fair Trading and Competition. The communications data are therefore unlikely in this case to constitute a useful basis for a dispersal recommendation.

3. Against this background, I recommend that ORRTA should not be dispersed.

SCIENCE RESEARCH COUNCIL

(388 staff in one building)

1. Unlike certain other Research Councils, SRC does not appear likely to undergo major changes as a result of the White Paper (Cmnd. 5046) on Research and Development and is likely to remain substantially unchanged in the foreseeable future.   The analysis of communications data suggested that while partial dispersal of SRC would not be appropriate, dispersal of the Council as a whole could be obtained at an acceptable trade-off between damages and gains, provided that the receiving location were a reasonably good communications centre not too far from London such as Basingstoke, Milton Keynes or Swindon.   A proposal for the dispersal of SRC as a whole was therefore discussed with the Council.

Communications Damage	Resource Gain	Link Weight
335	2,600	16·0

2. Because of difficulties in securing suitable accommodation in London, SRC was already considering the possibility of dispersal.   It is the Council's view that, subject to arrangements being made for meetings of the Council and its Boards and Committees to continue to be held in London, it can effectively carry out its operations away from London.   The Council is anxious, however, that the location should be conveniently situated for easy access to London and out of several locations which the Council has studied and discussed with staff there is a clear preference for Swindon, which also appears suitable on the criteria used in the Review.

3. I recommend the dispersal of the SRC to Swindon, facilities being provided for meetings of the Council and its Boards and Committees in London.

Communications Damage	Resource Gain	Average Trade-off
245	2,471	21·16

Given the immediacy of the accommodation problems with which the Council is faced so long as it remains in London, I also recommend that an early decision be given so that dispersal can take place without delay.

SOCIAL SCIENCE RESEARCH COUNCIL
(112 staff in parts of 2 buildings)

1. The analysis of communication needs suggested that dispersal could be obtained only at a marginally acceptable trade-off in gains and damage. However, a proposal for dispersal of the whole Council was put forward for discussion.

Communications Damage	Resource Gain	Link Weight
115	683	12·7

2. In discussion the Council presented the following arguments against dispersal. All major decisions are reserved for the Council and its Committees; separation of the Headquarters staff from the place where Council meetings are held would be achieved only at a high cost. The 200 or so Council and Committee members are recruited from universities and other bodies throughout the United Kingdom, and such recruitment would prove very difficult if the meetings were held outside London in view of the inconvenience that this would cause. Moreover, the Council does not operate through its own research establishments but through universities and colleges throughout the United Kingdom, through independent institutes which are almost exclusively in London, and through continuous links (often on a personal basis) with members of the social science community for whom London is a meeting place. For these reasons the benefits of dispersal would be obtained only at a high cost.

3. Against this background, I recommend that the Council should not be dispersed.

HER MAJESTY'S STATIONERY OFFICE
(481 staff in three buildings in London)

1. The communications study showed, first, that 52 per cent of the total link strength was between blocks within Headquarters and, second, that it would be desirable either to disperse the whole of the Headquarters under review, or none at all. A proposal, therefore, was made for the dispersal of the entire Headquarters still in London

Communications Damage	Resource Gain	Link Weight
781	3,504	1·0

2. In response, HMSO argued that, if the entire Headquarters were to be dispersed, account would need to be taken of three points. The first was that as part of HMSO Headquarters had already been dispersed to Norwich, that city was the only receiving location for the remainder of Headquarters where there would be a gain in terms of management and administration to offset the communications damage from dispersal. The second was that dispersal would affect the Department's ability to maintain the high degree of service its customers had come to expect. A third point was that some staff would be needed in London to provide essential services and a liaison point. HMSO have since made the further point that their London Headquarters staff incorporates a relatively small element which, in the event of dispersal, must remain in London because it is concerned with duties which can be performed only in the London area.

3. The fact that the major part of HMSO Headquarters is already at Norwich makes that city a prime candidate for further dispersal of the Department; the relatively low value of the link weight greatly strengthens the case for Norwich. There is a sound case for retaining a bare minimum of staff in London to maintain essential services. The exact number will have to be identified by HMSO nearer the time of the actual move; but HMSO's present estimate is that, of the 481 staff covered by the review, about 100 or so might need to be retained for regional and essential Headquarters needs.

4. I recommend the dispersal of 380 posts in the London Headquarters office of Her Majesty's Stationery Office. In the circumstances every factor emphasises that this should be to join the main part of the Headquarters already dispersed to Norwich. I note that the Department would wish to retain in London the minimum number of staff required to maintain essential services and recommend that this should be agreed.

Communications Damage	Resource Gain	Average Trade-off
481	2,695	11·1

CENTRAL STATISTICAL OFFICE
(225 Cabinet Office posts in one building)

1. The study of communications showed that 63 per cent of the Central Statistical Office's total link strength reflected contact within the Office and analysis suggested that dispersal of the whole Office should be possible but at a comparatively unacceptable trade-off between gains and damage. Two proposals were put to the Department, one involving the whole Office and the other involving most of the Office but leaving behind a few senior officers (including the Director) who were particularly strongly linked to contacts in London.

Communications Damage	Resource Gain	Link Weight
328	1,400	9·1

2. In the course of discussions the second proposal was rejected as it would seriously impair contact between senior staff and the blocks dispersed and create an unmanageable division of the Office. The salient objections to any dispersal, even to a relatively nearby location, were first that the CSO is extremely closely linked to the Treasury at several periods in the year in connection with Budget and forecasting work, and second that geographical proximity to the remainder of the Cabinet Office and to the Prime Minister is vital in enabling the CSO to exert influence on the work of the rest of the Statistical Service as well as to respond to new requirements for statistical analysis.

3. Against this background, I recommend that the CSO should not be dispersed.

DEPARTMENT OF TRADE AND INDUSTRY

(9,290 posts in 40 buildings)

1. The communications study showed that the main areas of the Department's work were closely interconnected and that there was no large group of related Divisions which appeared suitable for dispersal in its entirety. However, there were some individual blocks of work of significant size where there appeared to be a worthwhile trade-off between damage and resource gains.

2. The Department was therefore invited to consider the implications of three levels of dispersal:

(1) Dispersal of 40 blocks of work with 4,234 posts, including part of Research Division; Minerals, Metals and Electrical Engineering Division; Safety and Health Division and the Mines and Quarries and Nuclear Installations Inspectorates; Export Services Division; Films Branch of Paper, Printing and Publishing Division; Tariff Division; part of Standards, Weights and Measures Division; Marine Division; the Director of Statistics and four Economics and Statistics Divisions; Accountancy Services Division; Building Grants sections of Regional Industrial Development Division; the Companies Registration Office; Accounts Branches of Finance and Economic Appraisal Division; the Export Licensing Branch of Overseas Finance and Projects Division; the Laboratory of the Government Chemist and the Distribution Department of the British Tourist Authority.

Communications Damage	Resource Gain	Link Weight
2,720	31,800	13

(2) Dispersal of 25 blocks of work with 2,581 posts, leaving in London the whole of Research Division; MME Division; Safety and Health Division and the Inspectorates; ESD Division; PSD Films Branch; Tariff Division; and the whole of Standards, Weights and Measures Division, though still including the large group of Economics and Statistics Divisions.

Communications Damage	Resource Gain	Link Weight
1,180	23,600	16

(3) Dispersal of 7 blocks of work with 1,535 posts, including only RID Building Grants; the Companies Registration Office; the Accounts Branches of FEA; Export Licensing Branch of OFP and the Laboratory of the Government Chemist, leaving the Department's main organisation effectively intact.

Communications Damage	Resource Gain	Link Weight
370	17,200	24

3. In discussion, the Department emphasised that the need was for more, rather than less, integration of its exceptionally wide range of functions, in order to accomplish the purposes for which these functions were drawn together when the Department was set up. It needed to be sensitive to the pressure of events in critical areas and capable of responding immediately to unforeseen circumstances, for example, the current counter-inflationary measures. The communications study showed high " peaking " of face-to-face contacts in about a third of the Department. Entry into the EEC would profoundly affect the current communications patterns.

4. As to particular areas of work, it would make no organisational sense to disperse just one " industry " division (MME) and part of another (PSD Films Branch).

5. A special costing exercise on the BTA Distribution Unit indicated that a move from its present purpose-built premises would be too costly to be worthwhile.

6. There might be scope for dispersing more work on the collection of statistics to the Business Statistics Office at Newport, but it was essential for a considerable part of the Economics and Statistics Divisions to be co-located with the policy divisions they served.

7. In Export Services Division the scope for dispersal was limited by the desire of successive Governments to develop export promotion facilities in one readily available area; and the largest Branch provided a " regional " service to London and the South-East.

8. A number of other areas was already under organisational review, notably the Research Divisions following the White Paper on R and D (Cmnd. 5046) and Safety and Health Division and the Inspectorates following the Robens Report.

9. In the case of the Companies Registration Office it would be necessary to retain adequate public viewing facilities in London.

10. The RID Branches' work would be substantially run-down before dispersal was due to take place.

11. In the light of these arguments, the Department was invited to consider a revised proposal for the dispersal of 1,800 posts (including about 270 common service staff). This figure was made up as follows: the Intelligence Service of the Export Services Division (145 posts), Marine Division (30), Economics and Statistics Divisions (250), Insolvency Service (60) (not included in the original proposals), RID (15), Export Licensing Branch (10), Companies Registration Office (500), FEA Accounts Branches (161), Laboratory of the Government Chemist (330–358, depending on the receiving location).

12. The Department was also invited to look again at the areas which were still subject to review, namely Research, Safety and Health and the Inspectorates, Tariff Division, Standards, Weights and Measures, Marine Division and Sea Transport, and Accountancy Services (a total of about

800 posts excluding common services), though it was not considered possible at this stage to put a firm, or indeed even approximate, figure to future possibilities in these areas.

13. It appeared that dispersal on the basis of the original proposals could be achieved only at the cost of extreme organisational damage and administrative anomaly. The figure of 1,800 posts is therefore recommended for dispersal from DTI, taking account, as it does, of the general and detailed points which the Department made in its consideration of the initial dispersal proposals. The possibility of further, unquantified, dispersal is excluded from this figure.

14. With regard to location, the Laboratory of the Government Chemist should preferably be located near to another relevant research establishment to enable common facilities to be shared; a location on the periphery of London would be desirable to avoid the need for keeping an outstation in London. In this way the whole staff of 358 could be moved. Location at Teddington, near the National Physical Laboratory, would be the most convenient for the Department.

15. The Economics and Statistics posts (about 300 including common services) should clearly join the Business Statistics Office (BSO) at Newport, which already houses a substantial block of the Department's staff. The Department also expressed a strong preference for the location of its other dispersed work in the Cardiff/Newport area. In particular, a close link is planned between the Export Intelligence Service (145 posts) and the BSO at Newport to match the registers and classifications of the two units in order to improve the quality of the public service it provides on a fee-paying basis. The FEA Accounts Branches (161 posts) and Marine Division (30 posts) also have a close affinity with work already located in the Cardiff/Newport area.

16. The remainder of the work recommended for dispersal by the Department—the Companies Registration Office (500 posts), the Insolvency Service (Audit Section, 60 posts), RID (15 posts) and Export Licensing Branch (10 posts)—could in principle be dispersed to a location more distant than Newport. However, under the Companies Act 1948 there is a statutory requirement that the Companies Registration Office shall be in England (or Wales); Scotland has its own Registrar and registration system; similarly, the Audit Section of the Insolvency Service discharges the Department's statutory obligations in England and Wales only. So these blocks must stay in England and Wales. Furthermore, to recommend that the remainder should be separately located would go against two important principles of the review: to ensure, as far as possible, that no Department's Headquarters is split between more than two locations and to create, in the receiving areas, blocks of work sizeable enough to make sense in management terms and to provide reasonable career prospects *in situ*. I advise that this work should also be dispersed to Cardiff/Newport.

17. I recommend therefore that DTI should disperse 1,442 posts to Cardiff/Newport and 358 to Teddington.

Communications Damage	*Resource Gain*	*Average Trade-off*
791	15,182	35·1

REGISTRY OF TRADE UNIONS AND EMPLOYERS' ASSOCIATIONS

(44 posts in one building)

1. The analysis of communications data suggested that the dispersal of the whole of RTUEA could only be obtained at a relatively poor trade-off between gains and damage to communications; partial dispersal of so small a body is not practicable. Accordingly, no dispersal proposal was put to the Registry.

Communications Damage	Resource Gain	Link Weight
82	265	7·0

2. The possibility of an increase in contacts with London-based organisations, as the provisions of the Industrial Relations Act become better known, is likely to make RTUEA even less dispersable than it appeared at the time of the study.

3. The Registry operates in a field of great political sensitivity. It is of recent formation and its prospects of achieving the desired level of registration would be damaged if it were moved from London. Much will depend on fostering and maintaining the goodwill of unions and employers' organisations.

4. Against this background, I recommend that RTUEA should not be dispersed.

HER MAJESTY'S TREASURY

(1,068 posts, almost entirely in one building)

1. The study of communications patterns showed that 70 per cent of the Department's link strength reflected contact within the Department and that 30 per cent reflected contact with other Departments. Frequency of contact was high, both within the Department (between senior officials and with Ministers) and with blocks outside the Department. Analysis of the gains and communications damage likely to result if the whole Department were dispersed (no sensible division appeared possible) showed that dispersal could only be achieved at a very severe price in terms of damage to efficiency. The measures were:

Communications Damage	Resource Gain	Link Weight
2,139	6,600	0·5

In the light of this, no dispersal proposal was discussed with the Department.

2. Against the background of the numerical evidence, I recommend that the Treasury should not be dispersed, either in whole or in part.

TREASURY SOLICITOR'S DEPARTMENT

(340 posts in five buildings)

1. The communications study showed that 48 per cent of the Department's link strength reflected contact within the Department and analysis suggested that some dispersal should be possible at an acceptable trade-off between gains and damage. It was accepted that the Treasury Solicitor would remain in London because he has to be immediately available for attendance on Ministers, and it was also accepted that Claims Commission Branch would continue to be co-located with the MOD. Two proposals were put to the Department for discussion.

(1) Dispersal of Bona Vacantia Division, Conveyancing Division and the Statutory Publications Office. Total: 182 posts.

Communications Damage	Resource Gain	Link Weight
104	1,400	9

(2) Dispersal of Conveyancing Division and the Statutory Publications Office. Total: 147 posts.

Communications Damage	Resource Gain	Link Weight
73	1,100	24

2. The Department's main objections to the proposals were, first, the problem of recruitment to the Legal Class in any location other than London, second, the transitional difficulties likely to be caused by legal staff resigning or retiring prematurely because of dispersal, and third, increased management problems in continuing the necessary practice of posting staff throughout the Department if the Department were split in two. The nature of the duties performed by the Editor of the Statutory Publications Office made it necessary for him to remain in London, and the Department considered that unacceptable damage to efficiency would be caused if he were separated from his staff. The Department also stressed that, though comparatively infrequent, contacts with legal staff in other Departments were important, tended to arise at short notice and the Departments concerned at any one time varied greatly.

3. Against this background, I recommend that the Treasury Solicitor's Department should not be dispersed.

UNIVERSITY GRANTS COMMITTEE
(119 staff in one building)

1. The communications study showed that almost half the contacts of UGC staff were with universities throughout the United Kingdom, while contacts with London-based organisations such as DES and the Research Councils formed a relatively small part of the total pattern of contact. The smallness of UGC precluded consideration of partial dispersal, but the analysis of communications data suggested that dispersal of the whole organisation (if to a location not too far from London) would result in a degree of communications damage which was not so great as to make such a proposal unreasonable.

2. Accordingly, a proposal for dispersal of UGC as a whole was put forward for discussion.

Communications Damage	Resource Gain	Link Weight
205	925	8·3

3. The UGC argued that it would be very difficult for it to manage its staff unless it remained co-located with the bulk of DES, since, for staffing purposes, it is effectively a division of DES and it is unusual for an officer to make a full career within the UGC alone.

4. The UGC also felt that dispersal would have serious adverse effects on the work of its committees and sub-committees. The members of these, often of some eminence and outside Government service, might be unwilling or unable to serve if UGC were not in London. At the same time, it would not be practicable for the meetings to be held in London if the staff of UGC were not also located there.

5. Finally, the UGC argued that London would continue to be, as at present, the main centre of higher education in this country. There are in fact indications that UGC contacts with London-based bodies (Government and otherwise) are on the increase.

6. The arguments against dispersal put forward by the UGC have considerable force. Severe problems of staffing and career management are likely to arise if UGC were at any distance from DES—a Department for which no dispersal is recommended. The committee work of UGC would be likely to suffer as a result of dispersal, even to a good provincial communications centre.

7. I recommend that the UGC should not be dispersed.

APPENDIX 10

EXAMPLES OF WORK RECOMMENDED AND NOT RECOMMENDED FOR DISPERSAL

Introductory Note by Sir Henry Hardman

1. As a result of my enquiries I am convinced that, while there is scope for dispersal, especially to relieve pressures on the London office estate and the recruitment of junior staff, London as the capital city is the natural and most efficient home for a substantial part of the Headquarters work I have reviewed. Dispersal above a certain level must seriously impair efficiency. I give below some examples of work* recommended for dispersal, and some contrasting examples of work not so recommended, but I should make some general points first.

2. The first of these must be caveats. On the one hand, the examples are expressed in terms chiefly of the results of the communication study results so that, for instance, we learn that 76·7 per cent of a block of work's contacts (*i.e.* face-to-face contacts) may be with other blocks within the same Department and the rest with agencies outside. Plainly, such a presentation compresses within the space of a simple measure, and of a very few words, the reality of the business which staff in a Department conduct with their Ministers, seniors and colleagues and with people and organisations outside Government: it is indeed a pale reflection of such characteristics of business as urgency, the need to consult with colleagues and others immediately or the need to give an immediate response to a call for information or assistance from an individual or an organisation. On the other, it should be borne in mind that, if efficiency were the only consideration, much of the work I am recommending for dispersal would be undisturbed; in other words, the work covered by my recommendations is not dispersable in any absolute sense, but only in relation to other work, tied to London even more strongly, and to a desire to create new employment opportunities elsewhere.

3. Attention has already been drawn to the nature of London as the capital. It is, I think, worth repeating, lest the point should be lost sight of, that London is the seat not only of Parliament and numerous national institutions but also of many local government institutions, of employers' associations and trades unions, of the headquarters of major business concerns, of the major banking and business concerns, of the High Court, of the principal organs of the Press, radio and television, of the Embassies and High Commissions of foreign and Commonwealth countries as well as of myriad national bodies which are located in London and do business with Government. " It is being concentrated ", as Dr. Johnson observed, " which produces high convenience."†

4. I should also emphasise the convenience of London as a travel centre. It is the place to which people from overseas visiting London on Government business can come most easily; to which people in the United

---

* The figures and percentages given in the examples relate to the organisation and staff in post at the time of the communications study.

† " The Journal of a Tour to the Hebrides with Samuel Johnson ", James Boswell, Collins 1955, page 35.

Kingdom can come most easily on Government business or on business of their own which brings them into contact with Government Headquarters Departments; and from which Government officials can travel most easily to different parts of the country and overseas. Accession to the European Economic Community will reinforce the position of London in this respect and the Government is bound to pay serious attention to the greatly increased need for the staff of certain Departments to visit Brussels and other European centres. The pre-eminence of London as a domestic travel centre is demonstrated in Appendix 11.

5. The significance of this is twofold. First, from the Government's viewpoint, nowhere else is as convenient a location for interdepartmental consultation at Headquarters level. If Headquarters work is distributed about the country, many consultations will still have to take place in London if staff are not to be burdened with awkward and time-consuming cross-country journeys. Second, it should be recognised that, from the viewpoint of central Government's clients and partners, visitors to London (*e.g.* a local government chief executive or a university member of a Government committee) will often combine several items of business, affecting more than one Department or more than one part of the same Department, in their visit. If taking the time to visit London, they will and do expect to make the most effective use of it. To the extent that the dispersal of Headquarters work hinders this, and impairs the intimacy of contact between officials and those with whom they do business outside London, the efficiency of Government must inevitably suffer.

6. I did not overlook the advances already made or still to be made by rail and air travel. These have brought several locations, such as Manchester, effectively nearer to London in terms of travelling time. But travel always imposes burdens and there is a limit to the improvement that can be made. Even if air services, for example, become as frequent as trains, they are diminished by travel between airports and city centres, so that up to three hours each way is still a realistic travel time for most destinations. And of course they are particularly subject to delay or cancellation in bad weather. By rail, even the Advanced Passenger Train is unlikely to bring the journey to Glasgow, say, to under three hours. A total journey time there and back of up to six hours adds very significantly to the length of the working day and even if full use is made of sleepers (which of course means taking staff's own time for official business and may be an optimistic assumption) the penalty is severe. Even if we take telecommunications into account (to a degree which is discussed in Appendix 7), we must expect a considerable proportion of journeys still to be necessary and this has a major effect on two main characteristics of Government work as described below.

7. The review is concerned chiefly, but not exclusively, with policy work in London headquarters offices. (Some aspects of non-policy work have been involved where these are not of a truly local/regional nature.) Dispersal will stretch and weaken a number of links including those:

between Ministers and dispersed officials

between officials at Headquarters and dispersed officials

between dispersed blocks of work and other Departments remaining in London

between dispersed blocks and their non-Government contacts, whether these are based in London or not.

8. The effects of this must be adverse. Ministers have to consider how much loss of efficiency they are prepared to accept. This applies to the service they get and to the service which their Department has to give. That service is not just to them but to others—perhaps most important, on the one hand, to Parliament and on the other hand, to the community at large. Three examples illustrate the issues:

(i) Ministers will be separated from officials to whom they are used to turning, and need to turn, for urgent and sustained personal briefing. Those officials may be separated from other sources or Government contacts that they need for support in helping them. To take a recent Home Office experience, we had the prison riots of August 1972 and the Uganda expulsion crisis. If the officials concerned had been dispersed from London, it seems surely likely that Ministers could not have responded to either issue as effectively as they did.

(ii) Relations with the legislature are chiefly, and will remain chiefly, conducted by Ministers. Speedy response is fundamental. This is not just a question of the occasional Parliamentary Question or the occasional Bill. It is the whole range of the demands and needs of the legislature. Removal of a Minister's supporting staff from London is bound to weaken the reaction to this.

(iii) Working contacts between Government and non-Government contacts based in London would be seriously weakened by dispersal. This is not just a question of formal meetings. These could still be arranged. But informal contacts matter just as much for the important sections of public life which are centred in London. (Examples of non-Government London-based contacts of some typical blocks of work are given below.) Nor is this just a question of the various organised bodies representing different interests of national life. It is the general public who would lose much contact through the removal of work from London. There has already been adverse criticism in Parliament of the decision to move the Immigration and Nationality Department of the Home Office from High Holborn to Croydon (Hansard, Vol. 823, 25 October, 1971, col. 258; Vol. 825, 8 November, 1971, cols. 78–80; Vol. 826, 15 November, 1971, cols., 44 and 45). Decisions to move the Passport Office and the Companies Registration Office would also attract criticism. These are very much aspects of Government which Ministers do not see day to day, but the public does. The damage from moving such work from London cannot be quantified, but it is none the less real.

9. There is another characteristic of Government which will be impaired over and above the linkages and contacts described in the preceding paragraph. This is the working together of a Department. In the White Paper on Reorganisation of Central Government of October 1970, the arguments were

set out for the importance of bringing together functions of Government which were related. "Bringing together" was used in that White Paper in the sense of bringing them within one Department under responsibility to a single Minister. It also has a very real physical meaning, as well as Departmental organisational sense.

10. The objective was to cut down the amount of interdepartmental argument and thereby to improve the quality of Government decision-taking. This is much less likely to be achieved if the bringing together of various policy interests is then subjected to a physical separation between the people who are dealing with those different interests. There must be less cohesion and unity in a Departmental approach—and that was the whole purpose of the creation of the present Departmental structures—if large areas of them are physically separated from each other.

11. Nor is this just a question of the top policy decisions dealing with different aspects of a Minister's responsibilities. It applies just as much to the support services. These—Economists and Statisticians are a good example—need, as far as is practicable, to be integrated with policy work. This has not yet always been carried out as much as all Departments eventually want it to be. The result is that the communication studies have often shown that such areas of work are tied less strongly to London than traditional administrative work. Accordingly, they show up in the communications data as being more dispersable. But if as a result all, or a very large part, of statistical work in Departments was separated out and dispersed this would undoubtedly impair the operation of Departments. The increased efficiency of Government operation and comprehensiveness of the approach of Departments which was the essence of the reforms in organisation of the October 1970 Reorganisation of Government would at least in part be frustrated. Ministers have to decide whether the gains from dispersal are sufficient to offset such disadvantages. These issues cannot be quantified in terms of figures. It does not mean that they are not real.

12. I have considered the argument that the substantial number of junior staff in the supporting grades to be found in London need not be there and that it would ease recruitment problems if they were not. I wholly accept the force of the latter point, but the first should be treated with caution. In the first place, with a few exceptions, such staff are not to be found in large, self-contained blocks (which were, after all, the main target of my predecessor, Sir Gilbert Flemming) but are distributed in small numbers about Departments, working in direct support of senior staff. I have made some proposals for the dispersal of large bodies of clerical work, although not without reservations, but it would not accord with my or with Departments' understanding of administrative efficiency to suppose that Departments could operate satisfactorily with this clerical support located somewhere else. Apart from this, the clerical grades do of course provide recruits for the higher grades and there is considerable managerial advantage in having the two levels alongside each other.

13. I have considered whether there is a case for dispersing small parts of Departments and small offices (*e.g.* two or three blocks of work from the Department of Education and Science and all the National Debt Office). In

196

such cases, I have had careful regard to the balance between the claims of efficiency and regional policy, judging the former in the light of the communications and management damage involved and the latter in the light of the number of posts which would be created outside London. I have in most cases concluded that the disadvantages in terms of lost efficiency would outweigh the advantage in terms of new jobs and that it would be a mockery of dispersal—dispersal for dispersal's sake—which would impose such penalties as to render it absurd in organisational terms and indefensible in terms of its effect on staff.

14. I have also considered the argument that the experience of the Scottish and Welsh Offices shows that Ministers can operate effectively in London separated from the rest of their staff. A study has been made of Scottish Office experience. It has certainly shown that the Scottish Office can and does operate. But it also shows that it is really the Ministers who operate for short periods separated from their Departments. Furthermore, they do this against a background where the mass of related policy decisions is being taken within one single decision-taking centre of operations. That centre is London. Certainly, Scotland and Wales operate well as decision-taking centres for what are issues confined to their own geographical areas. In this respect, however, they are operating as regions. To the extent that they are something more than regions they are tolerable because they are small. Britain is not a geographical federation. We should have a very different system of Government if it were. We are a small island, where many decisions need to be taken nationally. It is the taking of those national decisions and the efficiency with which they are taken which is the issue to be considered. The existence of Scotland and Wales is, of course, very real indeed in terms of regional policy and in terms of decisions on policies which affect Scotland and Wales. It is irrelevant in the context of the efficient operation of the national Government.

Examples

15. The Departments and other bodies reviewed were divided, for the purposes of the communications studies, into over 1,500 blocks of work. To exemplify all of these in a few cases is clearly not possible. However, the following 12 examples have been chosen in order to illustrate some of the differing patterns of communication found. Two examples are given for each of the six patterns of communication illustrated, one for a block of work recommended for dispersal and one for a block of work not recommended.

16. The examples discuss the typical frequencies of contact of staff in each block with staff in other blocks of work, either in the same or in other Departments, and with those outside central Government altogether. Where there are any other noteworthy features, such as marked preferences for increased contact or peak periods of high frequency of contact or information on the importance, growth or decline of particular links, then these are also mentioned (as they were also in the block of work reports, only more fully). In interpreting the data, care should be taken *not* to equate numbers of contacts with numbers of journeys if the parties involved are separated. A single meeting will often give rise to more than one

197

contact, depending on the number of other people present, and these meetings will often not involve the staff in the block travelling to a meeting but rather others coming to see them. In addition, some journeys can be arranged so that several meetings can take place on the same trip.

17. The six patterns, for each of which two examples are given, are:

  (i) Frequent contact with Ministers and senior officials

  (ii) Contact mostly within own Department

  (iii) Contact mostly within Government

  (iv) Contact mostly with bodies in London

  (v) Contact mostly with bodies outside London

  (vi) Frequent contact with the public.

Type (i)—Frequent contact with Ministers and senior officials

(a) *Example of block of work recommended for dispersal: Supplementary Benefits Divisions I and II, DHSS*

18. Each Division is the command of an Under-Secretary reporting to the Deputy Secretary (Supplementary Benefits). Division I is responsible for the assessment of supplementary benefits and the policy, procedures and casework which arise, whilst Division II is concerned with problems of the unemployed, welfare, reception centres and the homeless, liability to maintain, supplementary benefit appeals tribunals and is also responsible for the SB Commission's Inspectorate. The two Divisions were defined as one block of work, whilst the Deputy Secretary (Supplementary Benefits) and the Chairman of the Supplementary Benefits Commission were each defined separately as two more in order to see the strength of the links between each of them. The proposals put to DHSS included dispersal of the 142 staff in the two Divisions, together with the Deputy Secretary (SB) and the Chairman of the SBC (whose work is almost full-time).

19. All 72 staff in the Divisions at or above Higher Executive Officer recorded their contacts, plus 14 Executive Officers, who have contact with members of the public, either in London legal aid cases or as part of their duties in the SBC's Inspectorate. A total of 384 typical contacts a month were recorded for the 72 staff and a further 142 for the 14 EOs on duties described above. This is an average of just over 5 typical contacts a month for each staff member at or above HEO level and 10 a month for each EO. Averages are misleading here, however, because the two Under-Secretaries account for 157 contacts a month, 80 of which arise out of their daily contacts with the Deputy Secretary (SB) and the Chairman of the SBC. The average contact for each staff member in fact rises from just over one a month for HEOs to about 9 a month for Assistant Secretaries and 80 for the Under-Secretaries.

20. The range of contacts recorded was wide and included 43 other blocks of work within DHSS, 7 blocks of work in other Departments and 25 outside Government entirely. In terms of distribution of contacts, however, 68·6 per cent is with others in DHSS, 2·9 per cent with other Departments and 28·5 per cent outside Government entirely.

21. The contacts with the Chairman of the SBC (19·2 per cent) and the Deputy Secretary (SB) (9·2 per cent) are the largest single contacts within DHSS and, since the proposal would co-locate all of them, these contacts would not be affected. This is particularly important for the two Under-Secretaries who have daily contact with both the Chairman and the Deputy Secretary to maintain on policy matters raised by individual cases (there are about 120 cases a week raised by Members of Parliament) or policy questions in new legislation. Dispersal would pose problems for them of how to do this and, at the same time, maintain about 55 contacts a month with those remaining in London in order to consult or advise them on these or similar issues. These include Ministers and their private offices (12 contacts a month and 20 a month for all staff), the Permanent and the Second Permanent Secretaries (6 contacts a month) and the Deputy Secretary (WP and NI) (3 contacts a month). The other single large contact within DHSS is Insurance Division B (14 contacts a month for the two Under-Secretaries and 20 for all staff), which would be co-located with them under this proposal.

22. The contacts with other Government Departments are very slight. The largest contact is with the Registrar of Companies, DTI, and concerns a small part of the Business Section of Branch SB 4. The block report suggests that this work could be organised so that a small nucleus of staff could remain in London.

23. These same staff in the Business Section of SB 4 are also involved in contact with the public, which accounts for almost all of the block's contact outside Government. The block report suggests that this too could be satisfactorily reorganised as above.

24. At the time of the communications study the two Divisions, the Deputy Secretary (SB) and the Chairman were located in separate buildings, which the staff felt inhibited contact; they expressed strong preferences for more. All of these have since been rehoused in one building, but not Alexander Fleming House, the main Headquarters building, so that contacts with senior officials and Ministers are still somewhat inhibited.

25. There were no major peaks of activity, except for contacts with local offices at EO level on Commission Inspections. The block report stated, however, that there were unforeseeable short-term pressures (*e.g.* from strikes, television programmes and Press comment) often necessitating urgent face-to-face contact with Ministers and concluded that " a discretionary service operating in the social field must of necessity be sensitive and responsive to such stimuli ".

26. The proposed co-location of the two Divisions with the Deputy Secretary (SB) and the Chairman would assist the two Divisions in maintaining their contacts and the Chairman also, because his contacts are overwhelmingly with these Divisions and the Deputy Secretary, but it would have repercussions for the Deputy Secretary himself. He has contacts two or three times a week with the Director of Management Services and Information Division and weekly with the Permanent and Second Permanent Secretaries and the Deputy Secretary (WP and NI). (*Note :* The Deputy Secretary is now also responsible for all operational aspects of Social

Security, including the management of the field organisation (*i.e.* the two central offices at Newcastle and Blackpool and the regional and local office network). This covers contributory, as well as non-contributory, benefits and to exercise this responsibility he needs to be near the Regional Director in particular (an Under-Secretary post which did not exist at the time of the communications study).)

27. In discussion, DHSS argued that it was not sensible to disperse any of the major policy blocks in their entirety and that it was necessary to examine each to determine which posts must be retained in London to ensure that Ministers continued to receive an efficient service (see Appendix 9, Part 2). Although therefore the final recommendation is to disperse most of the Supplementary Benefits block, the Deputy Secretary may need to remain in London; in any event there would remain a small but fairly high-level liaison group—somewhat on the Scottish Office pattern—which would keep the dispersed officials briefed on current developments in London, maintain contact with those senior staff of the Insurance Divisions and the Regional Directorate who remained in London, and stand in to provide top-level support in an emergency. Senior officials from the block would travel as necessary to brief Ministers and maintain contact with officials in London, but it would be likely that in time their communications patterns would change, with less emphasis on face-to-face contacts and more on telecommunications and paper-flow.

(*b*) *Example of a block of work not recommended for dispersal; Southern and Western European Departments; Western Organisations Department, FCO*

28. This block of work comprises three sections, each headed by an Assistant Secretary (*i.e.* Southern European, Western European and Western Organisations Departments) and includes the Under-Secretary responsible for all three. The Southern and Western European Departments are responsible for political and bilateral economic relations with some 23 countries, whilst the Western Organisations Department is responsible for relations with NATO and related bodies, Western European Union and the Council of Europe. The total staff is about 53. (None of the FCO's political sections is being recommended for dispersal because the evidence shows that they must be near Ministers.)

29. All 25 staff at or above Higher Executive Officer completed questionnaires, plus another two below that level. They recorded a total of 1,819 typical contacts a month or an average for each officer of about 67 contacts a month. This was not uniform across the different grades, however, rising from an average of 35 a month for staff at HEO level to 77 at Assistant Secretary and 204 at Under Secretary level. By far the greater proportion of these contacts, amounting to nearly two-thirds of the total, is accounted for by daily contacts with other blocks of work within the FCO, the Ministry of Defence and with Embassies and High Commissions in London. Contacts with 92 different blocks of work were recorded. In terms of the distribution of the total of 1,819 contacts a month, 80·3 per cent is with others within the FCO, including the ODA, 12·1 per cent with other Government Departments and 7·6 per cent outside central Government altogether.

30. Within the FCO there are daily contacts with

Ministers and Private Offices
Permanent Secretary and Private Office
Deputy Secretary responsible for this block
Defence Department
Eastern European and Soviet Department
European Integration Departments (1) and (2)
News Department
Dependent Territories/West Indian/Atlantic and Indian Ocean
    Departments
Communications Department
Training Department.

Contact with Ministers and their Private Offices is the largest single contact recorded, amounting to 11·1 per cent of total contact (*i.e.* 201 typical contacts a month) and reflects the current pre-eminence of European affairs in British foreign policy; daily contacts with the Defence Department is a facet of that policy. Daily contacts with the Permanent Secretary and the Deputy Secretary arise from the daily meeting of all Deputy and Under Secretaries with the Permanent Secretary and, in addition, there are frequently separate meetings to discuss specific policy issues arising.

31. The block has no frequent contacts at senior levels with parts of FCO recommended for dispersal. Contact with the ODA is not very great and will not be affected by recommendations for dispersal of that part of the Department.

32. Contacts with other Government Departments are not great for any one Department or for any single block of work, with the exception of the Defence Secretariat Divisions 11 and 12 in the Ministry of Defence, which account for 85 typical contacts per month or 4·7 per cent of the total contact. Contact with these Divisions, responsible for overseas defence policy and political questions concerning NATO, CENTO, SEATO and other defence interests, is daily.

33. Contacts with bodies outside Government are chiefly with Embassies and High Commissions in London and are on a daily basis for some staff. Other contacts involve the senior officials of Western Organisations Department attending regular meetings of the bodies concerned in the capital cities of member countries.

34. The report for the block of work points out that a preference for greater contact with the Research Department, which is housed in five separate buildings, was expressed by several staff. The report also lists a wide range of other contacts, within and outside the FCO, which increase significantly at periods of crisis or peak activity.

Type (ii)—Contact mostly within own Department

(a) *Example recommended for dispersal: The Accountant and Comptroller General's Office, Customs and Excise*

35. The communications study covered the 74 London staff of the Accountant and Comptroller General's Office, including A and CG himself. The Accountant and Comptroller General is responsible to the Chairman of

201

H

the Board for the accounting and financial arrangements of the Department, including the auditing of payments received and made by officials of the Department; the auditing of accounts of dutiable goods in bonded warehouses; the inspection of accounts and of accounting procedures in Collectors' offices; the management of the General Account of the Commissioners and the A and CG's Drawing Account in the Bank of England; the preparation of periodical and annual accounts of revenue and voted expenditure; the preparation of annual and any supplementary estimates of expenditure. About two-thirds of the staff of the office are already dispersed to Southend and more are due to follow in a year's time, leaving staff in London to prepare Departmental Vote and Appropriation Accounts and Estimates, Banking matters, the maintenance of Head Office accounts, Inspection, and the training and overall management of the office.

36. All 26 staff down to and including Higher Executive Officer grade completed questionnaires. They recorded contacts with 30 different blocks, 26 in London (of which 24 were within the Department), 3 with Customs and Excise at Southend, and 1 provincial contact block. The total monthly typical frequency of contact recorded was 90, giving an average of less than 4 contacts a month for each officer. Apart from the A and CG himself with 34 contacts a month and his Deputy with 21 contacts a month, none of the other staff recorded more than an average of 2 or 3 contacts a month. None of the recorded contacts was on a daily basis.

37. The distribution of these total contacts was 95·6 per cent within Customs and Excise (64·6 per cent London and 31 per cent Southend) and 4·4 per cent with one other Government Department (Exchequer and Audit). The recommendation for dispersal of Customs and Excise is to move A and CG's Office to Southend, plus the Stores Branch and Valuation Division. This would have the effect of reuniting the two parts of A and CG's Office, the present separation of which was felt by staff to enable them to have only one-quarter of the contacts they would prefer. It would, however, leave the A and CG and his Deputy separated from the Personnel Divisions A and B, which is their greatest single contact at present. It is not very frequent, however, amounting to about once a week for the A and CG and two to three times weekly for his Deputy. The burden of travel would fall on the senior officers. In total the A and CG and his Deptuy would need to maintain about 28 and 15 contacts a month respectively with other parts of the Department remaining in London, whilst still maintaining contact with their own staff. These contacts are highly dependent on the issues of the moment. None of their other staff would have typically more than two or three contacts a month with London to maintain.

38. There are peaks of activity for some staff and for some of their contacts. These are principally with C & E Collectors in London and the provinces, involving an inspection team of one SEO and one HEO in daily contact during visits lasting two or three weeks. Other peaks involve daily contacts by the Deputy AG and one HEO with Personnel Divisions A and B and weekly contact between the A and CG and the Chairman of the Board.

39. There are a number of regular contacts at levels below HEO which the block of work report details. These involve messengers in daily contact with the Bank of England, the Collector, London Port, and the Joint

Stock Banks, and less frequent contact with others, in order to collect or deliver documents or cheques. The Department has proposed to retain a nucleus of about 20 staff in London on dispersal of the remainder of the staff to Southend in order to deal with these duties and to provide pay office facilities for staff in the London headquarters.

(b) *Example not recommended for dispersal: Schools Branch, DES**

40. Schools Branch is responsible for the exercise of all the Secretary of State's main functions under the Education Acts in respect of primary and secondary education in England. Total staff is 121 and there are two registries with 13 staff who service the Branch. The communications study covered 52 officers from Under Secretary to HEO level, who all completed questionnaires.

41. Contact with 50 different blocks of work was recorded, 29 within DES (including, for this purpose, the Schools Council) and 21 outside, including 7 other Government Departments. A total of 816 typical contacts a month was recorded, an average of 16 for each staff member a month. This average was not uniform across all staff, however, rising from 10 a month for HEO grades to 42 a month for the 4 Assistant Secretaries and 68 a month for the Under Secretary.

42. In terms of the distribution of the total contacts, 76 per cent are within DES itself, a fifth of this being with Ministers and senior officials of the Department, 20 per cent with agencies throughout the country and 4 per cent with others in London. By far the greatest contacts within DES, accounting for one-half, are with Information Division, Finance, Legal and Statistics Branches and with Architects and Building Branch. This reflects the need to consult the Legal Adviser and his staff on the interpretation and application of statutory provisions, and also the need for territorial teams, headed by Principals and covering maintained schools in different parts of the country, to consult closely with Finance and Architects and Building Branches on the merits of including major building projects in local education authorities' building programmes, the distribution of resources for minor building projects and the approval of minor building projects at voluntary-aided schools. Other contacts with these stem from the responsibilities of eight functional teams dealing with specialised aspects of the Branch's work on a national basis. One such aspect is, for example, general questions arising out of the supply of schools and the compilation of building programmes, whilst another is responsibility for work arising on the Direct Grant schools. A feature of the contact with Ministers is that it is not confined to just the head of the Branch but extends to all grades, reflecting the nature of the business in hand. This includes discussing with territorial teams individual appeals from parents to the Secretary of State, statutory appeals (arising out of the reorganisation of secondary education, for example) and matters of wider importance, *e.g.* the distribution of the

---

* Since the location review took place and the Composite Report on the Department of Education and Science was presented, there has been some reorganisation, including the establishment of a second Schools Branch; as a result, the Schools Branch which was reviewed is now mainly Schools Branch I, but not precisely as described in the note.

305375

H 2

school building programme among local authorities. One-sixth of the contact internal to DES is with Senior Inspectors located at Headquarters and involves both territorial and functional teams.

43. The contact outside the Department is chiefly with local authorities or with Her Majesty's Inspectors in the regions and involves mainly the Principal and HEO grades. There is a low level of contact with seven other Government Departments; for any one it does not exceed four contacts a month in total.

44. An important feature of the work of this Branch is that it deals with almost one-third of the Parliamentary Questions of the Department, three times as much as any other part of the Department. Similarly, in Debates it accounted for about one-quarter of the total involvement and is often heavily committed in new legislation.

Type (iii)—Contact mostly within Government

(a) *Example recommended for dispersal : Population Statistics Division, Office of Population Censuses and Surveys**

45. The Division is responsible for initiating, interpreting and advising on a wide range of demographic statistics including national, regional and local estimates of population; birth, marriage and fertility statistics; both international and internal migration. The communications study covered 36 staff in this block of whom nine, from Assistant Secretary to HEO, completed questionnaires. The Division is recommended for dispersal along with all other OPCS staff in London. There are already large parts of the Department dispersed to Titchfield and Southport; these include units of the Division responsible for collecting and processing data.

46. Contact with 33 different blocks of work was recorded, 8 within OPCS (including Titchfield and Southport), 18 with other Government Departments and 7 with others outside Government. These gave rise to a total of 163 typical contacts a month, averaging 18 a month for each staff member, but varying across grades from 5 contacts a month for HEOs to 24 a month for Principals and 26 a month for the Assistant Secretary. There was only one case of daily contact, involving one Principal and Census Division.

47. In terms of the distribution of this total, 58·5 per cent is within OPCS, including 8 per cent contact with Titchfield, 31·8 per cent with other Government Departments and 9·7 per cent with bodies outside Government. The contact with Titchfield is all at Principal level and amounts to 12 contacts a month. Almost half of the contact within OPCS is with Census Division (in connection with the extraction of statistics from previous censuses and, when appropriate, with the planning of future censuses) and with Social Survey Division in connection with either *ad hoc* or ongoing research studies on behalf of Government Departments. This brings staff also into contact with these other Government Departments, principally those concerned with social and economic problems, specifically

---

* At the time of the location review, there was only one Population Statistics Division. It has since been split into two Divisions, each headed by an Assistant Secretary. The varying nature and quantity of contacts have increased as a result of this further development and growth of work.

DOE, DHSS, DES and the Home Office. Contact is maintained with the Statistics and Research Divisions of those Departments but equally with Divisions having responsibility for policy (*e.g.* Regional Planning and Economics Directorates in DOE; Community Relations and Immigration and Nationality Departments in the Home Office). About one-third of the contact with other Government Departments is with the Central Statistical Office and with the Cabinet Office proper. Much of the contact outside Government altogether is with universities and other educational establishments, but it is infrequent.

48. There are no single contacts which would seem to cause great problems on dispersal, but a multitude of infrequent contacts with other Government Departments in London will mean that one Assistant Secretary has to maintain 14 contacts a month and at the same time 12 a month with other OPCS Divisions, plus contacts, of course, with staff in his own Division. The problems for the five Principals would be of the same order. It is further complicated by the fact that several of the blocks in the other Departments are themselves recommended for dispersal.

(b) *Example not recommended for dispersal : Defence Policy and Materiel Divisions, Treasury*

49. This Division is one of four blocks within the command of the Deputy Secretary, Public Sector B, and is responsible for controlling public expenditure:

(a) for defence purposes (other than on personnel) by the MOD, including the Procurement Executive, the DOE (works services) and the Atomic Energy Authority;

(b) by DTI on assistance to the civil aircraft industry.

19 of the 31 staff completed questionnaires, from the Under-Secretary down to Executive Officer level. Neither this nor any other blocks within the Treasury are recommended for dispersal, because of the unacceptably high levels of damage that would result.

50. All the contacts of this block are with central Government Departments. Of the 79 different blocks identified, 16 are within Treasury and 63 within other Government Departments, principally MOD (including the Procurement Executive), DTI, DOE, FCO and CSD. A total of 329 typical contacts a month recorded by the 19 staff represents an average of 17 for each staff member a month, varying between about 14 a month for HEOs to 22 a month for the two Assistant Secretaries and 152 a month for the Under-Secretary.

51. Of the 329 total contacts a month, 31·4 per cent are within Treasury and 68·6 per cent within the rest of Government. The striking feature of this pattern is the very wide range of contacts that need to be maintained by individual staff, most of them not recurring frequently but amounting in total to 44 different contacts for the Under-Secretary, about 20 each for the Assistant Secretaries and about five each for the HEO staff. These arise from the need to examine Departmental long-term programmes, including functional costings, annual estimates, individual projects and other activities

(*e.g.* sales of defence equipment). It also involves assessment of the adequacy of Departmental systems of control and management. This work brings staff into contact with a large number of blocks and senior officials in the Departments already noted. Because defence expenditure is provided within the Defence Budget and this Division is responsible for advising Ministers on the level of this Budget, staff, particularly the more senior ones, are heavily involved in meetings with other parts of the Treasury concerned with the Public Sector and with Ministers and their most senior officials. In terms of frequency of contact with these then, apart from one HEO having daily contact with MOD, the Under-Secretary has the most intense pattern involving contact two to three times a week with each of six blocks of work, five of them within the Treasury. The other staff see their individual contacts monthly and occasionally weekly.

52. The block of work report points out that defence and aviation policy matters, with significant financial implications, give rise to meetings at very short notice to brief Ministers in consultation with officials from FCO, MOD and DTI.

Type (iv)—Contact mostly with bodies in London

(*a*) *Example recommended for dispersal : Publication Division, Commercial Books, HMSO*

53. This block of work undertakes a provisioning function which is outside the publishing activities of the remainder of Publications Division. It is responsible for the purchase of commercially published books, periodicals (including annuals), maps, etc. required for official use by HMSO and Government Departments. The main work of the block involves editing the demands and placing orders with commercial publishers. The block, comprising 24 staff, is recommended for dispersal to Norwich along with the remainder of the headquarters staff in London and this would have the effect of co-locating all of the policy and executive work of the Department. It would still leave in London some 600 non-industrial HMSO staff engaged in warehouses, presses, bookshops and other services.

54. Five staff at HEO and EO levels completed questionnaires. They recorded a total of 175 contacts a month with 25 different blocks, 6 within HMSO, 12 within other Government Departments and 7 outside Government, but almost all within London. The one HEO recorded a total of 15 contacts a month, whilst the four EOs recorded an average of 40 a month each. This high average is due largely to daily contacts with four different blocks, two of which are warehouses within HMSO not recommended for re-location, a third represents visits from members of the public and the fourth commercial organisations in London. Dispersal will, therefore, present difficult problems for these staff unless the Department can reorganise their duties or provide a small London liaison office.

55. Nearly a fifth of the 175 contacts a month is with other HMSO blocks recommended for dispersal, nearly a third is with HMSO blocks fixed in London, nearly a third is with bodies outside Government and mainly London-based and the rest is with other Government Departments. There is no contact with HMSO staff presently at Norwich. Most of the contacts

of this block will be with London, therefore, on dispersal, in particular with these four daily contacts already noted. The relatively high contact frequency with non-Government organisations is the result of the daily contacts of one officer with commercial second-hand book dealers and private collectors, etc. in his role as " the HMSO second-hand book dealer ". The block report expresses doubt on whether this second-hand bookselling operation would be feasible in a dispersal location.

56. The block of work report recorded peak periods of contact lasting two or three months with MOD and other Government Departments whilst carrying out reviews of subscription arrangements for periodicals. A CSD report has recently recommended that Departments be made responsible for their own arrangements for periodicals, however.

(b) Example not recommended for dispersal : The Arts Council

57. The Arts Council's 134 staff were regarded as one block of work for the purposes of the communications study and 48 of the most senior staff completed questionnaires. The Council itself consists of a Chairman and, normally, 19 other members; it is supported by four advisory panels and other sub-committees. All members are unpaid and appointed as individuals. These members were all regarded as London-based for the purposes of the study. The Arts Council was constituted under Royal Charter in 1946 " To develop and improve the knowledge, understanding and practice of the Arts; to increase the accessibility of the Arts to the public throughout Great Britain, and to advise and co-operate with Government Departments, local authorities and other bodies on any matters concerned, whether directly or indirectly, with the foregoing objects ". The Council itself mounts art exhibitions at the Hayward Gallery (leased from the GLC) and also manages the Wigmore Hall, and the Serpentine Gallery in Kensington Gardens. (Staff of these places were not included in the communications study.) It is not recommended for dispersal because of the high level of damage which would result.

58. A wide range of contacts were recorded by the 48 staff and 54 different blocks of work were identified, most of them London-based. A total of 2,201 typical contacts a month was recorded, which represents an average of about 46 a month for each staff member. This already very high average rises to about 75 a month for the Under-Secretary and his five Assistant Secretaries.

59. In order to advise Council on the award of grants or subsidies, the permanent staff need to keep abreast of individual artists and, therefore, regularly visit them or other bodies where their work can be seen or their performance assessed. The most frequent contacts are thus performances in London (13·7 per cent of total contact) and individual artists, almost all in London (15·4 per cent of total). Contact with these and others in London amounts to 84 per cent of all contacts. The 16 per cent of contact outside London represent mainly meetings with subsidised bodies, including Regional Arts Associations, and performances given by these bodies.

60. Apart from the two London contact blocks already described there are other subsidised bodies, individuals or agencies in London who

together account for a further 11·9 per cent of total contact. The Hayward Gallery, in which the Council mounts exhibitions, other museums and galleries in London and the DES, the "sponsor" Department, account for a further 14 per cent of total contact. The last London contact is that with Council members, either individually or in committees and this accounts for 10 per cent of the total contact. For many staff these London contacts arise necessarily daily.

Type (v)—Contact mostly with bodies outside London

(a) Example recommended for dispersal : The Ordnance Board, MOD

61. The Ordnance Board, which comprises Board Members and 112 permanent staff, was regarded as one combined block of work for the purposes of the communications study. The Ordnance Board is an inter-Service, independent, technical trials and advisory organisation for the appraisal of the safety and effectiveness of weapons and weapons systems in which explosives are used. It is recommended for dispersal, along with large parts of MOD.

62. 72 staff down to and including Major level completed questionnaires and identified 158 different contact blocks. These are mostly within the Ministry of Defence, but located throughout the country. The contacts arise from the need to visit military or research establishments in order to inspect or discuss developments in weapons and weapon systems. Other contacts outside the MOD are chiefly with civilian contractors throughout the country.

63. In terms of frequency of contact, the total for all 72 staff was recorded as 703 a month or an average for each staff member of almost 10 a month. This average varied between 8 a month for the lower grades and 16 a month for the highest grades. In terms of distribution, the most striking feature is that, apart from the three blocks contacted most frequently (a total of 27·1 per cent of total contact), no other single block accounted for more than about 4 per cent of the total, i.e. 28 contacts a month over all grades. For no member of staff was contact with any single block particularly frequent, therefore. Contact with MOD headquarters staff or MOD establishments throughout the country represented about 86 per cent of total contact, whilst contacts with other Government Departments was about 1 per cent of the total, and those outside Government accounted for the remaining 13 per cent. This latter includes regular visits to Common-wealth and foreign military and civilian establishments where the buying of defence equipment and collaborative ventures with other nations are involved. In terms of location, 51 per cent were with blocks based outside London and 49 per cent within. The block of work report stated, therefore, that there was a need for the staff to be located within easy access to rail and air services.

(b) Example not recommended for dispersal: The University Grants Committee

64. The UGC's terms of reference are "To enquire into the financial needs of university education in Great Britain; to advise the Government

208

as to the application of any grants made by Parliament towards meeting them ; to collect, examine and make available information relating to university education throughout the United Kingdom; and to assist in consultation with the universities and other bodies concerned, the preparation and execution of such plans for development of the universities as may from time to time be required in order to ensure that they are fully adequate to national needs." The UGC comprises a full-time Chairman, a part-time Deputy Chairman, and 19 other members, assisted by 119 staff. There are a number of sub-committees, mostly concerned with particular areas of academic study. For the purposes of the communications study all of these were regarded as one block of work and 52 UGC staff, plus the Chairman and Deputy Chairman, completed questionnaires. The UGC is not recommended for dispersal largely because, although the damage to communications would not seem to be intolerable, it would raise serious staffing difficulties because its staff are seconded from DES and officers do not usually make a full career within the UGC alone.

65. 40 different blocks of work were identified as contacts by the 52 staff and the Chairman and Deputy Chairman, 26 of them with Government Departments (of which 11 were within DES) and 14 outside Government. A total frequency of 491 contacts a month represented an average of 9 a month for each officer, but this rose from 3 a month for HEO grade staff to 24 and 40 a month for the Chairman and the Secretary respectively.

66. In terms of distribution, 9·6 per cent of the contact recorded was with DES, 5·9 per cent with DHSS, 11·6 per cent with the Research Councils and a further 1 per cent with other Government Departments in London, thus bringing the total for Government contacts in London to 28·1 per cent. There is contact with other Government Departments outside London, amounting to 7·7 per cent of the total, with the Scottish Office (Edinburgh) and the Welsh Office (Cardiff), arising largely from the monthly Committee meetings of the UGC to which these Departments send assessors. The same is true of the contacts with the Research Councils. The contact with DES is predominantly with the Permanent Secretary and his personal staff, Universities Branch and Architects and Building Branch for reasons which are self-explanatory. The contact with DHSS is with Divisions on the Health Side in connection with Teaching Hospitals and Medical Schools.

67. By far the largest proportion of contacts are outside London, however. They arise from visits to Universities (49·6 per cent of total contact) and contacts with other bodies not in London (7·3 per cent). Because of this volume of contact outside London, the block of work report registered the conclusion that staff must be able to make ready use of rail and air services. For individual staff, and particularly for the Chairman and the 11 staff at and above Assistant Secretary level, the contacts with Universities are the only ones which are at all frequent. All other contacts, including those with particular parts of DES, are at a frequency of only once a month.

Type (vi)—Frequent contact with the public

(a) *Example recommended for dispersal: Immigration and Nationality Department (excluding B4 Division), Home Office*

68. The detailed functions of the block are very numerous, but briefly it is concerned with policy and casework relating to the entry and control of aliens and Commonwealth immigrants, with legislation on immigration control and with the application at ports of Acts and Orders relating to the control of persons entering and leaving the United Kingdom. For the purposes of the study, B4 Division was regarded as a separate block of work and the bulk of the Department as another. The main block has 519 staff, plus 192 in the registries which serve it. (The Department has recently moved to Croydon, without prejudice to the findings of this Review.)

69. 92 staff at or above HEO level completed questionnaires and recorded a total frequency of 626 contacts a month with 50 different blocks. This is an average of about seven contacts a month for each staff member. This average did not vary greatly between the various grades of staff, with the exception of the Under-Secretary, who recorded 33 contacts a month.

70. For these 92 staff, three contacts represented 66 per cent of the total contact:

	Per cent
(i) Members of the public	29·5
(ii) Immigration Appeal Tribunal and Adjudicators ...	19·3
(iii) United Kingdom Immigrants Advisory Service ...	16·8

There is a quite different pattern of contact for staff above HEO from the staff at that grade, as the table below illustrates.

	HEO (62 staff) per cent	Above HEO (30 staff) per cent
Members of the public	25	5
Immigration Appeal Tribunal and Adjudicators ...	17	3
United Kingdom Immigrants Advisory Service ...	16	1
	58	9
Metropolitan Police Office	4	—
Other Home Office blocks	2	13
	6	13
Parliament	—	2
Other Government Departments in London ...	1	8
	1	10
Other London contacts	1	2
	1	2
Total	66	34

71. At HEO level, contact with members of the public is very frequent and daily for many staff. Below HEO level there is even greater frequency of contact, for it is on Executive and Clerical Officer grades that the burden of dealing with about a quarter of a million personal callers a year to the Public Enquiry Office falls. This number has been growing steadily and is accompanied by an equally great load arising out of telephone and written enquiries. (These contacts were not included in the communications study or in the subsequent analysis.) The Chief Clerk estimated that some 75 per cent of callers were from within the Greater London Council area.

72. Above HEO level the contact is predominantly with a wide range of other Home Office blocks and those in other Government Departments. The most frequent of these are with B4 Division and with Ministers or their Private Office, amounting in total to 21 typical contacts a month each. The contacts with other Government Departments is principally with FCO (Migration and Visa Department; East African Department) on business which is self-evident. No single member of staff above HEO has contacts as frequent as daily and for most they are about once a week or less, the exception being the Under-Secretary who has contact two to three times a week with B4 Division, for which he is responsible. Under this recommendation to disperse these contacts would be unaffected.

73. Because of pressure on its central London accommodation the Home Office has already implemented plans to move Immigration and Nationality Department work to Croydon. This recent move has already aroused adverse comment in the House of Commons on the grounds of loss of public convenience. It will probably be essential to establish public enquiry offices in several major cities if the Department is dispersed to a less accessible place than London although the main public enquiry office (for 75 per cent of the callers) will need to remain in London. The Home Office have argued also that a move of the Department away from London would result in a loss of effectiveness. It may be necessary to retain some senior staff in London, but they would need to maintain frequent contact with their dispersed staff and it would be necessary to compare the damage and loss of effectiveness caused by such a split with that arising from dispersal of the whole.

(b) *Example not recommended for dispersal : Charity Commission (excluding Official Custodian), London*

74. The Charity Commission was involved in an earlier dispersal exercise which resulted, in 1970, in approximately one-third of the work of the Department being transferred to Liverpool. The work of the Department can be broadly classified as follows :

(a) Giving advice to and carrying out semi-judicial work for charities in England and Wales, giving advice on the constitution of proposed charities, assisting with local reviews of charities, compiling and maintaining a central register of charities, dealing with cases involving possible mismanagement or misconduct and dealing with matters of general policy concerning charities.

(b) The Official Custodian for Charities acts as holding trustee for charities, involving buying and selling securities, investing cash, remitting dividends received from securities held and attending to all other matters arising out of his custodial function.

211

When dispersal took place, the two parts of the Department were dealt with separately so that the London office now carries out the functions mentioned in (a) in respect of charities that operate nationally or have no defined locality or are localised south of a line from the Bristol Channel to the Wash and the Liverpool office carries out similar functions in respect of charities localised north of this line. The work of the Official Custodian's Division was divided functionally, so that the Liverpool office is now concerned mainly with the distribution of dividends received from securities held, while the London Office is concerned with the rest of its functions.

75. For the purpose of the communications study, the work of the London Office was divided into two blocks:

    (i) The Charity Commission (excluding the Official Custodian for Charities), London.

    (ii) The Official Custodian for Charities, London.

76. This account deals with the first of these blocks, which comprises 120 staff at or above Clerical Assistant level plus other supporting staff. 35 staff from the Chief Commissioner down to the HEO grade completed questionnaires and recorded contacts with 44 different blocks of which the following four accounted for more than a half of the 535 total contacts per month:

		Percentage of total
(a)	Charities, London...	26·7
(b)	Charities, South	14·4
(c)	Members of the public, London	8·8
(d)	Members of the public, South (excluding London) ...	6·2
		56·1

77. The block of work report emphasised the relationship of mutual trust that has grown up over the years between the trustees of the larger charities and the London office staff, to which the legal staff attach the greatest importance. Inaccessibility of the Commission to the 51,000 registered charities in London and the South would have adverse effects on the efficient administration of these charities to the ultimate detriment of the beneficiaries. Because most of those representing charities provide their services free and are in many cases ordinary members of the public, inaccessibility of the Commission and staff would not enable them to fulfil their general obligations under the 1960 Charities Act, which are to best promote and make effective the work of charities in meeting the needs designated by their trust. It also gives the Commissioners the general function of promoting the effective use of charitable resources.

78. The 83 contacts a month with the general public, representing 15·6 per cent of total contacts do not fully take account of about 600 visits a month by the public to inspect the register of charities which must, under the 1960 Act, be maintained and accessible. Contacts with the public take place mainly at Principal and HEO level and are for a variety of purposes, including the discussion of complaints.

79. The Official Custodian, London, is the only other block with which there is frequent contact. This amounts to 92 contacts a month or 17·2 per cent of the total. The contact is greatest at HEO level. That block of work has itself strong links with financial institutions in the City to enable it to properly invest monies on behalf of charities.

80. The five contacts already noted account for 73·3 per cent of total contacts recorded, the remaining 26·7 per cent being spread over 39 miscellaneous contact blocks. In terms of location 74·6 per cent of total contact is with London and 97·4 per cent with London or the South. Contact with Government Departments accounts for 8 per cent of the total, the largest being the Public Relations Branch of the Home Office (2·2 per cent) and the Litigation Division of the Treasury Solicitor's Department (1·5 per cent).

81. In terms of the distribution of contacts across individual staff, the overall average is 15 contacts a month for each staff member, but this varies from 40 a month for the Chief Commissioner and for the Commissioner for London to only about 10 a month for the three Deputy Commissioners. At HEO and Principal grades it averages 20 and 15 contacts a month respectively.

APPENDIX 11

THE LOCATIONS AS TRAVEL CENTRES

1. A comparison has been made between travel facilities to and from London and similar facilities between the locations under study. The comparison covers estimated travel times—by road, rail and air—to other major towns and cities.

Rail

2. Map 1 shows the British Rail passenger network in January 1972. The map shows how the inter-city network is based on radial routes from London; these give higher average speeds on journeys to and from London than obtain on journeys between other travel centres.

3. The analysis of rail times is based on the ABC Inter-City Rail Guide, supplemented where necessary by British Rail local timetables. The ABC Guide indicates the quickest cross-country routes and incorporates interconnecting services in its timetables. Table 11 (1) shows the average times by the fastest trains between locations. On some routes there are no interconnecting services and the time shown includes a waiting time of 30 minutes at all junctions where no connecting services are timetabled. This interval sometimes includes a journey between railway terminals. The numbers in brackets after travelling times in the table show the number of connections for which 30 minutes has been added.

4. The times shown do not include time taken in travelling to and from the stations at each end of a journey. No adjustment has been made for differing frequencies of service.

5. Examples of travelling time by rail between London and other locations, with the amount of working time this would leave in a normal working day (0900–1800) are given at Annex A. This clearly shows that, under present conditions, it is easily possible to travel from certain locations to London, have time for one or more meetings and return home the same day, while the more distant locations require either an overnight sleeper or a next day return journey.

Road

6. Map 2 shows the projected Motorway and trunk road network for the early 1980s. As well as the major towns and cities, most of the receiving locations studied lie on this projected network—much of which already exists. Because of their central positions, locations in the Midlands are best placed for road travel to and from Britain as a whole.

7. Table 11 (2) gives approximate road distances and travelling times between the locations. The estimates of travelling time take into account time taken driving to and from city centres, rest breaks during longer journeys and such other incidentals as time taken to find a parking place. Examples of estimated travelling times by road between various locations, with the amount of working time this would leave in a normal working day (0900–1800) are given at Annex B. The estimates are not precise and

the time taken to cover any distance will obviously be influenced by traffic and weather conditions. In general, however, the estimates are believed to offer a suitable basis for comparison.

Air

8. Map 3 shows the routes between United Kingdom airports on which there is at least one direct flight every working day. As with rail, London is the focal point for travel, although there is no daily flight between London and Plymouth. Map 4 shows similar routes to overseas airports. These maps are based on information in the ABC World-Airways Guide, November 1972. There are few direct flights to European airports from provincial airports because the airlines route most journeys through London.

9. The ABC World-Airways Guide 1972 shows that direct flights between locations with airport facilities and major centres in Britain usually take about one hour's flying time. The comparisons in Table 11 (3) have therefore been restricted to the *number* of direct flights to various destinations, including European cities. It is important to bear in mind that for some locations which do not have airport facilities it is possible to travel to and from an airport within reasonable distance by rail or road, *e.g.* Plymouth and Exeter, Basingstoke and London; Glasgow, which has an airport of its own, is also within an hour of Prestwick and Edinburgh (Turnhouse). The extra time taken to travel via another location has not been estimated. On the assumption that city centre to city centre journeys by air take about three hours, it is quicker by rail from London to Liverpool, Manchester, Leeds and Coventry, but quicker by air from Glasgow, Newcastle and Teesside.

General

10. The travelling times given are not intended to suggest that there is a direct comparison of different modes of transport. Choice of method of transport is not made on travelling time alone. Each method of travelling has advantages and disadvantages. This part of the report is therefore designed simply to provide information about the travel facilities available and average journey times using these facilities.

11. The rail times do not include the time taken travelling to and from railway stations, apart from interchanges during a rail journey. On air journeys the flight may be about 60 minutes but to this has to be added the check-in time of up to 30 minutes before departure time and also the time taken to travel between city centre and airport. We have therefore assumed for city centre to city centre journeys by air a total travelling time of three hours.

12. No reference has been made in this Appendix to probable future patterns of rail and air travel, as both are somewhat unpredictable and the future relation between them is as yet unclear. As far as *rail travel* is concerned, British Rail are thinking in terms of a two-stage acceleration programme on the principal " Inter-City " routes. In stage one, a number of high-speed diesel trains (HSTs) would be introduced from 1974 onwards, raising average speeds from London to Bristol, Cardiff, Leeds and Newcastle by 15–20 per cent; for example, Newcastle would be reached in three hours,

216

at an average speed of just under 90 m.p.h. as compared with 75 m.p.h. today. In stage two, Advanced Passenger Trains (APTs), travelling at speeds of 150+ m.p.h., would be introduced; these would be powered by electric or gas-turbine engines. By the end of the 1980s, the major routes would all be served by APTs. *There must, however, be very considerable question marks over the economics of the HST and APT systems, and over the technology of the APT.* Some working assumptions have been made about future patterns of rail travel in Annex A. It is, however, uncertain to what extent high-speed running will spread round the railway system rather than be confined to the most important " Inter-City " routes.

Examples of travel time by rail and of time left for business at destination

	1972 x					1980 $\frac{2}{3}x$					1985 $\frac{7}{12}x$				
	Dep.	Destination Arr.	Destination Dep.	Arr.	Working time	Dep.	Destination Arr.	Destination Dep.	Arr.	Working time	Dep.	Destination Arr.	Destination Dep.	Arr.	Working time
London–Edinburgh	08.00	14.13	12.00	17.55	−2.13	08.00	12.10	13.57	17.55	1.47	08.00	11.38	14.28	17.55	2.50
London–Glasgow	08.00	14.45	11.15	17.54	−3.30	08.00	12.31	13.27	17.54	0.56	08.00	11.56	14.01	17.54	2.05
London–Newcastle	09.00	13.14	13.57	17.55	0.43	09.00	11.50	15.16	17.55	3.26	09.00	11.28	15.36	17.55	4.08
London–Middlesbrough	09.00	12.19	13.35	17.24	1.16	09.00	11.13	14.04	17.24	2.51	09.00	10.56	15.10	17.24	4.14
London–Manchester	08.55	11.39	15.30	18.12	3.51	08.55	10.45	16.24	18.12	5.39	08.55	10.31	16.37	18.12	6.36
London–Liverpool	09.30	12.17	15.30	18.24	3.13	09.30	11.22	16.37	18.24	5.15	09.30	11.07	16.44	18.24	5.37
London–Birmingham	09.10	10.42	16.45	18.19	6.03	09.10	10.12	17.16	18.19	7.04	09.10	10.04	17.24	18.19	7.20
London–Cardiff	09.00	11.07	16.00	18.15	4.53	09.00	10.25	16.45	18.15	6.20	09.00	10.14	16.56	18.15	6.42
London–Bristol	08.45	10.42	16.15	18.11	5.33	08.45	10.03	16.54	18.11	6.51	08.45	9.53	17.03	18.11	7.10
London–Plymouth	08.30	12.50	13.00	16.30	0.10	08.30	11.24	14.09	16.30	1.45	08.30	11.02	14.28	16.30	3.26
Manchester–Newcastle	08.40	11.52	14.15	17.55	2.23	08.40	10.49	14.28	17.55	3.39	08.40	10.32	15.47	17.55	5.15
Plymouth–Leeds	08.30	15.29	10.30	19.20	−4.59	08.30	13.11	13.25	19.20	0.14	08.30	12.04	14.11	19.20	2.07

Annex B to Appendix 11

Examples of travel time by road and of time left for business at destination

Journey	Distance	Time*	Official time available in destination
Plymouth–Bristol	117	3·1 hrs.	2·8 hrs.
Glasgow–Manchester	214	5·3 hrs.	7·4 hrs.†
Glasgow–Newcastle	139	3·6 hrs.	10·8 hrs.†
Coventry–London	99	2·7 hrs.	3·6 hrs.
Coventry–Liverpool	106	2·9 hrs.	2·2 hrs.
Cardiff–London	153	3·9 hrs.	10·2 hrs.†

* Based on travel times in Table 11 (2).

† Where less than 2 official hours remain in a one-day journey, time allows for an overnight stay.

219

Table 11 (I). Rail travelling times in hours

Travel/Major Centres	London	Glasgow	Edinburgh	Newcastle	Teesside	Leeds	Manchester	Liverpool	Nottingham	Norwich	Birmingham	Cardiff	Bristol	Southampton	Plymouth
Glasgow	6·6	—	0·8	2·9(1)	3·8(1)	4·7	5·1	4·9	7·1	7·9(1)	5·8	6·6(1)	7·8(1)	8·3(1)	10·6(1)
Newcastle	4·8	2·9(1)	2·3	—	1·4	1·9	3·2	4·1	4·3(1)	5·7(1)	3·9	6·4	5·6	6·5(1)	8·7(1)
Teesside (Middlesbrough)	4·9(1)	3·8(1)	3·8(1)	1·4	—	2·4(1)	3·4(1)	4·2(1)	4·1(2)	6·0(2)	4·3(1)	6·3(1)	6·1(1)	6·6(2)	9·3(2)
Darlington	3·9	2·8	2·8	0·6	0·5	1·4	2·4	3·2	3·1(1)	5·0(1)	3·3	5·3	5·1	5·6(1)	8·3(1)
Leeds	2·8	4·7	4·1	1·9	2·4(1)	—	1·3	2·2	2·7	4·7(1)	2·9	5·3(1)	4·3	6·3	6·8
Central Lancashire New Town (Preston)	3·4	3·7	5·3	3·8(1)	4·7(2)	2·7(1)	0·9	1·2	4·9(2)	6·8(2)	2·5	4·7(1)	4·5(1)	5·1(1)	7·3(1)
Manchester	2·5	5·1	6·3	3·2	3·4(1)	1·3	—	1·7	2·2	5·4(1)	1·9	4·1	3·4	5·7(1)	6·4
Merseyside (Liverpool)	2·7	4·9	6·2(1)	4·1	4·2(1)	2·7	1·7	—	4·0(1)	5·4(1)	1·7	4·2	3·8	4·4(1)	6·4
Runcorn	3·0(1)	5·4(1)	7·1(1)	5·0(1)	5·1(2)	3·1(1)	1·6(1)	0·4	4·4(2)	7·0(2)	2·1(1)	4·2(1)	3·9(1)	4·7(2)	6·7(1)
Birmingham	1·7	5·8	6·3	3·9	4·3(1)	2·9	1·9	1·7	1·8	4·4	—	1·9	1·4	3·3	4·3
Cardiff ...	2·5	6·6(1)	7·9(1)	6·4	6·3(1)	5·3	4·1	4·2	3·9	5·4(1)	1·9	—	0·7	2·9	3·7(1)
Coventry	1·3	6·9(1)	7·4(1)	5·0(1)	5·4(2)	4·0(1)	2·2	2·2	2·9(1)	5·5(1)	0·6	3·0	2·5(1)	3·0(1)	5·4(1)
Norwich	2·2	7·9(1)	7·5(1)	5·7(1)	6·0(2)	4·7(1)	5·4(1)	5·4(1)	3·6(1)	—	4·4	5·4(1)	4·6(1)	3·9(1)	6·9(1)
Bristol	1·9	7·8(1)	8·6	5·6	6·1(1)	4·3	3·4	3·8	4·0(1)	4·6(1)	1·4	0·7	—	2·4	2·5

220

Swindon	1·2	8·3(1)	7·8(1)	6·8(1)	5·1(2)	5·1(1)	4·6(1)	4·4(1)	3·8(1)	3·9(1)	2·5(1)	1·4	0·8	2·9(1)	3·7
Basingstoke	0·8	7·9(1)	7·4(1)	6·1(1)	6·2(2)	4·1(1)	3·8(1)	4·0(1)	3·4(1)	3·5(1)	2·9(1)	2·8(1)	2·2(1)	0·7	4·3(1)
Milton Keynes (Bletchley)	0·8	7·7(1)	7·4(1)	5·8(1)	6·2(2)	4·1(1)	3·8(1)	3·6(1)	3·4(1)	5·5(1)	1·4	3·8(1)	3·2(1)	2·5(1)	5·5(1)
Plymouth	4·2	10·6(1)	11·6(1)	8·7(1)	9·3(2)	6·8	6·4	6·4	7·0(1)	6·9(1)	4·3	3·7	2·5	5·4(1)	—
London	—	6·6	6·1	4·8	4·9(1)	2·8	2·5	2·7	2·1	2·2	1·7	2·5	1·9	1·2	4·2

Numbers in brackets indicate the number of non-interconnecting changes, 30 minutes has been added to the travelling time for each such change.

Note: (i) The travelling times (to the nearest tenth of an hour) shown here are average times of the fastest trains shown in the ABC Inter-City Rail Guide, September 1972 (supplemented where necessary by British Rail local timetables).

Table 11 (2). Road mileages (lower figures) and travelling times in hours (upper figures)

Travel/Major Centres	Plymouth	Southampton	Bristol	Cardiff	Birmingham	Norwich	Nottingham	Liverpool	Manchester	Leeds	Teesside	Newcastle	Edinburgh	Glasgow	London
Glasgow …	11·0 / 472	9·9 / 422	8·8 / 371	8·7 / 368	7·1 / 295	8·8 / 375	6·6 / 273	5·3 / 214	5·3 / 214	5·1 / 206	4·3 / 172	3·6 / 139	1·6 / 48	— / —	9·3 / 398
Newcastle …	9·3 / 396	7·7 / 323	6·8 / 283	6·9 / 287	4·9 / 198	6·0 / 249	4·1 / 162	3·6 / 139	3·2 / 122	2·7 / 94	1·3 / 36	— / —	2·9 / 106	3·6 / 139	6·8 / 284
Teesside …	8·7 / 370	7·0 / 291	6·2 / 256	6·3 / 263	4·3 / 169	5·3 / 214	3·4 / 129	3·2 / 123	2·7 / 99	1·9 / 64	— / —	1·3 / 36	3·7 / 142	4·3 / 172	6·0 / 249
Darlington …	8·6 / 363	6·9 / 288	6·0 / 249	6·2 / 255	4·1 / 163	5·3 / 217	3·3 / 126	3·1 / 111	2·5 / 90	1·9 / 59	0·8 / 15	1·3 / 35	3·6 / 137	4·1 / 162	6·1 / 250
Leeds …	7·3 / 306	5·6 / 229	4·8 / 192	4·9 / 200	2·9 / 106	4·3 / 170	2·0 / 69	2·1 / 74	1·4 / 41	— / —	1·9 / 64	2·7 / 94	4·7 / 188	5·1 / 206	4·8 / 194
Central Lancashire New Town	7·1 / 296	5·8 / 236	4·6 / 184	4·6 / 183	2·9 / 109	5·2 / 212	2·7 / 98	1·2 / 31	1·2 / 31	1·7 / 54	2·6 / 94	9·3 / 396	4·4 / 175	11·0 / 472	5·3 / 218
Manchester …	6·6 / 275	5·1 / 208	4·1 / 162	4·2 / 165	2·3 / 81	4·6 / 183	2·0 / 67	1·3 / 35	— / —	1·4 / 41	2·7 / 99	3·2 / 122	5·0 / 202	5·3 / 214	4·7 / 187
Merseyside …	6·5 / 269	5·3 / 216	4·0 / 157	3·9 / 154	2·5 / 90	5·3 / 214	2·7 / 97	— / —	1·3 / 35	2·1 / 74	3·2 / 123	3·6 / 139	5·2 / 210	5·3 / 214	5·1 / 205
Runcorn …	6·3 / 263	5·0 / 204	3·8 / 150	3·8 / 150	2·3 / 79	5·0 / 201	2·3 / 81	0·8 / 13	1·1 / 25	2·0 / 66	3·2 / 120	3·6 / 139	5·1 / 209	5·4 / 221	4·8 / 193
Birmingham …	5·0 / 203	3·3 / 127	2·5 / 88	2·8 / 102	— / —	3·9 / 155	1·7 / 52	2·5 / 90	2·3 / 81	2·9 / 106	4·3 / 169	4·9 / 198	6·8 / 282	7·1 / 295	3·1 / 116

Cardiff ...	3·9 / 154	3·0 / 111	1·4 / 41	— / —	2·8 / 102	5·8 / 238	3·9 / 154	3·9 / 154	4·2 / 165	4·9 / 200	6·3 / 263	6·9 / 287	8·5 / 358	8·7 / 368	3·9 / 153
Coventry	5·1 / 208	3·1 / 119	2·5 / 92	2·9 / 110	0·9 / 19	3·5 / 137	1·5 / 47	2·9 / 106	2·6 / 94	3·0 / 110	4·3 / 172	5·0 / 203	7·0 / 292	7·3 / 306	2·7 / 99
Norwich	7·7 / 324	4·7 / 191	5·2 / 212	5·8 / 238	3·9 / 155	— / —	3·2 / 121	5·3 / 214	4·6 / 183	4·3 / 170	5·3 / 214	6·0 / 249	8·3 / 352	8·8 / 375	3·0 / 114
Bristol ...	3·1 / 117	2·1 / 74	— / —	1·4 / 41	2·5 / 88	5·2 / 212	3·6 / 138	4·0 / 157	4·1 / 162	4·8 / 192	6·2 / 256	6·8 / 283	8·5 / 359	8·8 / 371	3·2 / 122
Swindon	3·9 / 152	1·7 / 55	1·4 / 41	2·1 / 71	2·1 / 74	4·3 / 173	3·1 / 115	4·0 / 158	3·9 / 154	4·5 / 178	5·9 / 241	6·5 / 271	8·6 / 356	8·7 / 368	2·3 / 82
Basingstoke	4·3 / 169	1·1 / 27	2·2 / 78	3·0 / 113	3·0 / 111	4·2 / 165	3·7 / 142	4·9 / 200	4·8 / 192	5·1 / 209	6·5 / 270	7·2 / 303	9·2 / 393	9·5 / 406	1·7 / 54
Milton Keynes	5·3 / 218	2·7 / 97	2·8 / 104	3·4 / 130	2·0 / 68	2·9 / 108	2·2 / 76	3·9 / 154	3·5 / 136	3·7 / 145	5·0 / 203	5·7 / 236	7·9 / 332	8·2 / 348	1·6 / 51
Plymouth	— / —	3·8 / 149	3·1 / 117	3·9 / 154	5·0 / 203	7·7 / 324	6·1 / 254	6·5 / 269	6·6 / 275	7·3 / 306	8·7 / 370	9·3 / 396	11·0 / 471	11·0 / 472	5·4 / 222
London	5·4 / 222	2·3 / 79	3·2 / 122	3·9 / 153	3·1 / 116	3·0 / 114	3·2 / 126	5·1 / 205	4·7 / 187	4·8 / 194	6·0 / 249	6·8 / 284	9·0 / 382	9·3 / 398	— / —

Notes:

(i) The road mileages are based on Ordnance Survey Grid References.

(ii) Travelling times (to the nearest tenth of an hour) have been calculated using an average speed of 45 m.p.h. plus a constant of 30 minutes.

Table 11 (3). Comparison of Air Services

Travel Centre	Major Population Centres within a Daily Direct Flight	Number of Routes	European Airports within a Daily Direct Flight	Number of Routes
Glasgow	Edinburgh (1), Newcastle (1), Leeds (2), Manchester (4), Liverpool (2), Nottingham (2), Birmingham (3), Southampton (1), London (18)	9	Amsterdam (3), Dusseldorf (1), Copenhagen (1)	3
Newcastle	London (4), Glasgow (1), Cardiff (2), Bristol (2), Liverpool (2)	5	Amsterdam (1)	1
Teesside	London (3)	1	None	0
Darlington (using Teesside) ...	London (3)	1	None	0
Leeds	London (4), Glasgow (2)	2	Amsterdam (1)	1
Central Lancashire New Town ...	Nearest airports, Liverpool and Manchester (c. 1 hour's travel)	—		—
Manchester	London (6), Edinburgh (3), Glasgow (5), Cardiff (1), Bristol (1)	5	Paris, Amsterdam (2), Brussels (2), Copenhagen (1), Dusseldorf (1)	5
Merseyside (Liverpool) ...	London (3), Glasgow (2), Cardiff (2), Bristol (2)	4	None	0
Runcorn (using Liverpool) ...	London (3), Glasgow (2), Cardiff (2), Bristol (2)	4	None	0
Birmingham	London (1), Glasgow (3), Edinburgh (2)	3	Paris (2), Amsterdam (1), Dusseldorf (1), Brussels (1), Rotterdam*	5
Cardiff	Bristol (2), Liverpool (2), Newcastle (2)	3	None	0
Coventry (using Birmingham) ...	London (1), Glasgow (3), Edinburgh (2)	3	Paris (2), Amsterdam (1), Dusseldorf (1), Brussels (1), Rotterdam*	5
Norwich	None	0	Amsterdam (1), Rotterdam*	2

	Domestic		International	
Bristol	Cardiff (3), Liverpool (2), Newcastle (2)	3	Paris (1), Basle,* Rotterdam*	3
Swindon	Nearest airport Bristol (50 miles)	—		—
Basingstoke	Nearest airport Heathrow (34 miles)	—		—
Milton Keynes (using Luton) ...	Glasgow (1), Leeds (1)	2	None	0
Plymouth	None	0	None	0
London	Birmingham (1), Liverpool (3), Glasgow (18), Manchester (6), Leeds (4), Teesside (3), Edinburgh (12), Newcastle (4)	8	Paris (27), Amsterdam (14), Brussels (8), Dusseldorf (5), Copenhagen (10)	5

Notes:

* Not yet operational.

(i) The information in this table is taken from the ABC World-Airways Guide, November 1972.

(ii) The number of Daily Direct Flights is shown in brackets after each destination.

225

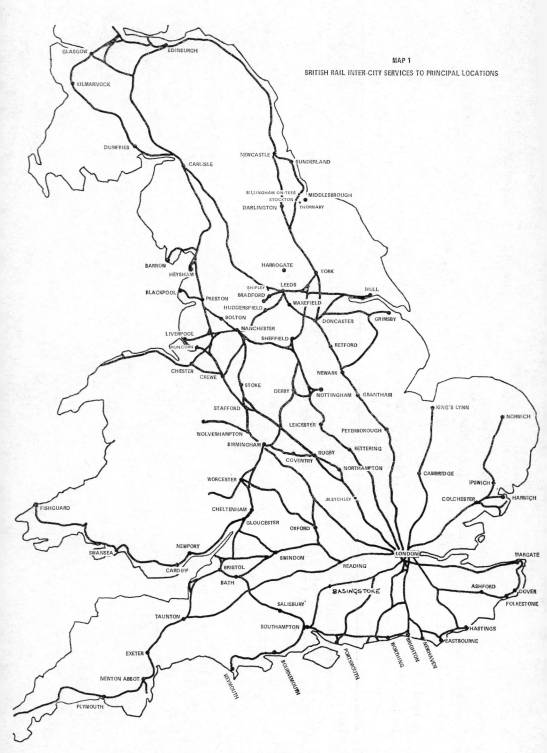

MAP 1

BRITISH RAIL INTER-CITY SERVICES TO PRINCIPAL LOCATIONS

MAP 2
MAIN ROUTES TO SELECTED LOCATIONS

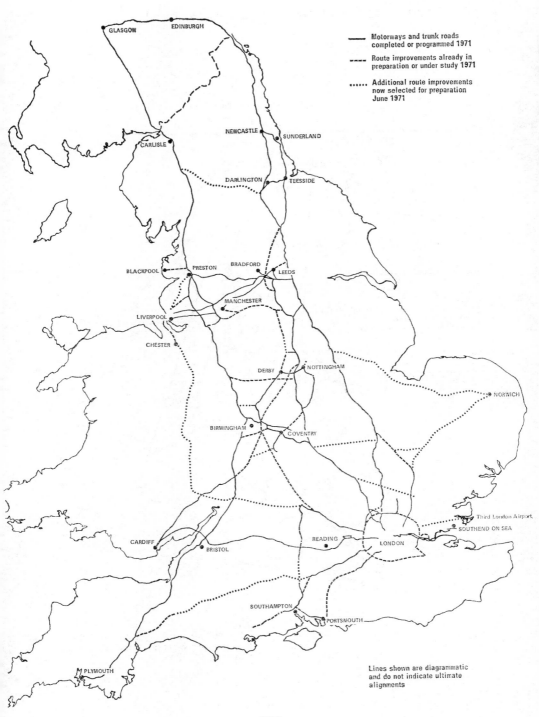

Motorways and trunk roads
completed or programmed 1971

Route improvements already in
preparation or under study 1971

Additional route improvements
now selected for preparation
June 1971

Lines shown are diagrammatic
and do not indicate ultimate
alignments

227

MAP 3

MAJOR GB INTERNAL AIR SERVICES(DIRECT FLIGHTS)

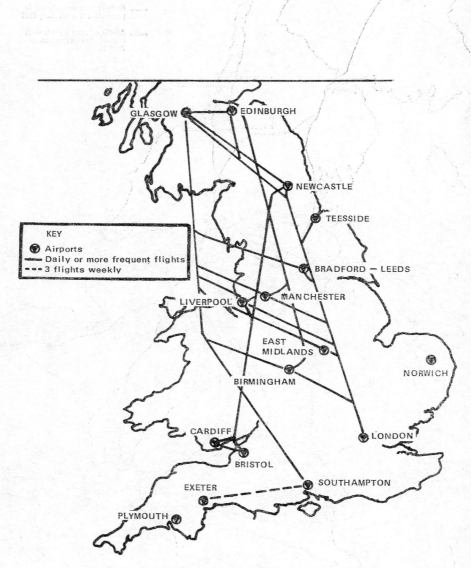

KEY

◉ Airports
—— Daily or more frequent flights
= = = 3 flights weekly

NOTE:
The information on this map is taken from the ABC WORLD — AIRWAYS GUIDE, NOVEMBER 1972.

MAP 4

MAJOR GB EXTERNAL AIR SERVICES (DIRECT FLIGHTS)

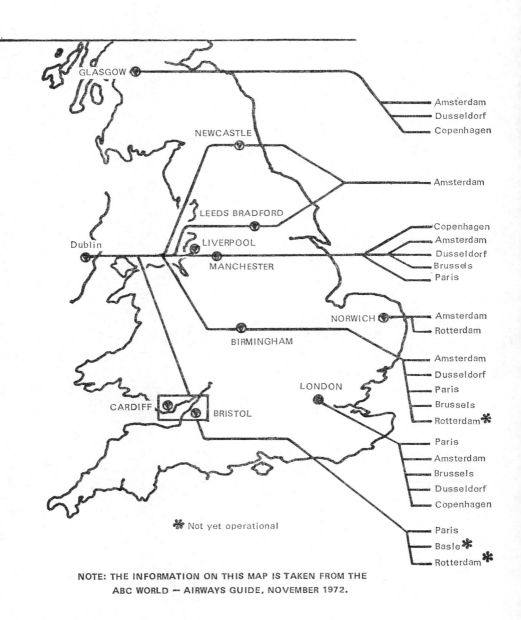

Not yet operational ✱

NOTE: THE INFORMATION ON THIS MAP IS TAKEN FROM THE
ABC WORLD — AIRWAYS GUIDE, NOVEMBER 1972.

Printed in England by Her Majesty's Stationery Office at St Stephen's Parliamentary Press
305375 Dd. 252024 K80 6/73